Certainly Uncertain

Praise for *Certainly Uncertain*

"Will Swain writes with the kind of curiosity that feels both down to earth and subtly radical. Drawing from decades as a science educator and a lifetime of lived inquiry, this book doesn't tell you what to think—it invites you into a richer, more compassionate understanding of how we come to know, believe, and make meaning."

—Renee Zukin, Educator,
Entrepreneur, & Author of *Every Day, I'm Brave*

"A thought-provoking deep dive into how we understand the world and what we come to believe about it. Presented with both humor and intellectual rigor. Highly recommend."

—Julianna K. Wilson, Ph.D. Entomology,

"Will Swain writes with wit, in an easy-to-read voice. He makes complex ideas understandable and interesting."

—Judd Lyons, Retired Major General and
former Deputy Assistant Secretary of Defense

"The book was as thought-provoking and clever as it was charming. Swain's ideas and arguments are intellectual, inclusive, and refreshingly insightful . . . and I learned more about Bigfoot than I ever expected!"

—Sean Strain, editor and former
vice president of Entrepreneur Press

"Mr. Swain's remarkable book encourages us to critically evaluate our thinking in a cultural environment where facts can be obscured by misinformation and political spin. In this massively entertaining and compelling book, he uses a variety of topics to explore the nature of our beliefs and their relationship to the nature of knowledge itself. I could not put it down."

—Mark St. Andre, Ph.D. Educational Psychology

Certainly Uncertain

RELIGION, FREEWILL, NATURE OF SCIENCE, BIGFOOT,

COLONIAL AMERICA, NEUROBIOLOGY, WAYS OF KNOWING,

CHRISTIAN NATIONALISM, EVOLUTION, GALILEO, PORTALS,

PIZZA, BIRDS, WITCH TRIALS, AND EPIGENETICS

THE LIMITATIONS OF KNOWLEDGE AND

THE UNCERTAINTY OF BELIEF

Will Swain

Waggle Dance Books
Iowa City, Iowa

ISBNs: 979-8-9954696-1-2 (paperback) 979-8-9954696-0-5 (hardcover)
979-8-9954696-2-9 (ebook)

Cover and book design by Molly Mortimer, Mayfly book design

Library of Congress Catalog Number: 2026907995
First Printing: 2026

Dedication

To my mom and dad. Their love, kindness, spiritual guidance, and humor helped shape my belief systems about the world.

Also dedicated to the three most important people in my life: Suellen, Henry, and Max.

Contents

Introduction

"You are gonna lose 'em," my son warned me after reading an early draft of my book. "You can't just start babbling about your life and your on-again, off-again interest in bigfoot."

"It's a hook!" I responded.

"I'm not sure that your hook is as interesting as you think it is," he bluntly criticized. "I think the readers might just think you're a crazy person when you launch into your bigfoot stuff. I think you need to start with a thesis statement of some kind so that people know why you are even talking about bigfoot."

Fair enough. Max's feedback was harsh, but correct. A small introduction before we begin talking about bigfoot is in order.

This book is about two questions: how we come to know things and how we form our beliefs. I want to explore the applications of these questions to our daily lives.

I use three major subjects as case studies for these discussions: God, evolution, and bigfoot. My motivations for choosing these topics are as deliberate as they are varied. For each of these subjects, the "ways of knowing" and the "areas of knowledge" are quite different. They are also good topics to explore the nature and development of our beliefs.

Of course, the other reason I choose these topics is because they interest me. More on those interests in a bit.

To me this book is not just an academic exercise. I have come to believe that metacognition about how we come to know and why we believe what we believe, are the most important and interesting topics that exist. All human arguments, at their core, are about how we come to know and what we believe.

It seems to me that humanity's agreed upon realities are fracturing. By that, I mean different people seem to live in different realities from each other. Conspiracy theories are common, each seemingly stranger than the last. I don't think this situation is entirely new, but I think it has become more pronounced in the last few decades. I did not want to write a book about politics, and this is not a book about political discord. Rather, it hints at the deeper philosophical underpinnings of this discord. My goal is to explore the important questions of how we can get to a place where we can understand the beliefs of others and how societies can have at least a somewhat agreed upon reality.

I realize that I might not really be equipped to answer these questions. But most jobs I have ever done have involved me jumping into situations where I was not quite ready. Historically, this is precisely how all problems have been solved. (The flip side, of course, is that incompetent people jumping in over their heads has also resulted in some real shit shows. So I admit that I am wading into these waters with some trepidation.)

I will start with the low-hanging fruit, the different "realities" around the subject of bigfoot. I developed a low-grade obsession with bigfoot for reasons I am about to explain. It also turns out that the topic of bigfoot is a reasonable entry point in the discussion of how we come to construct our own "realities."

So that is my somewhat rambling thesis statement. Hopefully it will get Max's seal of approval.

SECTION 1

Bigfoot

CHAPTER 1

Why Bigfoot?

Most people do not have much of their personal identity wrapped up in the idea of bigfoot. Bigfoot is viewed as a pop culture joke for many. Sure, lots of people "believe" in bigfoot, but it is *usually* a low-stakes discussion. The bigfoot phenomena is an excellent topic to explore science, truth, belief, and how we come to know what we know—without challenging anyone's personal identity.

To be clear, I don't think the topic of bigfoot is unimportant. If the sasquatch[1] are real flesh and blood animals, the implications of their existence are quite profound. But for most people, reexamination of their position on the existence of bigfoot is relatively easy because that position is not strongly held in the first place.

Bigfoot, as a subject, can serve as a jumping off point to discuss how we come to have beliefs about anything. So that is where we are going. Which is a long way from where we will start. Like everything I will talk about in this book, historical context is helpful. I will start this section with my personal history with the subject of bigfoot.

---

1.   In this book I'm going to flip back and forth between the term "bigfoot" and "sasquatch." I won't use the plural because "Bigfoots" just sounds weird. Bigfeet is even worse, and sasquatches is only a slight improvement. Assume I attend plural if the situation calls for it, in the same way we use the term "deer."

The Legend of Boggy Creek

In 1972, I saw a film that changed my life, or at least changed my elementary school life. The movie was *The Legend of Boggy Creek*. The "G" rating caused our parents to think it was ok to let third graders go see it by themselves. Our parents had obviously never seen this movie! Had they seen it, they surely wouldn't have let us watch until we had reached at least seventeen years of age.

The movie was terrifying. When I have mentioned this movie to men my age, many gave me the same response, "That movie scared the shit out of me!"

After the seven o'clock showing of the movie, my best friends, Bruce and Blaine, along with myself, made our way back to my house from the American Movie Theater in downtown Cherokee, Iowa. We ran from streetlight to streetlight, fearful of what lurked in the shadows.

The world was different after that movie. I didn't like to get next to windows at night. (There is a scene in the movie where bigfoot's hairy arm enters a window and grabs at Bobby Ford, who is sitting on a couch next to the window.) Even taking the garbage out to the curb at night became an act of courage. But I had it easy, I lived in town. My friends Bruce and Blaine lived on a 700-acre farm in the northwest Iowa countryside. They often had to go out, alone, sometimes into pre-dawn darkness, to do their chores.

Their land was mostly crops, but it had timber as well. When I'd go stay overnight, we'd pretend to hunt bigfoot, and we would work ourselves into sheer terror pretending to see bigfoot. "Did you see that?" "Something moved by that tree." "Did you hear that! It is getting closer; no, seriously!"

Gradually, the effects of the film wore off. We spent more time playing football or playing basketball in their hayloft than bigfoot hunting. (They actually had a basketball court in their hayloft. It was awesome!) We spent time swimming and fishing in their farm ponds. We were no longer obsessed with bigfoot, but the topic still came up now and then.

Bruce and Blaine's parents had a ranch in the Black Hills of South Dakota. In the summer, I would occasionally spend time in the Black

Hills with them. We would, of course, go looking for bigfoot among the ponderosa pines. In Iowa, bigfoot started to seem a little far-fetched, but in the wilds of the Black Hills, it seemed not only possible, but downright likely.

I remember hiking with them in the French Creek wilderness area one August evening. When we rounded a bend in the creek, we were met by an eight-foot-tall looming creature about forty yards from us. One of us gasped, and the other two froze for at least two seconds, our hearts in our throats. Over the course of the next two or three seconds, we gradually realized that this was not bigfoot, but rather, an eight-foot-tall, charred stump of an old ponderosa pine.

In October of 1980, the night before my first bow hunting season, I had a dream. I dreamt that I was watching a deer come down the trail and suddenly a bigfoot jumped out and killed the deer as I watched frozen with fear. In the morning, my dad woke me to go hunting. I didn't tell him about the dream as we drove in darkness to our hunting area. The early morning air smelled of the skunk-masking scent that my dad used as we gathered our equipment. My dad went off in the darkness toward his stand, and I pressed on with all the courage I could muster toward mine. The eastern sky was pale, but it was nowhere near light as I stood in the bean stubble at the forest's edge. I took a few steps into the frost-covered foxtail, which ran between the oaks and the bean field. I paused to listen. I forgot about bigfoot for the moment and was straining to listen for deer. I took a few more careful steps, the oak leaves crunched loudly in the still, predawn air. Suddenly, from under my feet, there was an explosion of sound and movement. I didn't see it, but after one or two very long seconds, I realized I had stepped on a pheasant. The old saying "You scared it more than it scared you" did not apply here.

In the late seventies, the Des Moines Register was running occasional stories about bigfoot sightings in Iowa. But the topic seemed to come up less and less throughout the eighties.

By the 1980s, my interest in bigfoot faded into nonexistence. I went to college, studied biology and film making, and to a lesser extent religion. I forgot about my elementary school interest in bigfoot.

In graduate school, I studied Science Education and then taught high school biology, physics, and chemistry in a little town near Iowa City.

My interest in bigfoot wasn't reignited until I went to visit my future wife, Suellen, out in Roseburg, Oregon. Hiking around in the dense Oregon rain forest brought back childhood memories of my interest in bigfoot. We decided to visit the Bigfoot Museum in The Dalles, Oregon, near the Columbia River. When we got there, we were told the museum had been recently demolished. All that was left was a hole in the ground where it had been. We both saw the humor in this: no museum, just an impression in the ground that hinted of something large that had once been there.

Shortly before we were married in 1997, Suellen bought me the book, *Where Bigfoot Walks*. This book didn't change my mind about the nonexistence of bigfoot. But it opened my mind to the *possibility* of the reality of bigfoot. The author, Dr. Robert Pyle, wrote about the topic with an open mind. He gave you the sense that he thought the jury was still out as to whether bigfoot existed.

Armed with cognitive skills I didn't have in second grade, I re-watched *Legend of Boggy Creek*. I was no longer terrified by this film. I now mostly laughed at the 1970s low-budget cheesiness.

One fateful day in the early autumn of 2004, while my wife was sitting in the same room watching *Judging Amy* or *ER* or some such show that that didn't appeal to me, I was sitting at the computer, bored. I had checked the weather, my stocks, my retirement account. So just for the hell of it, I googled bigfoot. I found the Bigfoot Research Field Organization (BFRO) website and began reading about various sightings. Iowa had several sightings from the late seventies and early nineties. Many seemed hokey, but a few struck me as oddly believable.

One sighting report came from a guy named Larry Wilson, from Minburn, Iowa. There was even an article from November seventeenth, 1979, Des Moines Register posted on the BFRO webpage.

I said to my wife, "Wouldn't it be cool to talk to someone who actually saw bigfoot?" She said, "Yep," and continued watching her show. I did a google search and found that Larry Wilson still lived in Minburn, Iowa, and more importantly, he had a listed phone number!

CHAPTER 2

Larry Wilson

S o, I had the number, but I did not call him. It is one thing to think about calling a stranger to discuss a bigfoot sighting, it is another to actually do it. The newspaper accounts I had read gave me the impression that Larry Wilson was a normal, reasonable person. But then again, you will not sell many papers with a headline "This Really Wacked-Out Guy Thought He Saw Bigfoot!" Even on the off chance that Mr. Wilson turned out to be normal, I thought about receiving my call from *his* perspective. How many wackos had approached *him* over the years? Had he been ridiculed by people after his sighting was published in the Des Moines Register?

I also thought that it was a very real possibility that the whole thing had been revealed as a hoax years ago. People who wanted to build a case for bigfoot were the same people that maintained the bigfoot websites. I imagined that these webmasters might not exercise diligence when it came to the removal of old sightings that were later revealed to be hoaxes.

As I tried to get the gumption to call Larry, I was nervous about it. I was also unsure what I would say to him. It would be many days later, when, like an awkward high school boy calling some girl for a date, I wrote down what I might say as an opening line: "Is this the Larry Wilson who saw bigfoot in 1979?" I crossed it out. Too blunt. It could be viewed as confrontational. For my next try I wrote, "Hello, my name is Will Swain, and this might sound a bit odd, but I'm curious about the possibility of a North American great ape. I read that you may have seen something in 1979." "Bigfoot" sounded a little crazy, where as "North American great ape" had a ring of legitimacy to it. When I felt ready, I plugged the number in, then I hit the call button.

"Hello"

"Hi . . . uh, my name is Will Swain, and, um, this might sound sorta odd, but I'm curious about the possibility of a North American great ape, and I read that you may have seen something in 1979."

On the other end, silence.

I continued, "Was this ever found . . . um, out to be a hoax?"

"No . . . no, it wasn't."

"Did people go on to see it more around there or what's the status . . . current story . . ." I fumbled around trying to say something that would lead into conversation but not lead to a hang up. I wished I wrote more than just an opening line.

He explained that over the years a few people told him they saw something around the same time he had. But they did not come forward immediately with that information. Other than these few well-after-the-fact sightings, no new sightings occurred. He himself only saw "it" the one time.

I then asked for the whole story of his experience that night.

I wish that I taped the forty plus minute conversation that followed. Unfortunately, I didn't, so I'll have to paraphrase the story Larry told me over the phone in October of 2004. What follows is that story from his 1979 sighting.

It was a cold November evening around 8:00 p.m. Larry sat in front of the TV reading a book. The *Barney Miller* show was on with the volume low. (Not that the show matters, but details sell the story!)

Larry was distracted by his dogs, who were outside barking like crazy. He got up and went out the sliding glass door from his walk-out basement to see what was causing the commotion. In the distance, he heard some coon dogs howling and assumed that was the cause of the ruckus. He told his dogs to settle down, and then he returned inside. The dogs continued to bark for a few more minutes, and once again, he walked back outside to tell them to pipe down. This time, when he listened for the coon dogs, he heard instead what he called a "swishing" sound. This "swishing sound" seemed quite distant, but it was clearly coming closer. Larry struggled with the description of this sound, but he said it was odd enough that he decided to go back inside and go upstairs where he could see better and listen. He peered into the darkness but saw nothing. So he cranked open the window, and then he heard it close!

"It sounded like a winded horse, but with much less frequency . . . and a little deeper and raspier."

At this point the breathing noises sounded about thirty-five yards from the house, and they moved along a row of eight-to-ten-foot pine trees. Whatever made the sounds moved right to left, or north to south, toward the area of his driveway and security light. He noticed that his dogs had stopped barking, and then he started to get glimpses of something big moving on the other side of the trees. He waited nervously, knowing that he'd get a good look when it came past the row of trees near the security light. When it emerged, he felt uneasy. It never looked toward him but started to walk east or down his driveway toward the road. He was struck by how it moved: as it glided along its long arms swung gracefully, seemingly almost in slow motion. Larry then moved to the south kitchen window to watch it as it continued to walk east, out of the cone of illumination provided by the single yard light. Larry quickly got his shotgun but couldn't find his deer slugs. He felt pretty rattled. He called the county sheriff and then found his pistol and loaded it.

It didn't take long for the deputy sheriff to arrive. The deputy sheriff, Craig Hien, wanted to look around. Larry wanted to look around as well, but first he asked if he could bring his gun. As Larry and the Craig left the house, a Dallas Center policeman pulled into the driveway. He had heard the call on the scanner. As they all looked around, the Dallas Center guy said, "Hey look at this." He pointed to a clear footprint in the frost. They were all struck by the size. Then, they found another, and another. They tracked "the thing" backward under the security light and back along the pines and out to where the grass met an alfalfa field. They found no tracks in the driveway. About this time, Larry's wife, Dixie, came home from an evening church function with their kids. She saw the police lights flashing and the cops carrying their guns and flashlights and thought someone had been killed. Everyone looked at the prints. Struck by the size of prints and the gait, they measured both the length of the prints and the stride length.

I wanted more details about how the thing looked. I asked about size. He told me that the only thing he had to gauge height was that it had walked past the clothesline pole which he had later measured at six feet. He said it was clearly taller than that, but how much taller was hard to say. If he had to estimate, he'd say, "Six-five or so." He added that the head was slightly cone-shaped, the arms were very long, and the gait was very fluid. I asked about hair color, and he couldn't say with any certainty. He couldn't even say with certainty if it was covered with hair. I asked about a smell or strong odor. "Nope," he said.

As our phone conversation finished up, I asked if he had any photos of the frost tracks, and he said, "No." The next morning, the frost had melted and with it all the tracks. He added that a few weeks later he did find part of a large barefoot track in a mole hill in his yard. He took a Polaroid of that track, which he sent to a bigfoot "researcher" in California. The guy blew up the photo and "analyzed" it. Larry got a reproduction of the photo back with the guy's notes on it.

My last question was, "Could I come see the area and meet with you briefly?" I told him I was going to be in that general area on Thursday. He politely agreed to meet with me on Thursday at 4:00 p.m.

Thursday

At this point, you might be asking yourself, why? Why, after my phone conversation, would I want to go to his house and meet him?

The conversation with Larry put the hook in me. I was intrigued. I felt confident that Larry was for real. Nothing he said made me think he was not sincere. He just seemed like a normal person who witnessed something he could not fully explain.

Two things you need to understand about me. One, I am a person who has a lot of curiosity. And two, I am an "in-person" kind of guy. I would rather go to a friend's house than call them. I still go to the bank to deposit checks. Sure, I could do it with an app, but I would rather just go to the bank. I know that makes me sound like I'm eighty-three years old, but I like seeing people in person. I had an opportunity to meet a person who saw bigfoot, and it was very close to where I was going to be on that very Thursday. The real question is, Why wouldn't you try to see him in person?

I was in the area because I was attending the Iowa Academy of Sciences fall conference in Des Moines. At that time in my life, I worked in the provost office at The University of Iowa, where I worked as the director of several pre-college academic programs. I attended this conference every year to get the word out directly to teachers about these educational opportunities.

The thing I like most about the conference is seeing people I haven't seen for a long time. When I worked in the Department of Biological Sciences, I ran seven HHMI (Howard Hughes Medical Institute) programs, including a research program for science teachers. I directed that program for nine years. Through this experience, I connected with several good science teachers across the state.

While at the conference, I thought about my own thinking. I found my unwillingness to tell any of my acquaintances at this conference that I was conducting a bigfoot interview kind of odd. I had told many of my friends, my parents, and in-laws that I was going to do this. Although my in-laws thought it was a little odd, my friends—none of whom believe in bigfoot—didn't seem to think it was all that odd. Or maybe they just thought that it wasn't all that odd that *I* would be doing this. My mother-in-law expressed some concern about me driving around rural Iowa talking to "weirdos" who thought they saw bigfoot.

At this point in time, I did not personally believe in bigfoot. I certainly entertained the *possibility* that the species existed, but that is a substantial step back from *believing* the species does *in fact* exist. In hindsight, I find it interesting that I felt any embarrassment about even admitting my interest in the topic. I felt so self-conscious that I didn't say a word about it all day.

At three o'clock, some exhibitors began taking down their displays, I quickly followed suit and packed up. On this cool, gray October day, I took the Perry exit on Highway 141 and then turned toward Grimes on Highway 44. I took this to the Raccoon River. I pulled off the road and attached a fresh battery to my video camera. I panned the area from my car seat. It was now drizzling and just a little foggy. The weather reminded me of the Pacific Northwest. *Fitting*, I thought to myself. I continued down the narrow, curvy gravel road. I occasionally caught glimpses of the Raccoon River through the river bottom timber. Some houses were scattered about, but the valley looked rural with a mix of forests and fields. I pulled into the driveway, looking for a name on the mailbox. I didn't see a name, but I felt confident I had the right place; his directions had been good. I walked toward the door, and Larry came out to greet me. He looked almost exactly as I imagined him. He was a big guy, about six foot one, mostly bald, and he walked with a slight limp. He greeted me with a smile on his face, he immediately seemed like a nice guy. He introduced me to his wife, Dixie, and the three of us sat in their kitchen. Immediately, I was drawn to his dog.

The month prior, I put my dog, Moose, to sleep, and honestly it just felt good to pet a dog. As we sat there, trying to figure one another out, I think it helped them to trust me when they saw that their dog liked me and that I liked their dog. Larry pulled out the picture of the mole-hill-track he took in 1979, and he explained that it was a reproduction of the original photo he sent to the bigfoot "researcher" in California. Larry explained that initially, the "researcher" had seemed knowledgeable about bigfoot, but after a few correspondences, the guy started talking about "bigfoot being linked to UFOs" and how they were "mining the Earth for resources." At that point, the "researcher" lost all credibility with the Wilsons. Larry quit returning his letters. Larry told me about other oddballs who showed up on their doorstep after the sighting. Not wanting to appear as an oddball myself, I told them I was skeptical about bigfoot—skeptical but open-minded. Larry acted as if he also felt skeptical, but at the same time, he knew he saw something that defied a simple explanation. A few weeks prior, during our phone conversation, Larry said, "It might have been a hoax; I'm just telling you what I saw."

He and Dixie also told me about sounds they heard a few weeks before the sighting. They described the sounds as loud, high-pitched wails, and on one occasion, like a woman screaming. These strange sounds happened a few times before the sighting and once about two weeks after. They were careful not to assume these sounds related to the sighting, but noted that they never heard the sound before, and they haven't heard them since.

I asked Larry to walk me through what he saw and heard that night back in 1979 while I shot video of the area. It was a recap of what he told me over the phone, but I now could ask specific questions as I looked at the actual terrain. It helped to see the details, like the window he looked out, the clothesline pole—which was still there—and the yard light. He told me that some things had changed in twenty-five years—the row of pines had been cut down, and they had built an addition and a deck—but I could easily visualize what had taken place that night.

I asked for clarification of the "swishing sound" that he described during our phone conversation as "a winded horse." He then attempted to imitate the sound. I once heard a bear in the woods very close to me; the sound Larry made reminded me of that guttural huff. (Since more people have heard horses than bears, I suppose his description is probably more useful.)

We went back inside. There we talked about his closest neighbor, who believed that Larry merely saw some lost hunter making his way back to his car that evening. Dixie interjected that this same neighbor had subsequently filled in the natural caves of limestone behind his house with dirt, apparently just to be safe.

As we talked, Larry became less guarded toward me. By the time I left, I was 99 percent sure that he was 99.9 percent sure that this had not been a hoax.

After talking to Larry, I read a lot of bigfoot sighting reports, and I watched several eyewitness accounts from documentaries. When I personally evaluate these reports, it always seems that there are only three options:

1. The person might not be telling the truth.
2. The person may have *thought* they saw a big biped that wasn't human, but they really didn't.
3. The person may have been a victim of a hoax.

(There is a fourth option as well, but it requires a leap into a different belief system.)

4. Maybe, just maybe, the person saw bigfoot!

1. Truthfulness

As I drove back to Iowa City, I spent those two hours replaying the conversation with Larry and Dixie in my mind. I was convinced, first and foremost, that they were telling the truth. My discussion with them occurred decades after the fact. They had no reason to lie, then or now.

The subtle ways in which the two of them interacted also bolstered their believability rating. When Larry said, "I couldn't find my deer slugs," his wife said, in a matter-of-fact way, that she had hidden them. I gave her a questioning look and she said, "We had four kids running around." The explanation was simple and to the point. They had a backstory for why he couldn't find his deer slugs. Either they were master thespians, or they were simply telling their story.

Also, when I briefly talked to Dixie separately, her account lined up with his. She added some details that he had not mentioned. She told me that when she came home and looked at the tracks in the frost, she said the tracks reminded her of her daughter's poolside tracks. I asked for clarification. She explained that her daughter had flat feet, just like whatever left the barefoot tracks in the frost. She also told me that Larry was really rattled by the experience and that this was out of character for him.

They only presented information. They didn't fill in the blanks. As Larry described everything to me, I noticed that he did not mention the hair color or length. When I asked about the hair, he said he didn't remember hair color, hair length, or if it even had hair. This matched what he said to me on the phone. His descriptions were consistent.

As he became less guarded, he admitted that he was afraid of what he saw the night of the encounter. He looked me in the eye and said, "You have to remember that at the time, this was petrifying. It really was."

2. Misidentification

Let's consider the possibility that Larry did see something, but he misidentified it. Perhaps, as the neighbor suggested, he saw a lost hunter. Larry had a good look at it, and he was pretty sure it wasn't a man, but there is no other animal that looks like what he saw.

We know it wasn't a hallucination because, well, hallucinations don't leave tracks in the frost.

So a man is really the only alternative explanation here. But the lost hunter hypothesis doesn't make sense. It would be an odd lost hunter: six feet five inches, barefoot, with flat feet, and making "heavy, winded-horse breathing" sounds. The closeness of the sighting, his description of the abnormally long arms, the cone-shaped head, the gait, and the dogs. The dogs that went quiet when "it" was in the yard. Misidentification of a lost person walking by simply made no sense to me.

3. Hoax

Perhaps Larry Wilson was the victim of an elaborate hoax. As I drove home that night, I thought about how someone could have orchestrated this hoax. He'd have to be a big guy to sell both the height and the stride. (I'm assuming guy, but it could be a woman. Either way six foot five makes that very unlikely.) This hoaxer would need a form-fitting hat to give his head a cone shape. He'd need to sneak into an alfalfa field at night, make heavy breathing noises, and walk by a dark house in the middle of nowhere with fake big feet attached to his boots—or just happen to have fifteen-inch flat feet and be barefoot. Then he would need to find a way home through the woods without being seen. All of this is technically possible, but somewhat absurd.

Oh, and in addition, he would need to alarm two large dogs and then hush them as he walked by. Maybe he carried two rib-eye steaks with him. The dogs do make the hoax explanation a bit tricky. But the part of the hoax hypothesis that bothered me most was the *why*. If this were a hoax, *why* would it be done outside a dark house in the middle of nowhere? There were no other houses around. For me to simply dismiss this as a hoax requires some major mental gymnastics.

After mulling this around while driving home that night, I decided that Larry Wilson *may* have seen bigfoot. I found myself saying "may." It was hard for me to definitively say, "He saw bigfoot." I still wasn't prepared to flat out believe. The idea that bigfoot might be a real species still left me off-balance. Surely something else made sense . . . but it didn't.

I was hooked. My wife and I talked about bigfoot every night for the next several nights. It became an obsession. As I explored the Iowa sightings more, I discovered that Larry was not alone in seeing bigfoot.

CHAPTER 3

Bigfoot and Epistemology

For several months, I obsessed with bigfoot. I read books by Peter Byrne, Robert Pyle, John Green, Jeff Meldrum, and others. I also watched several bigfoot documentaries, which ranged from okay to awful. I carefully weighed what people said. The "truth" seemed as elusive as bigfoot himself.

There was in fact a compelling case for the existence of bigfoot and, an equally compelling case that belief in bigfoot was all bullshit.

(Penn and Teller had a good series a while ago where they called out all manner of pseudoscience and other nonsense in a very convincing way. They had an episode about bigfoot, and they made an excellent case that it was all bullshit. The title of their series was even called *Bullshit*.)

In 2005, I left my job at The University of Iowa to return to teaching science in a small high school near Iowa City. My obsession with bigfoot did not completely subside, but I no longer had time for it. Then one day in 2005, while I was talking about the nature of science with my biology class, an idea suddenly occurred. Why not incorporate the topic of bigfoot into my teaching about the nature of science? The search for bigfoot seemed like an attention-grabbing hook and a good vehicle to explore many topics within the philosophy of science.

My goal was to use bigfoot as a case study for what constitutes "good" vs. "weak" evidence. How is evidence different from proof? How does science, as a way of knowing, differ from other ways of knowing? How does society dictate what science studies? How do scientists attempt to remove bias as evidence is gathered and analyzed?

It was almost a brilliant idea, but "bigfoot" became a distraction to the students. Some of these philosophical ideas around the nature of science seemed beyond the grasp of many high school sophomores. Students liked the "bigfoot part," but I struggled to communicate the nature of science concepts. Fun and engagement help in teaching, but they alone don't guarantee effective instruction.

Once, I was under my desk fixing a disconnected ethernet cable. As my students filed into the room, one student posed the hypothetical question to the class, "Is Mr. Sasquatch here, or is he out hunting bigfoot today?" I replied from under the desk, "Not hunting Sasquatch today, I'm just hanging out under my desk listening to students as they enter the room." I heard a whispered "oh shit," and then silence as students tried to remember if they had said anything that would get them into trouble.

Every year my "bigfoot-nature-of-science" unit improved a little, but it never achieved my full vision. A few years later, my teaching assignment changed to include a course in astronomy to ninth-grade students. At this time, I pivoted and began to use the story of Galileo as my go-to example for both the history of, and the nature of, science. I gradually abandoned the topic of bigfoot as a teaching tool.

But here I sit, twenty years after my first attempts, still trying to use the subject of the sasquatch to help explore the idea of how we come to know and believe.

Although whether bigfoot exists is a very low-stakes question, it is an interesting question. This is more than a philosophical issue; there is a definite answer. A compromise is not possible; it's a binary situation—we cannot decide that bigfoot is "somewhat real."

On binary questions like, "Does bigfoot exist?" we just want the answer key. But "a key" for this question doesn't exist, so we use available patterns and or logic to decide. Because we are busy people, the decision usually comes quickly. We don't have the time, energy, or interest to devote to a question about a big hairy critter in the woods. In short, we already have a lot on our plates, and this "mystery" doesn't make the cut as something we want to devote time to.

Interestingly, a lack of contemplation does not stop most of us from making a decision. And once people make that decision, they hold on to it tightly, as if they know the truth. And statistically, they have about a 50 percent chance of being 100 percent right or 100 percent wrong. Our confidence in our beliefs about bigfoot is likely disproportionately higher than it should be.

Strongly held unexamined beliefs interest me.

If you talk with friends, family, (or specifically in my case, hundreds of students) about the bigfoot phenomenon, one thing will become very clear: a lot of people *know bigfoot does not exist*. The other thing that is clear is that many other people *know that bigfoot is real*.

These observations lead me to consider that the reality of the sasquatch could be an excellent, low-stakes way to discuss what it means to *truly know* something.

Time to get into the weeds a bit.

"Do you believe in bigfoot?" is a different question than "Does bigfoot exist?"

The first question is asking about a *personal belief*.

"Does bigfoot exist?" is asking you about the reality of the world in which you live. Is bigfoot a species on this planet? Does bigfoot *in fact* exist?

The question, "Does bigfoot exist?" is a bit of a hot mess. It can only be *potentially* answered *in the affirmative*. Let me explain. *If* bigfoot does exist, this question can be answered by finding physical evidence that is subjected to review by anyone to verify its authenticity, then, and only then, can it be added to the canon of what we know as empirical knowledge. If this occurs, we could then answer the question: "Yes, bigfoot does exist."

However, if bigfoot *does not exist*, then this question *cannot be answered*, because nonexistence cannot be proven. I cannot prove that mice don't live in my house, even though I don't see them, or see evidence of them. The house is too large with too many hiding spaces to know, with certainty, that there are no mice—even if the assumption is reasonable. In science, we would call "nonexistence" a non-testable hypothesis.

That said, some might argue that science could simply start with the null hypothesis: We have not found bigfoot on Earth, or mice in my house, because they do not exist there. We are done. Closed question. The null hypothesis has support. Some scientists, and lay people, dismiss bigfoot using this logic.

This logic seems bulletproof until you realize that it shuts down inquiry. If you apply this logic to other phenomena that are not understood, you immediately see the problem. No sense looking for anything that has not yet been found. Why look for the cures for cancers, or the causes of any number of poorly understood mental disorders? Or why look for life on other planets? It has not been found yet, so it doesn't exist, case closed.

Science, as an area of knowledge, has always been about inquiry into the unknown. The whole purpose of the process of science is to investigate poorly understood phenomena.

I also think it is important to understand that the question as to whether bigfoot exists might not be a closed question. We could begin with the simplest hypothesis: The many tracks, sightings, and film, in particular geographical areas, are best explained by the presence of a hominid in these geographical areas. Those who argue that sasquatch exists, also stand on firm ground to claim they have evidence that supports *their* hypothesis.

Questions where people are on firm ground to hold differing beliefs are also interesting to me. It is important to recognize that your *beliefs* are not the same as *empirical knowledge*. Science starts with belief, or a hypothesis, and then attempts to refute that belief.

I believe it is important to dial back certainty when we are simply exploring possible hypotheses. If you have a little metacognition about what it means to know and how you came to your belief, it becomes easier to dial back unjustified certainty.

CHAPTER 4

The Bigfoot Question

If you were hoping to learn whether you were correct on the question of bigfoot's existence, then this book has probably been unsatisfying thus far.

I'm not the first person to notice that most people are more interested in finding the things that confirm their personal beliefs than they are in finding the truth. Let me throw you a bone here and explain why your beliefs regarding sasquatch are correct. I'll cover both possibilities in that I will make both the "bigfoot-does-exist" case, and I'll then make the case for the "nonexistence of bigfoot." If you are on the fence, try to suspend judgment until you have read both cases.

What follows are basically two position papers with differing views. My views have flip-flopped so much over the years that I am proficient in arguing either side of this argument. Years of debating the question of bigfoot's existence in my own head has given me an almost superhuman tolerance of bigfoot talk. However, if at this point in my book, you are showing symptoms of "sasquatch fatigue"—heavy eyelids, drifting thoughts, slight nausea (I have grown to recognize these symptoms in my wife and kids)—then feel free to grab a cup of coffee, get up and stretch, we can meet back in Chapter 5. You will have not missed anything critical to the themes of this book by skipping the next ten pages.

If, on the other hand, you find yourself a little intrigued . . .

The Case for Bigfoot's Existence

The only way to say for certain that something doesn't exist is to see everywhere at once. This approach is possible in, say, an aquarium, because it is small enough to see the whole thing. With a slightly larger scale, proving nonexistence is next to impossible. My example of "Mice don't exist in a house," is hard to prove to a skeptic. Claiming an animal doesn't exist in the boreal forest of an entire continent is not a claim that is feasible to test. I imagine my future readers, especially those in the "bigfoot-does-not-exist" camp, rolling their eyes.

I imagine them saying, "We can no longer say for certain that Santa, unicorns, or magical elves don't exist because you can't technically test for nonexistence? That is ridiculous!"

The slope is admittedly a little slippery, but there are some very important differences between bigfoot's possible existence and Santa, elves, or unicorns. Let's consider the Santa situation. (Very small children should skip this part.) If there is no Santa, then how did those presents get under the tree? Where did the cookies go? There is a solid, verifiable alternate explanation to the hypothesis that Santa is responsible. This hypothesis is simple, and it involves no flying reindeer or time traveling. The bigfoot situation is more complex.

We must start with the idea that bigfoot *could* exist, which is different from the argument that it *does* exist. For starters, there is physical evidence in the fossil record that bigfoot-like-creatures did exist! One such critter, *Gigantopithecus blacki*, existed from approximately 2 million years ago to nearly 350,000 years ago. Geologically and evolutionarily, that is very recent. The first fossil, a tooth of a *Gigantopithecus blacki*, was found in China in 1956. Since then, other teeth and three additional mandibles have been found. *Gigantopithecus was* likely a seven- to ten-foot tall, possibly upright, walking ape.

This animal walked while other Hominids inhabited the planet.

Is that remarkable? Yes, it is a remarkable fact. Are there still giant apes like *Gigantopithecus* walking around in remote forests? It is certainly possible based on the available data.

Gigantopithecus in the fossil record is not evidence that bigfoot exists. It is, however, evidence that it is possible to have a critter like the sasquatch. Such an animal *could* explain all the tracks and thousands of sightings. In addition to *Gigantopithecus*, there are several other upright walking apes, such as the *Paranthropus*, in the fossil record. It is possible that a big, upright-walking, nonhuman *could* exist because big upright walking critters *did* exist—and relatively recently—in the fossil record.

The hypothesis that claims bigfoot exists is supported by the following empirical facts.

1. Thousands of sightings of *something* that is big, (often seven- to nine-feet tall and of massive girth), hairy, walking, on two legs have been reported.
2. These "things" are purported to leave tracks, and we have *hundreds* of purported plaster casts of these tracks. Plus, hundreds more photos of these tracks. These plaster casts exist. The photos exist. This is physical evidence.
3. The First Nations people, who inhabited suitable habits for sasquatch, have names in their respective languages for the critter that many of us now call bigfoot or sasquatch. That is yet another fact. This bigfoot-like thing is often an important part of these native cultures.

To be fair, there are competing hypotheses to explain these facts, which I will discuss in the "bigfoot-does not exist" section. But those competing explanations are by no means conclusive.

Before I continue, I have a quick question. Am I convincing any skeptics to acknowledge the possibility of bigfoot yet? Because before we can examine our beliefs about anything, we first need to allow ourselves to dial back our certainty about our previously held beliefs. If you are still *certain* the bigfoot's existence is nonsense, then keep reading. I'm just getting warmed up!

When discussing bigfoot, the story is often told from a non-Native point of view. Discussion of this phenomenon from a purely Western viewpoint is misleading and inappropriate for a variety of reasons. I want to spend a paragraph or two sharing information about the First Nations people's experiences with the sasquatch.

The word sasquatch was coined around 1929. Sasquatch is an anglicized word that was somewhat poorly translated from the family of

Salishan languages. More specifically, it arises from the word "saesq'ec" from the Halkomelem dialect.

In native cultures, many tribes have a name for it, from the Yukon down to the Sierra Nevada mountains and everywhere in between:

Nuhu'ahn (or the woods man)	(Athabascans) Yukon River area
Bukwas and D'sonoqua	(Kwakiutl) Wild Man and Wild Woman, British Columbia
Saskehavas	(Coast Salish, Squamish, etc.) British Columbia & Washington State
Tintah-kwang xoya (or old man of the woods)	(Hoopa or Hupa) Northern California
Mayak Data (aka "Hairy Man" from 700ish year old Pictograph)	(Tule River) Sierra Nevada

Native American discussion of bigfoot is a little complicated because in some cultures, people consider it more as a spirit animal, as opposed to a physical creature. Other traditions describe it as a real physical creature, just like a bear or an eagle. And still, in other nations, there is little distinction between the physical and the spiritual.

Acting as though this phenomenon began when non-Native people arrived in North America is a false history. The story of the North American Sasquatch goes back many thousands of years.

Now, back to the evidence. In the interest of brevity, I will focus on two major compelling categories of evidence.

1. Physical evidence for the existence of the sasquatch in the form of footprints
2. Eyewitness testimony

Footprints

"There is no branch of detective science so important and so much neglected as the art of tracing footsteps" —Conan Doyle, 1891

In the non-native community, long before the tracks got widespread attention, "bigfoot" sightings were occurring. But the large bipedal hairy ape did not yet go by the name of bigfoot. Newspapers in the 1800s and early 1900s had accounts of bigfoot-like critters all over North America and Canada. In 1893, Teddy Roosevelt wrote about a bigfoot-like creature in his nonfiction book, *The Wilderness Hunter*. Plaster of Paris wasn't used to make a cast of tracks until the twentieth century. Historically, tracks began to get more widespread attention from the non-native community in the early 1900s.

In 1958, the most famous plaster cast was made by a man named Jerry Crew.

The Humbolt Times newspaper is credited with coining the name "bigfoot" in the story published with Jerry holding a plaster cast. This picture gave many Northern Californians their first glimpse of this phenomenon. Jerry saw his first track in early August and talked to a local taxidermist about how to best preserve a track. A few months later, he found and made the cast in the iconic picture. The article and photo were picked up by other newspapers around the country. Thus, the term "bigfoot" was born.

So sasquatch (1929) and bigfoot (1958) are two relatively recent terms for a very old phenomenon.

After the Jerry Crew story of 1958, other people from British Columbia to Northern California were making plaster casts or taking pictures of tracks they had found. Other tracks appeared in other parts of Canada and in other parts of the US.

In this section, I will argue that it is unlikely that the footprints are all hoaxed. Yes, some were hoaxes. That, too, is a fact. But it is *not* logical to assume that just because some were hoaxed that they were all hoaxed.

There were not just a few tracks. Dr. Gover Krantz (more on him in a moment) had a collection of 150 or more plaster casts at the time of his death. When he passed away, he left his collection to Dr. Jeff Meldrum,

Dr. Meldrum showing me his extensive plaster cast collection. Almost every tray in those two huge cabinets contains multiple plaster casts of tracks. (Photo credit to my wife, Suellen.)

Dr. Meldrum and I discussing the bigfoot phenomena in his office.
(Photo credit to my wife, Suellen.)

who now has a collection of over 300 plaster casts. (I know this fact because I went to Dr. Meldrum's office and personally looked at them!)

At this juncture, I may not have convinced you of the existence of bigfoot. However, it is important to acknowledge that there is a substantial amount of physical evidence supporting this claim. Saying that a flesh and blood bigfoot exists fits *a lot* of data. My goal here is not to convince a skeptic that bigfoot is real, but rather, to crack a skeptics *certainty* that any talk of bigfoot is just nonsense. I do acknowledge that for evidence to be worth anything, it must be scrutinized in a way that reduces bias.

Scrutiny of the Tracks

Dr. John Bindernagel, Dr. Grover Krantz, and Dr. Meldrum devoted much of their research time to the tracks themselves. The tracks are physical, and scientists like things which can be measured and scrutinized. It was the track of a particular bigfoot, one that had a clubfoot disorder, that first caught the attention of Dr. Krantz. It seemed so implausible that a hoaxer would correctly interpret the details of clubfoot anatomy that Dr. Krantz concluded that it was extremely unlikely that it would have been hoaxed.

Everyone who studies the tracks has noticed some patterns. The width to length ratio in alleged bigfoot tracks is somewhat consistent (and it is a different width to length ratio than is observed in a modern human foot.) We should also note an oversized big toe, (relative to a human) that often diverges, and an oversized heel. Hundreds of tracks sharing these characteristics is odd if you are under the impression—pun intended—that all the tracks cast from the 1958 through the 1980s are hoaxes. I would expect any competent hoaxer to be aware of these width-to-length ratios today. However, from the 1950s through the 1980s, it would not have been intuitive for all hoaxers to use a set of parameters like this. These ratios were not known and certainly not reported until much later in the bigfoot story. Given the almost endless variety of length and width ratios various hoaxers could have chosen, the fact that they nearly all settled on the same, very nonhuman ratio is quite remarkable, perhaps even unbelievable. This would require coordination of the hoaxing community from northern British Columbia down to central California.

The Metatarsal Hinge

One of the big contributions that Dr. Meldrum brought to the discussion was the foot anatomy of the midtarsal hinge required to support something the size of bigfoot. This feature allows the foot to bend closer to the heel than in a human foot. The tracks you get from a foot with a midtarsal bend are different from the tracks you would get from a less flexible foot, like our own feet. An animal with a midtarsal ridge would often push up the soil, sand, or mud in the center of the foot print as they walked.

It would seem remarkable, perhaps even unbelievable, that hoaxers would insert this piece of anatomy on tracks from all over BC and the Pacific Northwest from the 1950s to the 1990s. (Remember, Meldrum did not report his findings until the late 1990s.) The footprints with their midtarsal ridges, together with the odd length to width ratios, tell a pretty compelling story. It is difficult to dismiss this empirical evidence.

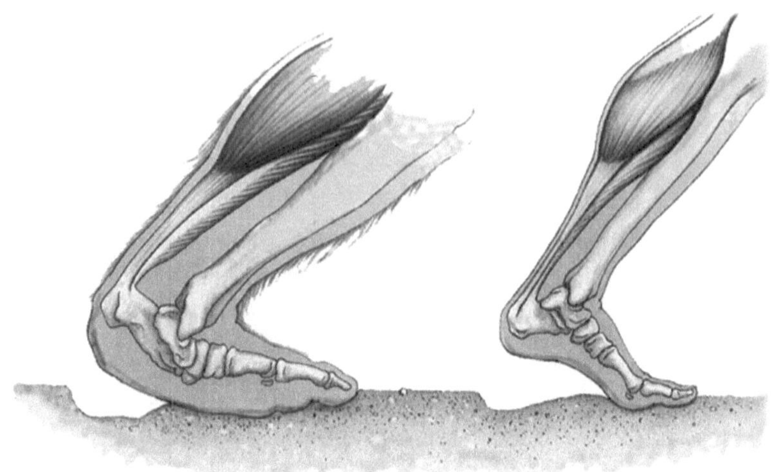

Jeff Meldrum's illustration of midfoot flexibility due to the presence of an anatomical midtarsal hinge. (Courtesy of Jeff Meldrum.)

Eyewitness Accounts

John Green was a newspaper reporter in British Columbia in the 1950s. He occasionally reported on various sasquatch sightings. From time to time, Green would talk to these witnesses, and after years of hearing similar stories, he began to wonder if this thing was real. He began to keep a file of the reports. After his file started to grow, he began to seek reports from other newspapers across British Columbia. By the late 1950s, he understood this was not just a Canadian story. He saw reports from Washington State, Northern California, and Oregon as well. Struck by the similarity of the accounts, he would later remark, "When you think of all of the things that people could describe, there was a remarkable similarity in what they did describe." John eventually put these sightings into a book called *The Sasquatch File*, published in 1973.

Skeptics will often categorically dismiss eyewitness accounts. I find this categorical dismissal to be rather odd. In court cases, eyewitness testimony could land someone in jail, or even on death row! Most of what we learn is not something that we saw, but something that was reported to us by an eyewitness. Just because someone thinks bigfoot is silly, doesn't mean that they can casually dismiss *thousands* of eyewitness reports.

It is noteworthy that the types of tracks observed indicate that the midtarsal hinge feature has been preserved over many years and across various geographic regions. (Courtesy of Jeff Meldrum.)

The other piece of historical context about Green's book is—and I think this is important—that prior to 1967, the witnesses had never seen a photo of a bigfoot. Their descriptions were stand-alone descriptions. The witness sighting reports came from British Columbia, Vancouver, places near Spokane, and Mount St. Helens, Mount Hood, The Dalles, and Willow Creek, California. In all of these places, what different people described would later fit the creature in the *Patterson-Gimlin film*.[2]

Thinking that these individuals were working together is quite absurd. When Green first saw the *Patterson-Gimlin film*, he said, "It looked quite similar to what I had imagined based on what had been described to me."

---

2. Though very interesting, I don't want to write about the Patterson-Gimlin film here. It's a big topic, and I feel like it would be a lot for an already longish section. I have written a blurb about the famous film in Appendix A. It is worth a read!

Another bigfoot researcher, Peter Byrne, had a different approach to gather eyewitness accounts. He set up a toll-free number, 1-800-BIGFOOT. He gathered over 1,000 eyewitness accounts of which he claims, "About a hundred of which seemed very credible."

Both Green and Byrne stated that the *quality* of eyewitness reports seemed to drop off after the *Patterson-Gimlin film*, even as the *quantity* increased. People were more likely to conflate something they saw or heard into the image of bigfoot they saw in that film. It became harder to separate the wheat from the chaff so to speak. There was no such confirmation bias prior to 1967, when just two individuals, Green and Byrne, documented literally *thousands* of sightings from the 1930s to 1967.

Using this evidence, I have convinced myself that bigfoot was, in the not-too-distant past, most certainly real! Bigfoot may still walk the Earth. Of course, this is my personal knowledge, based on lots of ways of knowing. This is different than collective knowledge or scientific knowledge, where the bar is much higher. (Personal knowledge, ways of knowing, opinions, facts, beliefs, scientific knowledge, etc., are all terms that we will unpack later.)

The Case against Bigfoot's Existence

This section is much shorter because it can be. The burden is not on skeptics to prove bigfoot doesn't exist; it is on those who insist the species is real to show its reality. Extraordinary claims require extraordinary evidence. A giant seven- to nine-foot-tall, hairy population of bipedal apes, or relic hominins, roaming through modern forests, is an extraordinary claim.

The evidence provided to date is compelling, but not definitive. The sightings thus far could be explained away in four different ways: conflation with archetypal myths, hallucinations, misidentifications, and/or hoaxes.

Yes, evolutionary evidence indicates that other large bipeds walked alongside our human ancestors. But this fact could explain why modern humans seem to be "hardwired" to fear, or least be predisposed to think, that there are other hairy men in the woods. These predispositions to believe certain stories could just be part of our psychological makeup, what Joseph Campbell refers to as archetypal myths. Many myths and folklore share commonalities, recurring motifs if you will. This could explain why we are so quick to interpret eyeshine eight feet off of the ground at night as a bigfoot, instead of the more benign explanation of a raccoon part way up a tree.

Many of the hallucinations and misidentifications could be tied to these archetypal myths. The archetypical myth explanation is a plausible reason as to why these sightings have such consistency in their descriptions.

Quick side story, that last raccoon example really happened to me! I was on my way to my deer stand shortly after I had interviewed Larry Wison. In the predawn darkness, deep into the timber, my head light caught a glowing pair of eyes about eight feet of the ground. It really got my heart a thumpin'. It took a long fifteen seconds to figure out that it was a merely a racoon part way up a tree!

When bigfoot enthusiasts make claims about the rich historical evidence in native cultures, this is also misleading. In many of these traditions, the distinction between spirit and flesh, is as blurry as the supposed "photographic evidence."

Hoaxing has occurred—this is an undisputed fact. Ray Wallace claimed that he made tracks by strapping big wooden feet to his boots and walking along logging roads. He later in life claimed he was the creator of the entire bigfoot hoax. So how can we know which cases are hoaxes and which are not?

Believers argue that the sheer numbers of sightings and tracks strengthen the case for bigfoot. Unfortunately for them, that is not how evidence works. It is not the amount of evidence that matters, it is the veracity or strength of the evidence. If there are many pots of weak coffee, and we combine them all together, the coffee does not become stronger. Now there is just a lot of weak coffee. Weak evidence is not strengthened by more weak evidence.

It is true that very few scientists are looking for sasquatch, but it is *not* true that very few scientists are looking for animals in remote areas. Researchers conduct a wide range of animal surveys in the remote wilderness. They look for black and grizzly bears; moose;

elk; whitetail, mule, and blacktail deer; snow leopards; wolves; wolverines; fishers; flying squirrels; and even rare wood bison. Many of these are very elusive, some are rare and nocturnal, and yet *all* have been captured on trial cameras or regular cameras. Logic tells us that *IF* a breeding population of large upright walking apes, is out there, we would have some very good photographic evidence of these things from researchers. We don't.

In addition, tens of thousands of private hunter trail cams monitor the woods. Not a single cam has captured a photo that is clearly a sasquatch. Even if you could explain away all the trail cam absences, sasquatches should at least leave some kind of sign. We should find piles of scat laying around. We should see trails, evidence from where they browse, or where they made kills—if they are eating other animals. But we don't see this evidence. Contrastingly, in areas where we find mountain gorillas, we see their impact on the environment: trails, areas where feeding has occurred, and scat. There should be lots of scat!

My wife and I had breakfast with Dr. Esteban Sarmiento, a primatologist who spent months at a time with lowland and mountain gorillas in their African habitats. Esteban was a research associate at the American Museum of Natural History, and he was also Fulbright scholar at Eduardo Mondlane University in Mozambique. I asked him about the impact of gorillas on their environment; specifically, if they left trails. Estaban's reply was a resounding, "Yes, obvious trails. Where the undergrowth is thick, they are better described as obvious tunnels through the brush."

The lack of this obvious sign, points to a lack of a sasquatch. At the very least, the lack of sign points to a population so small as to be unsustainable.

Sure, non-believers can't prove that sasquatch does not exist, but the burden is on the believers. The axiom: "Absence of evidence is not evidence of absence" is true, but only to a point. There comes a time when the towel must be thrown in. Perhaps that time has come?

If you are feeling a little confused about what you believe, well, welcome to my world. The people who believe in bigfoot have a solid case. The people who do not believe in bigfoot also have a solid case. I have been wrestling with this topic, and forcing my family to wrestle with it, for decades now.

I have had to make my peace with uncertainty, which is not easy. At the end of the day, my answer is, "I have no idea whether it still exists, though I believe it once did exist." That statement is merely my *personal belief*. We, as a community of humans, don't have evidence strong enough to put bigfoot's existence in the canon of *shared knowledge*. We collectively, do not *know* that it exists. We also don't *know* that it does *not* exist. There is really no answer key here yet, and there may never be. In this particular case, uncertainty is appropriate. In other cases, we do, in fact, collectively know that something does exist, or we collectively know the explanation for some phenomena. This begs the question, "How do we know?"

How Do We Know?

CHAPTER 5

What Does It Mean to Know?

I'll let you in on a little internal dialogue I am having with myself. On one hand, I want to write about epistemology—the study of what it means to know. On the other hand, I would like people to read my book. These two goals might be at odds with each other.

I must admit, epistemology is one of those words that makes me feel smart when I say or write it, but when I read it, I feel sleepy. I get bored fast when I read the work of the classic, or even the modern, philosophers. The jargon and the long run-on sentences with five million qualifiers to everything exhaust me.

Therefore, I will sidestep most of epistemology. I will not delve into the subject any deeper than needed. I'll try my best to not go too deeply "into the weeds."

I will start the discussion about epistemology with "the theory of knowledge." The theory of knowledge is one framework that epistemologists can use to explain how we know. "To know" is a hard concept to define. "To know" could be applied in the context to know a person or a place.

I want to focus on a different "to know." I want to focus on "how we know that something is." The framework used in the International Baccalaureate's Theory of Knowledge course is the simplest explanation that I have found to solve the "how do we know that something is" problem. Within this framework, there are eight separate "ways of knowing." Here is the list:

Sense perception
Memory
Imagination
Logic/Reason
Emotion
Faith
Intuition
Language

In Appendix B, I have elaborated on each of these "ways of knowing." Some might find a more detailed explanation of these terms useful.

These eight "ways of knowing"—I think I can be done with the quotes around ways of knowing now—allow us to gather information about the world. How do we know the temperature outside? How do we know our parents love us? How do we know where we went on vacation last year? When we accumulate any new knowledge, that new information helps us confirm or confront our belief systems. All these intertwined ways of knowing work together to help us make sense of our reality.

Personal knowledge and shared knowledge are also two important categories of "how we know something is." What the temperature is outside at a given location could be—and often is—shared knowledge, whereas do our parents love us, where did we go on vacation last year, or is it wrong to kick a puppy is personal knowledge. A lot of what we know is personal, but knowledge that the square root of sixteen is four, for example, is shared knowledge. That mathematical answer doesn't depend on the person, or depend on their beliefs.

All ways of knowing have limitations and strengths.

Types and Ways of Knowing

Notice that "science" is not on the list of ways of knowing, even though science is often taught as a way of knowing. I used to teach science as a way of knowing. It was not a horrible mistake, I have made worse, but it's still technically an error.

So why isn't "science" on the International Baccalaureate (IB) Theory of Knowledge course's ways of knowing list? After all, it does appear on other epistemological *types* or *areas* of knowing lists. At first, that might seem like a contradiction, but it is not. *Ways of knowing* are subtly different from *types* or *areas of knowledge*. This distinction was lost on me until I tried to tackle the project of writing this book. I guess I'm still not done learning new things.

Broadly, scientific knowledge is an *area* of knowledge, not a *way* of knowing. When I introduced my high school students to the nature of science, a branch of epistemology, I developed my own ways of knowing list. While my version closely resembled the International Baccalaureate's established list, I incorporated several modifications that I believed were erroneously omitted from their framework. (Sometimes I am too cocky for my own good.)

The reason that science is not on their list is because science is a unique process that requires *all* of the other ways of knowing. Science is not just memory, not just sense perception, not just logic, not just faith, but science employs a combination of all ways of knowing. The process of science, importantly, uses specific methods of inquiry that are designed to remove bias. Bias poses the greatest obstacle to the uncovering of empirical truths.

We can consider the "ways of knowing" in the same way we think of food groups: sensory is the grain, intuition is the meat, logic is the dairy, language or authority is the veggies, etc. In this analogy, faith is like the mixing bowl. We must have a mixing bowl to make anything. Faith in the idea that we can discover the truth. Faith that there are patterns in nature that follow rules. Faith that we can figure out these natural explanations for physical phenomena. Without this faith in these ideas, science cannot even begin.

To put science on the ways of knowing list is akin to putting pizza on a list of the major food groups. Pizza *is a food*, but it is *not a food group*. Pizza is a particular type of combination of foods that is delicious. Science is not just another way of knowing, but it is a specific combination of all the ways of knowing. It's a broad area that leads to a kind of knowledge that is more reliable than any individual way of knowing.

The various "recipes" for this knowledge pizza are analogous to the scientific methods we use. Notice "methods" is plural. There is not just one scientific method, just like there is not just one type of pizza. That said, the different methods for slightly different disciplines are subtle. The commonalities are more striking than the differences.

In addition to scientific, other areas of knowledge, like historical and mathematical, also use multiple ways of knowing. In general, the areas of knowledge are used for shared or collective knowledge, and the individual ways of knowing are used for our personal knowledge. I am sure the folks of International Baccalaureate will be very happy to know that they now have my seal of approval!

CHAPTER 6

The First Pizza of Empirical "Truth"

Who made the first pizza of shared empirical "truth"? Some say Aristotle. He is often called the father of science because he used sense perception to gather information about our world and logic to decipher it. The practice of testing our reasoning through observation marked the inception of empiricism. It makes some sense to call Aristotle the "father of science," but I don't. Empiricism in and of itself is not science. Also, the lag between Aristotle and the Age of Enlightenment was a little over 2,000 years. Maybe we could call him the great-grandpa of science?

Where were we? I got distracted. Oh yes, "the father of science" is not Aristotle . . .

I'm going to give the title of "father of science" to Galileo Galilei. I will argue that the first "truth pizza" was rightfully made by an Italian.

The reason I give the nod to Galileo is that he was the first person to assert that one could *apply* Aristotle's idea of using data from observations to get to a previously *unknown truth*. It is one thing to have an idea, and another to use it. Not only that, but he set the wheels in motion to replace a previously entrenched system for deciding what is "the truth."

If I am being perfectly honest, and I am, I personally believe that science has many fathers and a few mothers. Science did not appear one day fully formed, as if written on tablets that were handed down from the divine. Science is a human endeavor that came about through several paradigm shifts throughout human history. The process of science gradually evolved into the endeavor that we currently call scientific inquiry.

Kepler and Newton contributed by incorporating more mathematics into their model building to make those models better at predicting phenomena. In the early 1800s, statistical methods were devised to eliminate sources of bias from the analysis of datasets. I won't walk you through the entire history of bias removal (mostly because I don't know the complete history). I do, however, know enough to say that scientific inquiry evolved into the practice that it is today over a period of a few hundred years.

That said, for the sake of storytelling, it is easier to pretend one person was the was the "father of science." And Galileo's contribution to this process was certainly a game changer.

Many teachers and textbooks portray Galileo's major contribution as his claim that the Earth orbits the Sun, which challenged the prevailing beliefs of the Church at that time. Although that's true, it really misses the entire point. First of all, Copernicus was the first person to propose *that* idea. In fact, most history books refer to the proposal of the heliocentric theory (the idea that the Sun is the center of the solar system) as the "Copernican Revolution." Copernicus did have the idea; he did publish his idea in a book, but he offered zero evidence for it, died many years later, and almost *nothing* happened as a result. I would argue that he didn't cause much of a "revolution."

It wasn't until about one hundred years after the death of Copernicus that Galileo would *use evidence* to refute the idea that the *Sun* went around the *Earth*. Galileo did adopt Copernicus's idea, *but* had Copernicus not existed, Galileo would have come to the same truth, because that is where the data led him.

That is an important thing about truth, it is *independent* of the discoverer. To quote particle physicist Dr. Savos Dimopoulos, "I was drawn to science and mathematics, because here, truth does not depend on the eloquence of the speaker, truth is absolute."

In my worldview, fundamental empirical truths do exist. The *Earth* goes around the *Sun*. We know this truth. It is not an opinion. It is a

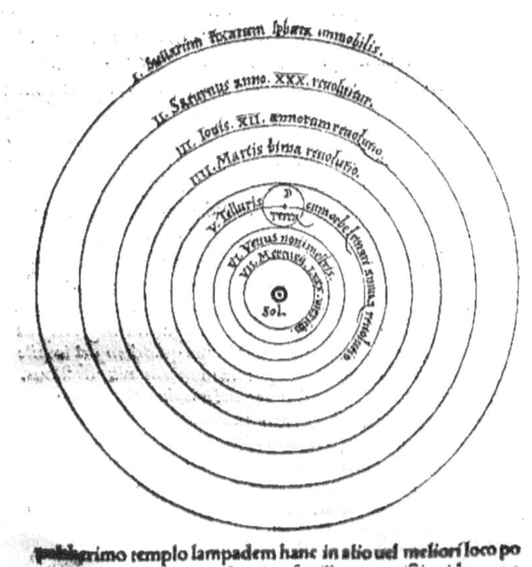

Copernicus's model of a heliocentric solar system. (From Wikimedia Commons.)

fact, or an objective truth. We know this fact, in part, because of Galileo. If Copernicus did not exist, this truth would still be true.

Copernicus is like Indiana Jones in the movie *Indiana Jones and the Raiders of the Lost Ark*. It seems like Indiana Jones is central to the story, but he really isn't. "If Jones doesn't exist, the Nazi's still get the Ark, they still open it, and their faces still melt, and then the Ark is still lost again." (Courtesy of Amy Farrah Fowler, on *The Big Bang Theory*.)

More than discovering the orbital relationship between the Sun and the Earth, it was Galileo that put forward a new attitude, a new philosophical stance. This new way of thinking paved the way for a new process—the new process of science. It had implications that were much more important than the mere discovery that the Earth went around the Sun. The "objective truth" that our Sun is a fixed point in our solar system doesn't really matter nearly as much as the new attitude. The idea that we, mere humans, can use a process to discover "objective truths" about the universe. The idea that the *universe has rules* and *that humans can discover them*, was a monumental attitude shift. It seems so obvious now, but remember, this was a *very new* idea.

The ancient Greeks thought that violent storms resulted from the anger of the gods. The Mayans and the Incas thought gods, not physical patterns and natural laws, controlled the rains and celestial objects in the sky. These views were prevalent worldwide. Even hundreds of years after the "Golden Age of Greece," The Holy Catholic Church, along with the rest of the world, felt that the heavenly bodies could, and did, move *however God wanted them to move*, so there was no point in trying to find or understand the patterns.

Galileo is important because he brought us these two new and important *attitudes*.

1. The universe obeys patterns that can be understood through simple observations and reason.
2. Empirical evidence is *more important than authority* when it comes to the discovery of "objective truths."

These two beliefs were critical to the birth of science as a new *type* of knowing. By the 1700s, monotheistic religions came to view God differently. God was now viewed as the master clock maker, but it was the job of humans to figure out how that clock worked. Understanding the universe was no longer viewed as a threat to religion. The 1700s began the period in human history known as "the Enlightenment."

So now you know a bit about why Galileo gets credit for the first truth pizza, but the entire story of Galileo is even more informative about the nature and history of science.

I believe if you are going to understand the relationship of different ways of knowing and areas of knowledge, you must understand the history of Galileo's last years on this Earth.

CHAPTER 7

The Story of Galileo

Many years after Copernicus died, Galileo and another guy, Kepler, noticed his work. (So I guess Copernicus is slightly more important than Indiana Jones.) In 1609, Galileo, a mathematician, heard of the invention of a telescope. He acquired some lenses, did some simple optics calculations, then ground and polished the lenses. He then built a telescope for his own use. He turned the scope to what was then referred to as "the heavens," and very quickly he made some important observations.

1. He could see the Moon wasn't a perfect circle, but it had mountains and valleys.
2. He saw that Jupiter had "things" next to it. He saw four of them. He then watched them for several weeks. He could see that these objects circled Jupiter. We now call these "things" moons.
3. He saw that Venus had phases, like our Moon. But watching Venus over the course of several months, he saw that unlike our Moon, the apparent size of the different phases changed dramatically. Venus appeared largest in the crescent phase and smallest in the gibbous phase.

The first two observations contradicted what was taught by the Catholic Church at the time. The Church, together with much of the global community, had accepted Aristotle's model, which illustrated that all celestial bodies orbit the Earth in perfect circles. This model

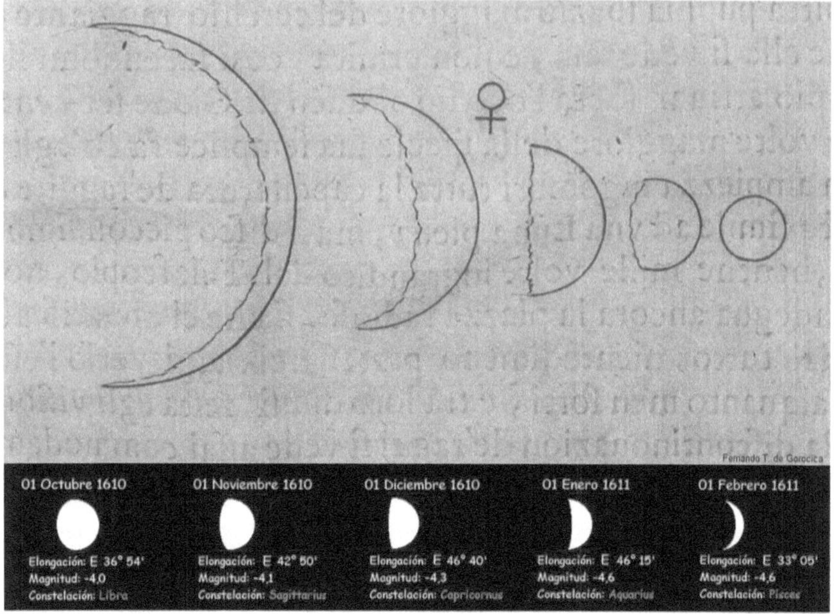

Galileo's sketches of the relative size and phases of Venus. This data refutes the idea that Venus orbits the Earth. Something that orbits the Earth in a perfect circle would not change in relative size. (From Wikimedia Commons.)

seemed to make sense since God, who created mankind as the pinnacle of his creation, would naturally place the Earth and mankind at the center of creation. This is a great example of how our belief systems impact our observations.

Aristotle, along with the Church (despite their lack of direct affiliation), maintained the belief that the heavens were perfect.

(Just a quick FYI, in case you don't have a good feel for historical time.) Adherence to Aristotle's conceptual model of "the Heavens" (350 BCE) was widespread well over 400 years before the Holy Catholic Church even existed, even longer if you define the official start of the Church with its split from Eastern Orthodox. Aristotle's model was later modified, and slightly improved in terms of predictive ability, by Ptolemy (150 CE, or if you are old school, AD), but I'm going to just call it Aristotle's model, to simplify.

The church viewed "the heavens" as the domain of God, and since God was perfect, it made logical sense that the heavens were perfect as well. In addition, Aristotle and many of the Greeks believed in the

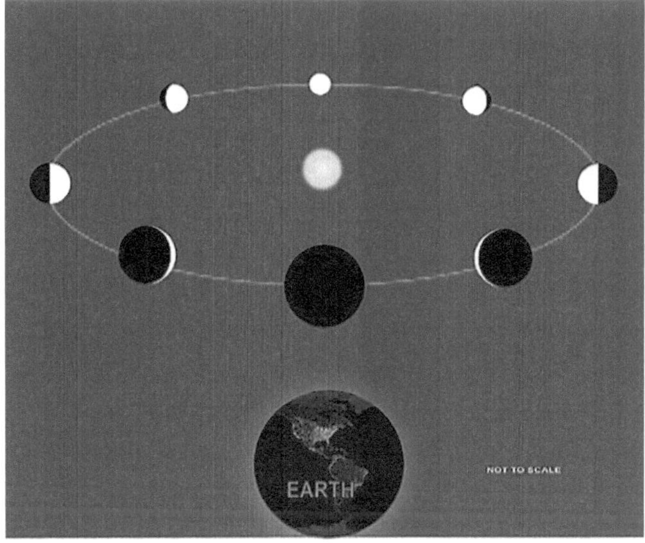

If Venus goes around the Earth, then its distance to the Earth does not change over time. However, if Venus goes around the Sun, then its distance to the Earth does in fact change. When it's closer to the Earth, it will appear larger and will be in the crescent phase; further from the Earth, it will appear smaller and its phase will be closer to full, or the gibbous phase.

perfection of the heavens for geometrical reasons. (The Greek thinkers loved their geometry.)

Galileo observed that the Moon was pitted with craters and mountains like the imperfections on the Earth. This went against the current thinking of perfection in the heavens. The observation of objects moving around Jupiter conflicted with the official doctrine that everything specifically revolved around the Earth.

Galileo's third observation was the most problematic. Why was the apparent size of Venus changing as the phases changed? If Venus went around the Earth in a perfect circle, then this observation made no sense. The distance between the Earth and Venus should not change. If there is no change in distance, then why such a *drastic* change in the apparent size of Venus? The Moon doesn't change size when its phases change.[3]

If Venus orbits the Earth, its relative size should not change. But

---

3. Technically, the Moon occasionally appears *slightly* larger since it, like all satellites, has an elliptical orbit. So occasionally it is slightly closer to the Earth. Thus, the occasionally slightly larger "supermoon."

if Venus goes around the Sun, the *apparent* sizes of Venus *would* need to change, because the distance between Venus and the Earth dramatically changes. If something is farther away, it looks smaller. And, of course, that's what Galileo saw. His observations were a 100 percent match to what would be expected if the model of a Sun-centered solar system was correct.

The three bits of data that Galileo gathered through his little telescope were all *compatible* with Copernicus's Sun-centered model. And more importantly, his ideas were *incompatible* with Aristotle and the Church's Earth-centered model of "the heavens."

In 1610, Galileo released his book, *The Starry Messenger*, in which he presented evidence supporting the heliocentric model and detailed how it disproved the geocentric (Earth-centered) theory.

This was a bold move by Galileo. Just ten years prior, in 1600, an astronomer named Giordano Bruno was burnt at the stake for making the same claim in the nearby city of Rome. (Public stake burnings were more common back then; the Catholic Church is much more mellow these days.)

Why wasn't Galileo burnt at the stake? Throughout human history, justice has always treated the rich and famous with more generosity than the poor and less famous. It also helped that Galileo was friends with Pope Urban VIII. In the early 1600s, a mini-renaissance was happening across Europe. Against this backdrop, Pope Urban VIII desired to be known for a "more enlightened" papacy. He and Galileo even had conversations about this. Galileo was wealthy and had powerful friends, so he got special treatment.

That said, Urban VIII was not thrilled with Galileo's book. *The Starry Messenger* was an affront to the teachings of the Church. But support of the heliocentric model over the geocentric model wasn't what bothered Pope Urban VIII the most. His annoyance stemmed from the fact that Galileo used his observational data and logic to show the veracity of his claims. History books often missed this subtle point. Galileo used a new combination of ways of knowing, to challenge the assumptions given to us by authority—in this case, the Church. The new process of science challenged the authority of the Church as the sole way that we can acquire knowledge for physical and testable questions.

So here is the important part: In 1610, *all natural phenomena were explained by the Church*. Science did not yet exist. In Pope Urban's mind, human-created proof denied faith. Not only did Galileo's book teach something different than the Church, but his process of *evidence gathering*, coupled with *logic and reason* was being used to refute the Church's adopted model of the view of the universe. In Urban's mind, this *new process* undermined the authority of the Church and was therefore a threat.

Galileo, luckily, was only verbally reprimanded and told not to write on this topic again. However, Galileo's book began to cause a bit of a stir as it became popular. So, in 1616, six years after its publication, the Church formally banned *The Starry Messenger*. Galileo was issued a formal injunction, which officially forbade him from writing or promoting the Copernican heliocentric view of the universe.

The Church also *now banned* Copernicus's one-hundred-year-old book. (Again, no one cared about Copernicus until Galileo came along.)

The faith and authority of the Church was colliding with a new way of knowing. Even in its infancy, science showed itself to be a plausible alternative to authority and faith as a way of knowing. This marks the start of a paradigm shift.

The debate *on the surface* was between the heliocentric (Sun-centered) and geocentric (Earth-centered) models of planetary motion. But the real issue, the core of the debate, was this: What is the best method to get to objective truth? Is it the process of science, the new pizza? Or is it faith, the mixing bowl—which was filled with a big dose of papal authority?

So imagine this scenario: You are having an argument with someone. It could be a spouse, a boss, or a coworker. You know you're right. You are certain of it, and as you are making your best points, you are asked to just drop it. It just kind of eats at you. This is where Galileo found himself. It was an itch he could not scratch. He desperately wanted the injunction of discussing the Copernican view to be lifted. He would love to write about the topic again.

The Pope and Galileo talked past each other with different arguments. The Pope argued against Galileo's assertion of proof. The Pope was threatened by the process of science. Galileo, on the other hand, focused on the particular question of whether our solar system was heliocentric or geocentric.

During this period, Galileo still had a friendship with the Pope, albeit more strained. They still spoke. The Pope explained to him the dangers of claiming proof. Galileo argued that the Church was losing credibility by not allowing an open discussion. The Pope eventually decided to compromise. He told Galileo that he may discuss the ideas, but only "hypothetically," without evidence or claims of proof.

In Galileo's mind, this was an opening, but it was also a problem. How do you write about your seemingly correct claim without your evidence? How do you convince people of something—hypothetically?

What he did was both genius and stupid. He wrote a book that had three fictional characters in a debate. Two debated the evidence, and the third character weighed the evidence but did not come to any conclusion.

It was brilliant, because the evidence could be offered hypothetically and without a conclusion. However, to think he could pull this off without putting his life at risk, well, that was stupid.

He titled his second book, *Dialogue Concerning the Two Chief World Systems*. Galileo printed it in 1632, sixteen years after the injunction. However, during those sixteen years, the political climate had changed. Catholicism faced challenges from protestant countries to the north. The "mini-renaissance" of the late 1500s was fading, so many in the Church felt a need to push back on any challenges to its authority.

To make matters worse for himself, Galileo gave the character who supported the Church's Earth-centered model a dull voice, and the person who offered the Copernican, or Sun-centered, point of view an articulate voice. This made perfect sense from a literary point of view, but this made no sense from a "don't piss off the Pope" point of view. Furthermore, most scholarly texts of the day were published in Latin. Galileo published his new book in Italian, which brought his case directly to the people.

Pope Urban VIII was not amused. He viewed Galileo's book as a political and personal betrayal. Galileo was arrested and stood trial. (The trial is portrayed in an excellent docudrama entitled "Reach for the Stars" on the BBC series *Days That Shook the World*.)

Galileo's trial was really a show trial. The Church did allow Galileo a lawyer. Galileo also broke no laws in the writing of his book. To prosecute Galileo, the court really needed a confession of heresy, but Galileo did not confess.

Galileo was old and not feeling well after months of imprisonment. When the prosecution had hit legal dead ends against Galileo, the Pope authorized torture as the next step.

Okay, now for the big payoff: Galileo folded and retracted his claims and said that "the Earth, not the Sun, was the center of the universe." *Religious authority and faith were shown to be the superior ways of knowing in all things!*

The end!

Wait, what?

You might be thinking, *But wait, that's not how that story ends. You left out the feel-good Hollywood ending.* Yes, I left it out because it did not exist.

Galileo was imprisoned for the last ten years of his life as he gradually went blind and died alone. Galileo's "truth" was, in fact, defeated by the Pope's authority and faith. "The father of science" died defeated. The process of science lost. The Church "proved" that the Sun is not at the center of our solar system after all.

That ending bothers us because we know Galileo was right! We know the "truth." It upsets our sense of truth and justice. It is an upsetting story.

Often, an apparent defeat paves the way for future victories. While that statement doesn't lessen the personal tragedy of Galileo's persecution, it can give us some comfort when the world seems to be punishing the heroes and rewarding the villains.

Galileo's loss contributed to a growing recognition that authority and faith were less effective than empirical methods for answering testable questions. The world came to understand that the best way to understand a phenomenon was to gather evidence and then to try to refute possible competing explanations. This area of knowledge would later be called scientific inquiry.

The assertion that all celestial bodies possessed "perfect" geometric forms and that everything orbited the Sun was ultimately disproven by empirical evidence. No one needed faith or authority to see these facts. These are simply empirical truths.

Was Galileo's model perfect? No, it was not. In science, it's not only acceptable but downright encouraged to change a model as you get more data. The tentative nature of science is one of its strengths. Galileo's model was not proven, but the Church's model was refuted. It did not really matter if the Church's authority accepted this truth, it was an objective truth.

In my opinion, the switch to science, as a new way to understand physical and testable questions, begins with *The Starry Messenger* and *The Dialogue*. Yes, Galileo's "truth" was outlawed. But the Church's banning of Galileo's new insights did not alter their validity.

The scientific process that Galileo used was in its simplest form. The process of science gradually evolved to become a better and better way of knowing. Trust in science as a way of knowing began to improve as the process improved. The resulting paradigm shift took time.

The historical period referred to as "the Enlightenment" is generally considered to begin around the year 1700. The term "scientist" wasn't even coined until 1834 by William Whewell, 202 years after *The Dialogue* was published. In the early 1800s, bias removing standards for the practice of science were formally laid out. The following century would see a science-caused societal transformation on a scale that is difficult to fathom.

CHAPTER 8

The Nature of Science

In the Fall of 2020, I asked a group of ninth-grade students how they defined science. Most of them responded by describing topics: study of biology, chemistry, geology, medicine, engineering, etc. Others described science as just a long list of facts discovered by scientists. One student defined science as "an alternative to religion to explain things."

I loved this answer because it was such a great starting point for a conversation about what makes science different from other ways that we gain knowledge about our world.

The relationship between science and religious belief is complex to be sure. Four hundred years ago, Galileo and the Pope could not resolve their issues. The friction between religion and science festered for hundreds of years. In some religions and or denominations, this feud it is still festering. (FYI: On October 31, 1992, Pope John Paul II admitted that the Catholic Church mistreated Galileo and formally apologized for his persecution.)

One of my goals with this book is to resolve some of the misconceptions that plague discussions about science and religion. First, it's important to define the precise terminology found within scientific fields. It is difficult to discuss any topic unless we have a common, agreed-upon language.

Language of Science

Sometimes words mean different things in different contexts. For example: "Lit" could be the past tense of to set fire, "lit" can mean drunk, "lit" can be slang meaning awesome, "lit" can even be an abbreviation for literature. Context matters. When I hear millennials saying things like, "That is so fire!" or "He is so lit!" it takes me a moment, or three, to figure out what they are saying.

Language is critical to understanding the nature of science. Some words have very specific meanings in a *scientific* context. To add to the confusion, these same words often have different meanings outside the scientific context.

This tiny section includes a list of a few important definitions. I almost feel like I need to apologize for including a list of definitions, but people misuse these words so often that their misuse interferes with our understanding of the larger concepts. I want to ensure that we possess a common language before we explore the nature of science further.

Science: A process crafted over the last several centuries to remove bias and refute hypotheses regarding physical, testable phenomena.

Theory: A grand unifying explanation that can tie several different scientific concepts together. In some cases, scientific theories help explain the scientific laws. To become a theory, the explanation must be supported by the available evidence—gathered in a way designed to reduce bias. It must also not be refuted by any evidence also gathered in a way designed to reduce bias.

Hypothesis: A possible explanation of some phenomena.

Laws: Universal relationships between variables under certain conditions.

I want you to notice that a theory is *not* just a guess in this context. Theories are *unifying explanations*. A hypothesis is not a *prediction*. Scientific laws are very limited. This is not always the way that people think about these terms. We'll come back to these terms later, but at the very least I wanted to introduce them.

Educational research says a person needs to hear a new term an average of sixteen times before it enters their vocabulary. I will not come back to this sixteen times; I will just assume you are well above average.

Limitations of Science

The best path to understanding the nature of science starts with explicitly understanding its limits.

The process of science can only answer certain types of questions. Questions such as which song or movie is the best, cannot be tested. Similarly, questions regarding the nonexistence of anything cannot be tested.

In addition, ethics and many matters of faith are not testable through the methods of science. That does not mean that we cannot *know* right from wrong, but science is of no use to us in this endeavor. We use other ways of knowing—such as intuition, emotion, even imagination (which helps with empathy)—to help us decide right from wrong in matters of ethics. Logic and reason are also helpful in ethical arguments.

Science cannot tell us right from wrong, but we can use information gathered through the process of science to help us understand the realities around an issue. Just because science does not speak to ethics, *does not* imply that science is not ethical.

In addition to ethics, science also can't study the supernatural. Science is limited to *physical, natural* phenomena. This doesn't mean that scientists cannot be religious or even believe in ghosts. Many scientists are Hindu, Muslim, Christian, etc. However, when scientists study natural phenomena, they don't accept the first supernatural explanation they come to. That would stop a lot of inquiry (and for most of human history, it *did* stop *most* inquiry). When a scientist—or a layperson who understands science—hears a bump in the night, they first eliminate all the physical, non-supernatural causes.

Speaking of ghosts, a few years back, another high school student asked me if I believed in ghosts. (I've been asked this question more than once. I gradually learned to respond to this question with some clarifying questions.)

I responded, "Are you asking what does the established canon of science think about ghosts? Or what do I personally think about the likelihood of ghosts?" I then followed up with, "The enterprise of science doesn't think much about the topic of ghosts as they are not physical phenomena. But if you are just asking me what I believe, I don't believe in ghosts." Then I would add, "I am uncertain about my claim. It is not a fact. It is just my personal belief—and my justification for my belief is not that strong."

I tried to make several points with that very disciplined and, admittedly, oddly specific answer. I attempted to point out the type of questions that science can and can't address. I attempted to point out the differences between belief and testable empirical knowledge. Thirdly, I tried to avoid endorsing, or belittling, a belief that I do not hold. Lastly, I want to role model uncertainty when there is a lack of evidence or when a question is not testable.

I think it would help people understand the nature of science if more scientists and science teachers would be somewhat ridiculously specific about the limitations of science. Saying that ghosts are not real, and pretending that this opinion is a science fact, is off-putting—especially if the person you are talking to happens to believe in ghosts. More importantly, when scientists or science teachers take a scientific stand on non-testable, non-physical phenomena, they are misrepresenting the nature of science.

Methods of Science

It is a common practice to teach the scientific method as follows. We begin with a hypothesis, and then we design an experiment to test that hypothesis. A good experiment compares two sets of data where only one variable is changed. Then we repeat the experiment many times to ensure that the results were not due to chance. That is a pretty good description. If you had a good teacher, that is likely how you were taught. But that is not how science is *always* done.

Throughout my time as a science teacher—frequently in rural schools—I taught a wide array of subjects, including geology, astronomy, physics, chemistry, environmental science, biology, and research methods. If college-level teaching is thrown into the mix, I also taught human biology, ecology, and evolution. Most scientists are specialists, whereas I have taught and studied science from the vantage point of multiple disciplines. I can tell you that the "method" that is broadly referred to as the scientific method, is not just one method. "Scientific method" should be plural. Teachers often teach that there is just *one* scientific method, so as not to complicate things. I think that is appropriate when teaching in the younger grades. But, according to the National Science Teacher Association guidelines and the Next Generation Science Standards, before students leave high school, they should understand that scientists can use many variations of a scientific method.

Sometimes we collect data first, and *then* we come up with a hypothesis. Sometimes we have difficulty controlling variables. (Galileo could not tweak Venus's orbit to see what would happen, for example. There could be no changing of variables there.) Sometimes the replication of an entire experiment is difficult (particularly in medical research), so we compensate by enrolling multiple participants in a single experiment to help us statistically validate the results from just one trial. In this case, each participant acts as a separate trial within that one experiment. There are several other variations on this theme.

No matter what scientific method researchers use, the way the data is gathered and analyzed must meet some rigorous, bias removing, systematic methodology. The aim is to always strive to remove personal bias in the process. Controlling variables helps to remove bias, while statistical analysis of the data to ensure results are not due to chance also helps. Other steps might include conducting multiple trials or the offering of a placebo to ensure there is no "placebo effect" in a clinical trial of a treatment.

Only after that is done can the researchers now invite other scientists to prove them wrong by reviewing the experiment and analysis of data. Those reviewers must also adhere to systems that are designed to remove *their* own personal biases.

In science, researchers set out "to disconfirm" the explanation of the phenomena we are testing. To *disconfirm* might seem like a weird approach, but it is the only way science can effectively operate. Researchers don't seek to *prove*; they seek to *disconfirm*. It is a last man standing situation. The idea that cannot be disconfirmed wins.

In the language of science, researchers are attempting to *refute* a *hypothesis*. Scientists work to disprove their ideas and the ideas of others. This process is an important and unique way that we, as a society, can get to an empirical truth. Thomas Huxley wrote that science is a discipline where "beautiful hypotheses are slayed by ugly facts."

Many, especially outside the discipline of science, are under the false impression that scientists aim to prove their ideas. Rather, scientists seek to disprove their ideas. It takes a long time and lots of hypothesis killing before something emerges as the idea that cannot be refuted. Therefore, it takes a long time for knowledge to enter the canon of what we collectively call "scientific knowledge." I feel that the importance of understanding the methods and the language of science cannot be overstated.

I have talking about the *area* of knowledge called science, but notice how much I use other ways of knowing like intuition, language, and even imagination when I try to communicate ideas.

Strengths of Science

Precisely because of its methods, science is a vast improvement on any of the individual ways of knowing. From Galileo (1630) through the "Age of the Enlightenment," roughly the late 1600s to early 1800s, science has evolved.

All of what we know and understand about the physical world is a direct result of the gradual human invention of the process of science. Engineering applies the empirical knowledge obtained through the process of science to solve problems. Engineering, in turn, produces technologies. The industrial revolution early (1900s), the atomic age (mid-1900s), and the revolution in biotechnology (1950s) all stem from the invention of the methods of science.

Forget engineering and technology for a moment and just marvel at what we have recently come to understand just in the last one hundred years. We, as a collective group of humans, now accurately understand atoms, the movements of our solar system and galaxies. We understand our circulatory systems, endocrinology, and our immune systems; protons and neutrons down to the levels of the quarks, leptons, and bosons; the molecular basis for cancer, diabetes, HIV, cardiovascular disease, and some mental illness. We understand our own DNA, and how it codes for proteins. We have figured out how to get clean energy from splitting atoms. We understand thousands of interspecies relationships within ecosystems. We have figured out how honeybees communicate and make decisions. I could go on and on. This is just a smattering of a smidgen of what science has revealed about natural phenomena.

While I was sitting in a coffee shop correcting physics papers, I overheard some young college aged kid blathering on and on about how scientists don't know what they are talking about. It took lots of self-restraint to suppress the urge to get involved in an argument with a stranger. The irony of comfortable, well-fed people, with access to remarkable health care on their wireless laptop computers and smart phones, shouting from a soapbox about the evils of science was almost unbearable. Science, and its offspring, engineering and technology, have profoundly impacted the world in a positive way.

CHAPTER 9

Misconceptions about Science

Oddly, some non-scientists often portray the work of scientists completely backward. They are portrayed as a group working together as some part of a biased agenda, collaborating to prove something. Some politicians and pundits refer to climate change, for example, as "yet another example of science promoting biased propaganda." That sentence sounds very strange if you know something about the nature of scientific inquiry.

Science is a special process that has many safeguards used to eliminate all possible biases. "Biased and science" go together about as well as grapefruit juice and freshly brushed teeth.

Mistrust in science has been around since its inception. I will talk about the origins (circa 1920) of American mistrust in science in a later chapter. Recently, mistrust in science has gotten more complicated—and dangerous.

Frontier Science vs. Established Science

Some of the mistrust in science comes from deliberate political tactics, but much of it is far less nefarious. A lack of a distinction between two overlapping categories of science—frontier science and established science—is partially responsible for this mistrust. I recently watched an interview with Dr. Neil deGrasse Tyson where he made the distinction between these two categories of science. I have always known about this difference, but I had never heard anyone explicitly make a distinction between the two—and I think it's important.

Frontier science refers to research currently underway, emerging concepts awaiting review, or newly published discoveries. Established science, by contrast, pertains to theories or explanations that have remained unchallenged by credible refutation for extended periods, often spanning decades or centuries. These include ideas such as Newton's laws of motion, or the Earth is a sphere, or the Sun is at the center of our solar system, or the gravitational theory. I concede that all science, even established science, is technically always tentative, but overturning of established science is far less likely than the overturning of frontier science.

Part of the process of doing science involves the tentative findings reported as frontier science. Unfortunately, these tentative findings can and do frequently change.

Let me give a specific example. When non-scientists hear a journalist say, "*Scientists think that* small amounts of alcohol are good for you," and then weeks or months later they hear, "Scientists *now* think that *any* alcohol may increase risk of cancer," the non-scientists are left confused. One possible conclusion is that "the scientists" keep changing their minds because they don't know what they are talking about! This situation feeds the mistrust of *all* science.

Another obvious problem with the phrase "scientists *think* that. . ." is that it puts scientists as the main part of the discussion. What an individual scientist thinks or believes does not matter. They are a relatively unimportant part of the discussion. A better way to report the finding is with the phrase, "evidence shows that . . ." It is a subtle, but important, difference. Furthermore, "scientists *think* that . . ." gives the incorrect impression that scientists are a like-minded group working to prove something. Those in the media, not familiar with the language of science, sometimes use language that inadvertently causes distrust in science.

Let me give you another example of problematic reporting of frontier science. In the early days of the COVID crisis, we first heard about washing your groceries, then we heard that COVID was mostly airborne, and then that it only entered our bodies through the nasal cavity. Later we were told to wear face shields; that they are better than masks. Later, the message was that face shields provided less protection, or that the cheap masks are not really doing anything, you need the N95. All of these are examples of reporting of frontier science. But these conflicting messages made many people think that scientists did not have a clue. This conclusion was even more likely for those who did not respect the process of science to begin with.

Others reacted to this frontier science in the opposite way. They hung on every headline, and they were in a constant state of fear. This group expressed frustration toward people who did not "accept the science," even though that science was only at a preliminary stage. Researchers tested many hypotheses, and most of them turned out to be wrong. This, quite frankly, is business as usual in science. But because people were dying, and hospitals were full, the science was being watched closely by people who didn't normally watch the process unfold. The drama took on a life of its own.

These two groups, both with misconceptions about science, were at each other's throats. The misconceptions about science itself, specifically about the difference between the canon of scientific knowledge and frontier science, made it difficult to have a calm public discourse.

In addition, individuals held different beliefs and values. What seemed like an argument about science had, at its core, an argument about risk tolerance, about imposing risk on others, or imposing your feelings of risk tolerance on others. This was also a discussion about public good vs. personal rights. It is very hard to have a discussion when we cannot even agree about what we are discussing. People were talking *past* each other, not *to* each other.

Combine that confusion with the nasty people who like to throw gasoline on divisive fires for their own personal gain and you get a real mess. The mess caused an even deeper political division in our country, and even less trust in science as a process.

While frontier science is a legitimate part of actual science, its findings do not have the same credibility that you will find in established science. When we conflate frontier science with established science, it diminishes the credibility of the canon of knowledge that we have obtained from established science. "Newton's laws state that . . ." is different from "A new study shows that . . ."

The actual process of science moves at a snail's pace. To the untrained eye, it seems like scientists cannot make up their minds, therefore, some people jump to the conclusion that scientists don't know what they are talking about. Or, worse yet, that they are a group of political pawns.

Post COVID, particularly in America, there was a growing sense that we needed to just tune out the "noise" and rely on our personal knowledge. That we should trust our intuition, our faith, our emotions. It was almost as if people were saying, "Do what our gut tells us we should do. Never mind what the science says!"

Those who find the actual scientific facts to be at odds with their own personal agendas exploit the public confusion regarding the scientific process confusion. Certain political or religious groups that do not hold "established science" in high regard in the first place were the first to be exploited (or be manipulated by) the lack of clarity regarding the "frontier science" during the pandemic.

At this point, it is worth noting that science, as a process, was heroic. Using the process of science, we developed a reasonable understanding of COVID-19 virus in less than a year. Scientists created and tested vaccines in just a little over a year. That's remarkable.

But the reporting of COVID science, coupled with people's misunderstanding of that reporting, caused mistrust in the very process that saved hundreds of *thousands* of lives. Misunderstanding and mistrust in science—in this specific case, refusal to get vaccinated—likely resulted in almost as many deaths as the vaccines prevented. Understanding the nature of science has real-world implications.

The Human Element in the Process of Science

Another limitation of science is that science is done by humans, and humans are fallible. Failures of individuals, including scientists, will inevitably occur in any human endeavor. It is important to remember that the failure of a scientist is not the failure of the process of science.

Occasionally, some scientists think they are experts in areas that are *outside their fields of study*. Of course, scientists are entitled to their opinions, but outside their field of study, they have no more authority than non-scientists. As an example, I will once again turn to the topic of bigfoot.

CHAPTER 10

Scientists and the Sasquatch

Dr. Neil deGrasse Tyson, famous astrophysicist and excellent science communicator, describes belief in the sasquatch as "untenable." He puts the "belief in bigfoot" in the realm of "pseudoscience."

The most famous primatologist in the world, arguably, was Dr. Jane Goodall. On NPR's *Talk of the Nation / Science Friday* in 2002, she commented on the sasquatch saying, "Well now you will be amazed when I tell you I am sure they exist..." She went on to explain her logic based on discussions she had with aboriginal peoples about their accounts of seeing sasquatch.

Another excellent scientist, Dr. George Schaller, was the world authority on mountain gorillas. He says regarding sasquatch, "I am neither a believer nor can I reject all the evidence and conclude that an apelike being does not exist. Large, unrecognized creatures may still roam remote forests. The question of existence remains open."

I mention the *opinions* of Dr. Schaller, Dr. Goodall, and Dr. Tyson to make a subtle point about the expertise of scientists. Expertise in science does not transfer from topic to topic. PhDs are experts because they focus on an area. Good scientists have excellent analytical skills. I am sure there is a temptation for them to speak on any topic as if they have some expertise. (I'm not even a PhD scientist, and here I am writing a book about bigfoot, God, the nature of science, evolution, and epistemic responsibility, so I understand the temptation to assume you have some expertise beyond your field of study.) All I'm saying is that when it comes to bigfoot, I would rather hear from a large primate field biologist than an astrophysicist. Dr. Tyson is a genius, an excellent astronomer, and certainly has a right to any opinion he may hold. But when he speaks about sasquatch, his expertise no longer applies.

That said, just because Dr. Jane Goodall was convinced, doesn't mean you have to be. She was stating her opinion, which is fine. But as a primatologist, her opinion carries more weight than Dr. Tyson on this topic. But she was still just a scientist stating a belief, not a scientist stating a scientific fact. Schaller states uncertainly. Still, this is just his opinion. But again, because of his work with large, recently discovered primates, his opinion has some credibility. Regarding black holes, I would defer to Dr. Tyson over Goodall or Schaller.

To the credit of all three of these scientists, they all express that they are not relaying *scientific facts*. They all say they are stating their "belief" or "an opinion." The public, and some scientists, need to understand that just because a scientist gives an opinion, does not mean that it is a scientific fact. We especially need to understand that scientists speaking on topics outside their field of expertise, are in no way speaking for the scientific community.

CHAPTER 11

Three Men and a Sasquatch.

Grover, Jeff, and Paul

Grover Krantz was an anthropologist at Washington State University and was the first academic in the US to openly give serious consideration to the bigfoot phenomenon. His interest in the topic started in 1963, and after almost thirty years of study, he published his book, *Big Footprints*, in 1992—revised and reprinted as *Bigfoot Sasquatch Evidence* in 1999. Grover's work was not well-received by his peers. According to Grover, "My university supports my research on the sasquatch, they don't fire me."

Dr. Jeff Meldrum was an anatomist and a physical anthropologist who studied the evolution of bipedal locomotion at Idaho State University and was a well-respected academic in his field. (Dr. Meldrum passed away recently, in September of 2025.) Dr. Meldrum was one of the few academics who seriously considered the potential existence of bigfoot.

Dr. Meldrum's understanding of evolution, the nature of science, and bigfoot made him an obvious person for me to contact as I embarked on the journey of writing this book. I sent him an email, and he graciously agreed on a time to converse.

Our conversation began as you might expect, with me asking him about how he got interested in the topic of bigfoot. His story follows:

One fateful day in early of 1996, Dr. Meldrum and his brother drove from Boise, Idaho, to the neighboring state of Washington to visit fellow anthropologist Grover Krantz. He had recently investigated a video shot in Northern California that may have captured a bigfoot. This video investigation rekindled his youthful, but latent, interest in the subject of bigfoot. Dr. Meldrum was not a bigfoot believer, nor had he ruled out the possibility of its existence. But, just like any scientist worth their salt, he was curious.

When Jeff and his brother arrived at Krantz's lab, they were both intrigued by Dr. Krantz's collection of plaster casts and his interpretations of the foot anatomy of those casts. On their way back to Boise, the brothers thought, why not drop in on Paul Freeman, the very person who had made several of the casts they had just examined. Paul Freeman lived in Walla Walla, Washington. After all, his home was right on their way home. I want to note that their visit was an unannounced, impromptu, drop-in.[4]

When they arrived at the door, they lucked out and found Freeman at his home. After some introductions and pleasantries, he invited them inside for a visit. They began talking about the circumstances of the casts that Jeff and his brother examined early that day in Dr. Krantz's lab. Freeman then revealed that he, earlier that day, found some newish big footprints in the mud! Freeman offered to show the Meldrum's those tracks if they had time. The Meldrum brothers were caught a little off guard. (It is important to repeat that this was an unannounced, impromptu, drop-in.) Nevertheless, this coincidence seemed suspect. But, since they were already there, they really wanted to go have a look for themselves.

So within hours of deciding to visit Paul Freeman, Jeff and his brother now stood on a farm access road, looking at a long set of tracks in the mud near Walla Walla, Washington.

---

4.   I don't want to devote too much time to discussing Paul Freeman here as it would slow this narrative, but I will put some info about Paul Freeman in Appendix C. One could, and someone has, written an entire book just about Freeman!

It seemed very unlikely that Paul Freeman hoaxed this for a variety of reasons. Could it be that that they were looking at actual bigfoot tracks? Could Dr. Meldrum just ignore this evidence?

Here I interrupted Dr. Meldrum's story to ask, "I remember reading that Grover got some flak from the scientific community for looking into the bigfoot phenomenon. Have you received any backlash?"

Dr. Meldrum laughed and said, "Most definitely."

He explained that Dr. Krantz warned him. Krantz said that people's opinions on this topic are stronger than you can imagine. Even exploring this could get you into hot water with your colleagues.

Dr. Meldrum, if not naïve, was perhaps overly idealistic about the integrity of some of his fellow scientists. He recalled thinking something like, "Sure, it happened to Grover, but I don't think that would be much of a problem for me."

It was no longer the mid-sixties after all; surely people had mellowed out regarding the study of sasquatch. So, although he heard the warning, he wasn't too worried. In addition, at that point in time, while talking to Grover, he wasn't even sure this bigfoot topic was worth his time.

Back to Meldrum's story.

As Meldrum stood on the muddy road staring at the tracks, Meldrum explained, "it was like I had two imps on my shoulders, one warning me about my career, saying that the mere study of this might turn him into a laughingstock. The other imp was cultivating my curiosity. How can you be interested in hominins and bipedal evolution and not even look at this? The tracks are in the mud right in front of your face. You cannot simply ignore this."[5]

The "imp of curiosity" won. Soon after, Dr. Meldrum decided that looking into the bigfoot mystery would become part of his hominin research. It quickly became clear that Grover Krantz's warnings were not overblown.

---

5. The story doesn't really end here. After the Meldrums and Paul say their goodbyes, the Meldrums didn't leave. Instead, they headed into town to the hardware store to get some plaster of Paris and return to the site to make casts and look around more. They found another set of tracks that went through a drainage ditch that Paul seemed to be unaware of. It was dark before they finally left and headed back to Boise.

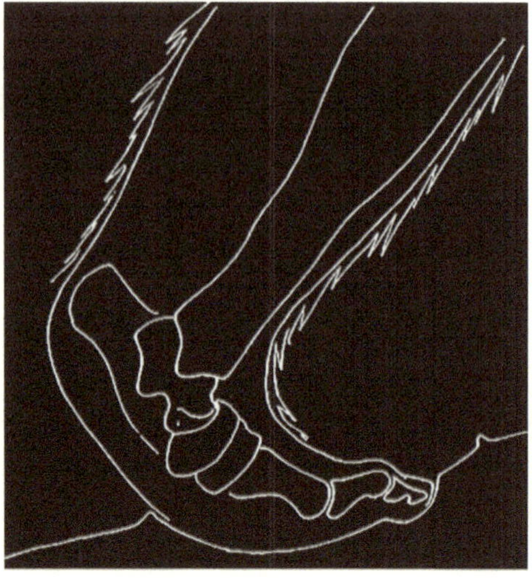

Jeff's photo of a half-of-a-track from the trackway shown to him by Paul Freeman. This track is a the front part of the foot with toe slide. Whatever made the track, apparently slipped a bit as it went up steep incline. The illustration shows how a flexible mid-tarsal break would result in this half track. Earlier in the trackway, the tracks were all full tracks. (Courtesy of Jeff Meldrum.)

A few colleagues within his own department—and curiously some colleagues from other departments with no expertise in any life science field at all—became extremely critical of Dr. Meldrum for looking into this phenomenon. He was denied travel money to conferences; his tenure and promotion reviews were sabotaged by his critics on various committees.

Political infighting in university departments is not terribly unique. However, this situation differed somewhat, as individuals contended that *the subject of study* was not acceptable. They weren't attacking his research; they were censoring his choice of inquiry. They refused to even accept the possibility that sasquatch might be real. Dr. Meldrum did achieve tenure and promotion to full professorship, but his public acknowledgment that he had an interest in the bigfoot phenomenon was definitely a hinderance.

So why do some otherwise perfectly logical people in the scientific community find the study of bigfoot so objectionable? (Dr. Meldrum has some ideas about why he met resistance. I will share his ideas in the chapter "Human Evolution.")

Science as Societal Immune System

I use the following analogy to help me explain the objection to certain subjects of inquiry. For this analogy, I think of human societies as superorganisms. Don't think of people as individual people; instead, think of entire cultures as individual organisms—a superorganism if you will. Different people have different roles within these superorganisms, but the culture itself lives or dies because of how the culture of a particular society functions.

In some cultures, a bullshit detector gradually evolved. In this analogy, the methods of science act as the bullshit detector. The way science functions within a culture is analogous to an organism's immune system. Science protects those cultures from ridiculous practices like burning witches or drilling holes in people's heads to let the demons out. Science helps cultures find empirical truths to help people make good decisions and to hold a similar view of reality. Just as an individual's immune system protects them from bacteria and even more insidious viruses, science protects societies from pseudoscience in its various forms. So science (the bullshit detector) is analogous to the immune system of a developed culture.

Occasionally, an individual's immune system finds *itself* under attack. AIDS and cancers, like Leukemia, for example, target the very cells that allow our immune system to function. In the same way, there are also certain people who attack science itself. They attack science because people knowing the "truth" is not always in *the attacker's* best interests. Charlatans promoting pseudoscience to discredit real science present a very real problem in modern societies. Scientists need to diligently fight off these charlatans.

Hyper-vigilance can be a good thing, but it can also be taken too far. Our own immune systems sometimes overreact to non-threats like a little bit of pollen or a little peanut protein. We call this overreaction an allergic reaction. A different but similar problem occurs when our immune system sometime freaks out and attack our own cells! For example, in the case of rheumatoid arthritis, a person's healthy synovial cells get attacked by their own immune system.

In much the same way, in advanced cultures, science itself is on a hair trigger to defend itself. And occasionally, this very sensitive trigger goes haywire. The scientific establishment attacks its own (other scientists), perceiving a pseudoscience threat where there is no pseudoscience threat at all. Often, this attack comes from scientists outside the field in question. This "autoimmune response" damages the integrity of scientific endeavors as it results in the censorship of inquiry into any area that could be *perceived* as pseudoscience. Some scientists can misidentify their own colleges as a threat because of their choice of inquiry. I'd argue, and I am arguing, that pseudoscience is not defined by what is studied. *Poor methodology* is what differentiates real science from pseudoscience.

In 2023, Katalin Karikó won the Nobel Prize in Medicine alongside Drew Weissman for their research that led to the development of mRNA COVID-19 vaccines. Only eight years prior, in 1995, Karikó had been demoted with a pay cut, partially because her mRNA research was deemed "unlikely to go anywhere" and, importantly, "did not attract enough grant funding."

In the highly competitive world of science, *scientists* who don't understand the *nature of science* are occasionally the worst enemies of the process of science. They can end up suppressing legitimate topics of scientific inquiry.

Dr. Krantz, Dr. Meldrum, and Dr. Karikó have experienced this unwarranted censorship firsthand.

If scientists understood both their personal limitations—and those of science, as an area of knowledge—they could improve how they communicate with the public and become better collaborators with other scientists. Unfortunately, these self-appointed pseudoscience watchdogs, eager to speak on topics outside their fields, harm the process that they aim to protect. It is very important that these "watchdogs" try to keep their hubris in check.

Belief

As a science teacher, I obviously think that science is a very important area of knowledge. As a student of the nature of science, I also respect the limitations of science. And as a human being who thinks about his thinking, I understand that I construct my personal reality using many different non-science ways of knowing.

I must confess that I find writing this section of the book, the part about belief, more difficult. For all my droning on and on about the importance of accepting uncertainty, I must admit that I am more comfortable writing about subjects where an answer is discoverable and testable. The types of questions which involve beliefs are many, and they are very important questions.

I am hoping you will enjoy the switch from the relatively narrow discipline of science to the ginormous topic of belief. What are beliefs? How do beliefs differ from areas of knowledge and ways of knowing? Where do beliefs come from? I find these topics as fascinating as they are difficult. Maybe the questions interest me because the answers are so elusive, and sometimes, kind of blurry. If you haven't already noticed this about me, I find illusive, blurry things fascinating.

My intention here is not to challenge your beliefs. Instead, my aim is to explore the nature of our personal beliefs and the origins of those beliefs.

CHAPTER 12

What Does It Mean to Believe?

I was shopping for a dryer many years ago with my wife, and for a reason that I cannot remember, I wanted a gas dryer. My wife asked me, "Is there even a gas hookup in the basement?"

I had looked a few weeks earlier, and yes there was. She was pretty sure there wasn't a gas line, but she didn't *know* there wasn't. I wasn't just pretty sure, I *knew* there was. I could picture it in my mind clear as day. The gas pipe came down along the stud opposite from the stud that held the 220 outlets for the very electric dryer that we were replacing. Luckily, my wife trusted me, and we bought the gas dryer. When we brought the dryer home, I went downstairs to show her the gas line. It wasn't there! Clearly, someone had snuck into the house and removed it while we were out shopping for the new dryer. Nothing else in the house was touched. A strange act of vandalism indeed! I was perplexed; I am still perplexed to this day.

I included that little true story as a starting point for discussion of the difference between what we know and what we believe. Spoiler alert, the distinction is a bit messy.

Sometimes we are sure we *know* something—and yet we do not. Our conviction to our claim is not the best predictor of its reliability.

Everyone has heard someone say they know something that *we know* is incorrect. At times, we are just being too casual with language; we say we "know" when we should use the term "believe."

Using the more technical language of epistemology only slightly improves this situation. In epistemology, there is an acknowledgment that the phrase "to know" can have different levels of veracity or trustability. Knowledge, as a term, is *not* interchangeable with *factual* knowledge. When a philosopher says, "I know that . . ." they are not necessarily about to tell you a fact. Philosophers concede that all knowledge is tentative, but factual knowledge simply has a very high degree of reliability or veracity.

CHAPTER 13

Definitions

We need to agree on language before we embark on a tour of our own thinking. Yes, definitions can be a little tedious, but I think gaining an understanding of the terms belief, knowledge, fact, and faith is more enjoyable than say, unloading the dishwasher or folding laundry.

Belief

A belief is a propositional attitude of truth.

When you are declaring what you think is true, you are voicing a belief. A hypothesis, for example, is a belief about a possible explanation. We are not declaring something *is* true. We are saying we think an explanation *could* be true. Implicit in the use of the term belief, is the feeling that we are not a 100 percent, or perhaps not even 55 percent, sure. Belief is more like an opinion about what is true. Use of the term belief requires some humility.

Knowledge

Knowledge is more complicated. As you might expect there exists more than one accepted definition of what it means to have knowledge. As you will remember from our earlier discussion about the Theory of Knowledge, there are eight different "ways of knowing":

sensory, memory, intuition, language, emotion, imagination, faith, and logic. These ways of knowing can be combined to make more complex types of knowledge, such as scientific, mathematical, or historical knowledge. These three latter *types or areas* of knowledge are more trustworthy than any of the individual eight *ways* of knowing from which they came.

Part of the reason that knowledge is so hard to define is that the veracity of different kinds and types of knowledge is highly variable. We use the word "knowledge" to describe what we remember about the presence of a gas line; we also have knowledge that the Sun is at the center of the solar system. I know the Sun is at the center of our solar system, and I knew there was a gas line dryer hookup in my basement, but only one of these claims is correct.

Knowledge might come from our memory, or it might be derived from reason or logic. It is not absolute, rather it is probabilistic in nature. By that I mean, knowledge is not 100 percent certain. Established scientific knowledge, such as pathogens cause infectious diseases or knowledge that an object in motion stays in motion unless a force acts on it have a very, very high probability of being true. On the other hand, knowledge from intuition is much, much lower on the reliability scale. All knowledge can and should be subject to change when we get more information.

This graph above is simply a qualitative visual representation showing relative levels of trustworthiness or veracity of these types of knowledge. I could have attached error bars on these bars to indicate differences in individuals. For example, the trustworthiness of *memory* in an Alzheimer's patient is lower than the trustworthiness of *memory* in a healthy friend. I decided to split the difference and simply profess that *memory*, as a way of knowing, is not as reliable as say, the established canon of *scientific knowledge*. But *memory*, on average, is more reliable than *imagination* or *intuition* as a way of knowing—at least on average. If you have not already done so, it may be a good time to revisit the definitions of the various ways of knowing in Appendix B.

I am talking around the problem of defining knowledge, but I still have not actually defined it. I'm going to start with a definition of knowledge which is given from the perspective of a third party. With

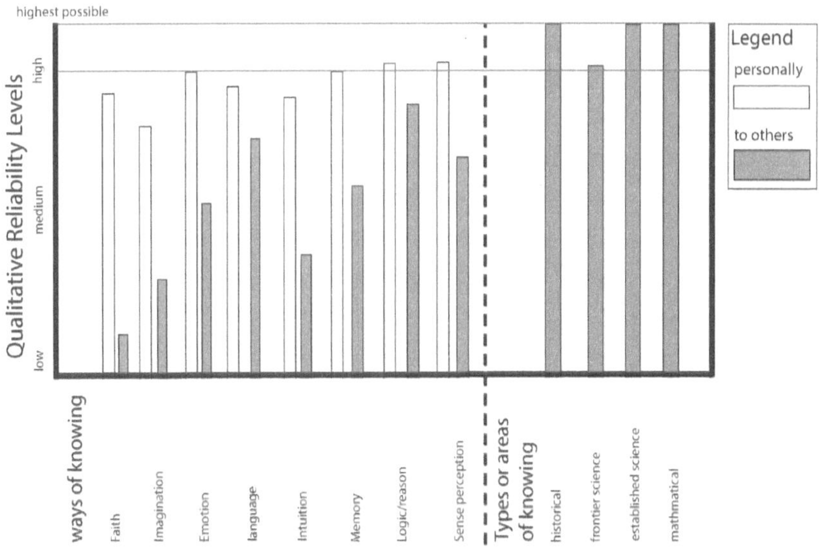

This is a qualitative chart of the relationship between a way, or a type, of knowledge and its level of reliability. This chart illustrates that different kinds of knowledge have varying levels of trustworthiness. Since it is qualitative, no scale or units are provided on the y-axis. On the x-axis, we have ways of knowing. The first bar is reliability to an individual person, I also put a second bar on each way of knowing, to indicate how much reliability the way of knowing has to a third party. I also plotted types or areas knowledge on the graph. (I designed and sketched this graph; my son Henry then used his graphic design skills to make my vision look more professional.)

this definition, we are answering the question, "Does a person have knowledge?" According to this definitional approach, we must meet three criteria: a person must believe a thing is true, they must have justification for the thing being true, and the thing must be true in order to qualify as knowledge. I know the Sun is at the center of the solar system: I believe it, I have justification for thinking it, and it is true. Therefore, I have knowledge of the Sun-centered model of our solar system.

To know something does not mean we are necessarily talking about facts or object truths. I know I love my wife: I believe it, I have justification for thinking it, and it is true. I know I had granola this morning: I believe it, I have justification for thinking it, and it is true. In these two examples, I use different "ways of knowing." In the example of my love for my wife, I'm using emotional knowledge. In the granola example, I am using sense perception and memory as ways of knowing. While these both *feel* like objective truths or empirical facts, I would have difficulty proving these statements to a skeptical third party.

I think it is important to consider that most of life's questions depend on less reliable types of knowledge. When we ponder ethics, value judgements, political ideas, relationships, aesthetics in music, art, literature, religion, or any kind of faith, they all come down to some non-rigorous ways of knowing.

It is interesting, and somewhat problematic, that for the biggest slice of the knowledge pie, we use the least reliable ways by which we acquire knowledge.

For most things that we ponder, the best we can do is to offer a propositional attitude of truth—a belief. Individuals tend to assess the accuracy of their own knowledge more favorably than an external third party might. A third party would call most personal knowledge, beliefs. For example, if a future version of myself had Alzheimer's disease, I might *know*, based on memory, that I had granola for breakfast. But my sons, Max and Henry, might say, "He *believes* he had granola. But we really don't *know* what he had for breakfast."

Humans have knowledge about a wide variety of things, and this knowledge helps us make sense of reality. But we often forget that not all knowledge is created equally.

Facts

In everyday language, facts refer to knowledge with a very high level of reliability.

To achieve the level of reliability, which I will call factual, the knowledge must go through a bias removing process to increase its level of reliability. Types of knowledge like historical, scientific, or mathematical go through such a process to give us facts.

Even though "facts" or "objective truths" are *not* terms that philosophers typically use, I *believe* they are useful terms. These two terms serve to differentiate knowledge with extremely high levels of veracity from knowledge with lower levels of reliability. Knowledge of what someone, other than yourself, had for breakfast is inherently different from knowledge regarding the relationship of the Earth to the Sun in the solar system.

I understand that all knowledge is tentative, but at some point, we can use terms like "fact" to describe knowledge like the Earth orbits the Sun. I *believe* it is confusing *not* to call knowledge that has attained the highest possible level of verification, a *fact*. I also *believe* it's important to make *a* distinction between knowledge generated from intuition or memory from knowledge generated by established scientific or mathematical methods. In my opinion, using the term fact for these areas of knowledge clarifies conversations.

Sometimes, the confusion between "facts" and "beliefs" is accidental. It's simply a product of somewhat ambiguous language.

Unfortunately, many times the confusion itself can be a purposeful product. For example, when a lawyer wants the jury to entertain doubts about facts, he/she may purposefully muddy the waters between what is fact and what is opinion in the interest of getting their client out of paying the fine or doing the time. When you are bested by facts, one course of action is to insist that the established facts are in doubt. This happens with political spin all the time. Unfortunately, when we don't distinguish between facts and beliefs, we are particularly vulnerable to manipulation.

I *believe* teachers, scientists, mathematicians, and historians should use the term fact when referring to established mathematical, scientific, or historical facts. Pearl Harbor was bombed on Dec. 7, 1941. The square root of sixteen is four. The heart is an organ that pumps blood. These are three facts.

I also believe that the term "fact" should not be used in the gray areas, such as frontier science and preliminarily findings. The term "fact" should not be applied to any particular individual *way* of knowing, regardless of an individual's level of certainty.

That last sentence was easier for me to write than it is for me to implement in my own life. I must admit that I often voice "facts" that are merely my strongly held beliefs. Throughout the process of writing this book, I improved my usage a bit, but I still can't help myself from time to time. My son, Henry, has called me on this more than once.

Recently, I put on my old curmudgeon Rick Beato hat, and I boldly stated, "It's a fact that the music of '80s and the '70s was better than the crap that passes as music today!"

Henry was quick to retort, "Dad . . . that it is not fact, it's just your *opinion*." My face contorted and my blood pressure rose—but he wasn't wrong. Fostering epistemological awareness in my kids sure takes the fun out of me bombastically stating my views!

I understand that there is an infinitesimally small possibility that data could overturn facts. It is *possible* that the *fact* that the freezing point of pure water at one atmosphere of pressure could change in the future due to some unknown force. But it is appropriate, at this time in history, to call the freezing point of pure water at one atmosphere of pressure, a known fact.

Faith and Beliefs

According to the theory of knowledge, faith is one of the seven "ways of knowing." Faith can be defined as belief without evidence. But while the reliability of faith is low, the importance of faith is very high. In fact, some of the most important things "we know" are matters of faith. Religious faith is the most obvious example, but we all have faith in many ideas.

Another distinction I need to make is between faith and belief. They are often lumped together but they have subtle differences. Faith is a particular type of belief, in the way that bananas are a particular type of fruit. All bananas are fruits, but not all fruits are bananas. Faith involves reliance and trust, whereas belief is simply something that one takes to be true. (Even though we may not be able to prove it to a skeptical third party.)

Faith, as a way of knowing, has a low level of veracity, and it does not require physical evidence. I think that is an important distinction to say that "no evidence" is not the same as "without justification." Justification does not need to be physical; it could just be sound logic.

Faith lives around the edges of *all* knowledge. For example, the science of geology requires a faith in the idea of uniformitarianism. Uniformitarianism is the idea that geologic events that happened in the past are still happening today and the events that are happening today also happened in the past. It is important for understanding geology that the idea of uniformitarianism is true. It makes perfect sense, and so far, it seems to be true. However, uniformitarianism is very difficult, and perhaps impossible, to prove. (Even though there is very, very strong justification for having faith in this idea.)

Early in the Enlightenment period, which ran roughly from 1685 to the early 1800s, when the first "scientists" thought that the laws of nature were discoverable, this was initially a leap of faith. It still is. But now, I would argue, there is a good deal of very compelling physical evidence that adherence to a scientific process yields discovery. That said, doing science still requires some faith.

Faith in a particular result, on the other hand, introduces bias. Bias is the sworn enemy of the scientific process. Furthermore, science has sought to differentiate itself from many types of faith, particularly faith in authority. In science, evidence and the process itself rules.

So, as you can see, science and faith have a complex relationship.

An important subset of faith is religious faith. The story of Galileo and the Pope Urban VIII is just one example of the complex history between science and religious faith. Science seeks to understand the natural, physical world. While religious faith explores the spiritual. Religious faith and science should drive in two separate lanes divided by a substantial median.

It is, for example, difficult for science to form and test hypotheses around ideas like love, forgiveness, relationships, ethics, and the afterlife. Many, perhaps most, of humanity's concerns are not physical in nature.

Science and religion *should* get along like peas in a pod because they address different aspects of humanity. Most religious leaders incorporate knowledge which originates from the scientific way of knowing into their worldviews, and many scientists have an interest in some form of spiritual realm. They *should* understand the powers and limitations of these separate realms. The operative word in the preceding sentence is the word "should."

Unfortunately, according to a few denominations and individuals as well as a few scientists, science and religion are involved in a war. There is no need for a conflict between these different realms of knowledge and belief.

CHAPTER 14

Pitfalls of Beliefs

We have no choice but to rely on beliefs for most of life's questions. Unfortunately, beliefs are problematic for three reasons:

1. No checks and balances on beliefs.
2. Beliefs spread quickly.
3. Beliefs are specific to certain groups.

No Checks and Balances

Beliefs are not generally held to a code of acceptable standards. As with almost all such statements, there are some exceptions. When a belief becomes *obviously* harmful, the larger society will attempt to discredit that way of thinking. We see this with arrests of cult leaders, like Charles Manson. He and his followers were not simply entitled to their own beliefs. Nor were the Nazis. Many Nazis needed to be killed to end their aggression and to end that horrible belief system. Other than these extreme examples, societies generally do not have a mechanism to hold harmful beliefs in check.

Speed of Transmission

Another problem with beliefs is the speed at which they spread. Anyone can write a letter to the editor or post their beliefs on Facebook.

This enables beliefs to spread much faster than facts. The process to form beliefs is very, very fast. The process to test and refute hypotheses and screen for bias is painstakingly slow. As a result, bad information and odd beliefs can travel much faster than facts or rational thought.

Specificity to Groups

Beliefs are not universal, but groups of people can have common beliefs. Often these groups live in the same geographical areas.

Established scientific and mathematical facts, on the other hand, are not specific to a group. These facts transcend cultural beliefs. Everyone accepts that the freezing point of water is zero degrees Celsius or thirty-two degrees Fahrenheit at standard atmospheric pressure. It doesn't matter if you are Christian, Muslim, Hindu, Buddhist, atheist or agnostic, or republican or democrat. Water freezes at zero degrees Celsius or thirty-two degrees Fahrenheit at standard atmospheric pressure because it is a property of H2O. It has nothing to do with your culture. The square root of sixteen is four, in Paris or Des Moines. These are facts, and as such, are not specific to a group or geographical area.

What makes this especially hard to untangle is that our beliefs are usually part of elaborate belief *systems*. These belief systems reside in our minds, or more accurately, in our brains.

Beliefs and Belief Systems—an Overview

Let's start with a one-sentence definition of "belief system." A belief system is an ideology or set of principles we use to interpret our everyday reality. A belief system could be thought of as the screen through which we view our perceptions.

Why do bad things happen to good people? Why do sunsets and stars look so beautiful? What happens to our souls after we die? Where were our souls before we were born? Do we even have a soul? Does my dog feel emotions like I do?

Our belief systems help us make sense of these and many other questions. We use our belief systems to help guide us through our world. They help interpret that which we perceive.

Core beliefs and values are our modus operandi. They dictate how we prioritize things in our lives. Things like: money, God, family, compassion, truth, our country, personal friendships, or the protection of the natural world. These core beliefs act as glue to hold all our individual beliefs together in one coherent system. These nodes in the synaptic web constitute the values on which we are unwilling to compromise.

Most of us have a mixture of these core values that we hold on to very tightly. Examples might include loyalty, kindness, following the teachings of Christ, the elimination of suffering, or following Sharia Law. Others could include the search for power, ambition, status, public responsibility, or personal freedom. These core beliefs and values are the nodes on this interacting web of beliefs that we hold as our personal identity. Of course, different people have different nodes. The entire web constitutes the individual's belief system.

The above description is not metaphorical; belief systems are physical things. To some, this may seem like an odd claim. How can something as ethereal as a belief be physical? Like all cognition in the brain, synapses that are used are reinforced, and those that are not are pruned back. These physical and complex networks of interacting neurons form our belief systems. If these webs are somehow broken, the beliefs the individual holds are altered.

As I was researching for this book, I read an interesting paper entitled, "The underpinnings of religious beliefs: evidence from brain lesions" in the journal *Frontiers of Behavioral Neuroscience* (2022). This was a unique longitudinal follow-up of American male combat veterans who suffered traumatic brain injury, or lesions, to specific parts of their brains. The database was big enough to allow for the controlling of variables such as age, educational level, and even pre-injury intelligence levels. The study followed veterans for *50 years* after the injury occurred. In the *final phase* of the study (from 2008–2012), "169 participants (134 with specific brain injuries, and 34 with no injury) were assessed for executive functions, social cognition, personality, as well as large battery of tests dedicated to religious beliefs, including fundamentalism, God-Image, and mystical experiences.

This study seemed to show that brain structure was correlated to belief systems. Specifically, the results showed that two brain injuries were related to religious belief, and one type of injury was linked to fundamentalist religious views. The lesions in question were in the ventromedial prefrontal cortex and the dorsolateral prefrontal cortex. (In layman's terms, the injuries were located within two—slightly different—places within the part of your brain that is located above and behind the bridge of your nose.)

For ventromedial injuries, subjects had a significant increase in their personal relationship with God. In terms of social cognition, this group also exhibited more empathy and a stronger sense of personal control. This was even more pronounced when the right side of the ventromedial prefrontal cortex was damaged.

Damage to the dorsolateral part of the prefrontal cortex was correlated to mystical experiences and fundamentalist views. It also correlated to decreased executive functions and decreased flexibility of thinking and openness.

The data showed a direct correlation between types of brain lesions and particular religious beliefs systems, as well as other aspects of personal belief systems. The data in this article supports the notion that beliefs are physical characteristics of a person's brain.

Another way to study the relationship between physical neural networks and belief systems involves looking at specific psychiatric disorders.

In Capgras syndrome, patients think a loved one has been replaced by a look-alike, double, or imposter. It is a very weird and very sad disorder (for them, and I would imagine for their family members as well). Brain scans show that people with this disorder all have damage to a very particular region of their brain. This study provides more evidence that types of beliefs can be correlated to specific physical structures in the brain.

Neurologists now understand, from these examples and countless others, that belief systems reside in your brain as a web or a net of neurons. The cortex, the prefrontal cortex, and the entire limbic system intertwine, forming this net. Our central values and beliefs form the nodes of this network, while specific beliefs—like trustworthiness, openness to the mystical, empathy, vulnerability to fundamentalism, and attitudes toward freedom and responsibility—reside in specific parts of this web. The whole network of neurons makes up our belief systems.

But how do these neural nets form in the first place?

CHAPTER 16

Where Do Belief Systems Come From? (Nature)

Since beliefs reside in our brains, understanding belief systems involves a smidgen of knowledge about brain development.

At birth, much of the wiring of our brains is already complete. But the part of the brain called the cerebral cortex undergoes massive growth in the first several years of life. Language acquisition in early life is nothing short of phenomenal. Here, during ages zero to five, we begin to form our systems of belief. Some of our wiring depends on our DNA, and our early experiences also determine some of this wiring.

Between the ages of thirteen to around the age of twenty-two, we undergo another huge spurt of brain growth. This spurt of brain development occurs in a part of the brain called the prefrontal cortex. What we experience—and even our consumption of alcohol—will help or hinder the development of that part of our brain. Our notion of self-identity, reasoning, risk assessment, and basic executive function all develop in our prefrontal cortex. By the end of age twenty-two, most people have their core values and their system of beliefs firmly in place. Individual beliefs may change, but the entire belief *system* is somewhat robust at this point.

Genetics

Upon conception, we receive twenty-three chromosomes from each of our parents. Which twenty-three chromosomes we get, matters. These chromosomes impact our personality, our learning style, and even our beliefs. Some of the wiring of our brains is simply genetic.

Children come out of the womb with different genes and therefore different temperaments and personalities. If you are a parent of more than one child, you don't need me to tell you that. We know *intuitively* that some temperaments are at the very least partly genetic. My sons could not be more different in personality from each other. My wife often says, "Man if we could put them in a blender we would have one great kid." They of course take offense to this. Well, at least one of them does, the other, predictably, finds it amusing.

When I taught genetics as a biology teacher, I thought it would be fun to have my own genome sequenced. That year for Christmas, my wife purchased a DNA test kit for me through the company "23andMe." Some people fear getting their genome sequenced because they may find they are predisposed to some horrible ailment. But, for whatever neuronal network reason, I am in the "I'd-rather-just-know" camp.

I am not at all sure what I was expecting to learn from the test, but I am oddly excited to share one result whenever I get the chance, mostly because it amuses me, and also because I think it makes me sound cool. It turns out, according to the test, that I have the muscle composition found in "elite power athletes." Interesting side note, I weighed ninety-eight pounds in high school, and I was horribly uncoordinated. When I wrestled, I had a record of two wins and thirteen losses. I spent so much time on my back in the middle of wrestling mats that I joked about my detailed knowledge about the ceilings of the gymnasiums in our conference. "Elite power athlete" are three words that would have never been used to describe me.

That said, my genetic makeup likely influenced, at least in part, why I enjoyed cross country and track in high school. My success in these sports likely influenced my self-esteem and peer interactions. That success likely influenced my beliefs about my physically capabilities. Which, in turn, influenced that part of my belief system. Perhaps my genes get some credit for the belief that if I work hard, I can improve. If I was not predisposed to success in the running sports, would I have developed these beliefs?

In studies of identical twins—children with identical genetics—who were separated at birth, we find remarkable similarity in temperament and personality. This provides strong evidence that our genetics are at least *part* of the temperament/personality formation equation. And, by extension, because our temperaments and our personalities affect the beliefs that we come to hold, our genetics affect our belief systems.

CHAPTER 17

Beliefs and Nurture

During two periods of elevated brain development—from birth to the age of five, and a good chunk of ages fourteen to twenty-two—our parents are often an omnipresent part of our environment. (A lot of development also happens from ages five to fourteen as well, but it is just relatively less than these other two periods.)

Either intentionally or unintentionally, our parents donate their beliefs to us—along with their genes. They bombard us with *their* belief systems as our brains develop. This immersion has a huge influence on our brain development. Often, children adopt the beliefs of their parents. But sometimes, particularly if the relationship between child and the parents was strained, some adopt *the opposite* belief systems of their parents. Either way, it's an influence.

Whether or not we picked up on our parents' political party, political apathy, or religious denomination, we likely adopted many of their *core* values.

In late adolescence, friends often become more influential to us than our parents. In high school, my friends Bruce and Blaine shaped some of my religious views. Just out of high school, my friend Fred challenged some of my more homophobic views. He also shaped some of my political views. He illuminated the atrocities occurring in Central America and South America under the pretense of fighting communism. Gaining different perspectives as we meet more people is what growing up is all about. *All* of my close friends influenced who I am and what I believe.

Geography Is Part of Our Nurture

Where we live also plays a significant role in the formation of our belief systems, particularly in the case of political belief systems. Today, in the United States, the rural, urban, and suburban political divisions are stark. Look at a map on election night and it almost seems like the county in which we live determines our party affiliation. Some of this is due to policies, but it is also marketing. The political culture wars intentionally pit rural against urban.

When we are surrounded by people who think a certain way, that way of thinking gets normalized. This normalized way of thinking gets incorporated into our belief systems.

I once believed that my naturally contrarian nature made me resistant to the effects of local influence. I like to think of myself as a freethinker who does my own thing, resistant to the political winds around me. When I am around liberals, I tend to argue the conservative point of view. When I am around conservatives, I tend to make the liberal case.

However, I became more aware of my own errors in thinking during the COVID mess. I taught in a rural school, in a very politically conservative area. Deep into the pandemic, my school had no mask mandate. This policy preceded the availability of vaccines. In addition to myself, only two or three other teachers and maybe ten total students wore masks at my school.

During the same time, I lived in a more liberal town about fifty miles away. In that town, it seemed as though everyone wore masks. Mask wearing had become normalized. If you went to the grocery store and left your mask in the car, you could almost feel the glares. Those glares served as a reminder to turn around and get your mask.

I eventually had a conversation with Tim Bartels, the principal of the school. Tim did not wear a mask, but he was an awesome person and leader. I told him that I felt increasingly uncomfortable in this mask-free environment. As usual, he was great. He told me he would advocate for a change in the school's policy to the school board. He kept his word, and the board put a mask mandate into effect in December of 2020.

Then in the spring of 2021, I received a vaccination, and about this time, Iowa's conservative governor put pressure on schools to lift all mask mandates.

And here is the important part, after I received my vaccination, and after the mask mandate was lifted, I conformed to two different social norms. I stopped wearing a mask at my school, but in the more liberal town of Iowa City, I did not go out without my mask. I realize that my behavior is inconsistent and nonsensical—which is, of course, my point.

As social creatures, we tend to incorporate the beliefs of the culture in which we are immersed. My surroundings shaped my beliefs and actions.

The degree to which geography plays into our belief systems depends on our personalities. Some of us like to fit in, others like to stand out. Particularly, if you are a "fit-in" type of person, your community will impact your beliefs a great deal. Even a contrarian such as myself felt the impact of my location. The influence of my environment on my beliefs appeared to be inevitable.

CHAPTER 18

Entanglement of Nurture and Nature

The relationship between nature and nurture is deeply interconnected—calling them "entangled" barely captures how closely linked they truly are. These two causal agents are so deeply intertwined they cannot really be separated.

To illustrate entanglement of nature and nurture, I'll begin with an example using the neurotransmitter called dopamine. The release of dopamine—often referred to as the "enjoyment transmitter"—in the brain enhances activity within the engaged neural network, thereby reinforcing and strengthening that specific network.

Let me give you a specific example, let's say you are good at chess. When you play, you often win. Winning causes a release of dopamine, so you feel happy. The more satisfaction or enjoyment you get from a thought process, the more likely that you will repeat it. Gradually you get better at chess because you play it more.

Now imagine in this example that, as a result, you spend time with others who play chess, start studying various openings, and maybe even get a chess coach. You just changed your environment! This shows how a genetic predisposition (nature) could alter your environment (nurture). Playing chess and studying the game can cause a rewiring of your brain, making you better at chess. You just changed your brain's nature!

Another look at the causal link between nature and nurture comes from a relatively new and very interesting field, the field of epigenetics.

Epigenetics

Epigenetics is the study of how our environment—our *nurture*—can cause molecular level changes to our *genetics*, our very *nature*.

Epigenetics gained traction as a topic a couple of decades ago after a fascinating study on the survivors of the Dutch Hunger Winter. The Dutch Hunger Winter was a period of famine that took place during the end of World War II when the Nazis blocked food supplies to the Netherlands. By the time the Dutch were liberated in May of 1945, more than 20,000 people had died of starvation. Pregnant women were particularly vulnerable, and the famine impacted the physiology of the unborn children for the rest of their lives.

When the children of those mothers reached middle age, they had higher LDL cholesterol and triglyceride levels. They also suffered higher rates of obesity, diabetes, and cardiovascular disease. When scientists investigated why, they found that these children carried chemical marks, or methylations, on their genes that affect gene expression. Those who did not have mothers who were starving did not have these methylations on their genes, and therefore did not have higher rates of high cholesterol, diabetes, or cardiovascular disease. These changes could be seen even sixty years after the Dutch Hunger Winter!

Unlike normal genetic changes, epigenetic changes do not change our DNA sequence, per say, but they can change how the gene is expressed, or how our body reads the DNA sequence and turns the DNA code into specific proteins—or traits. In other words, our personal *genetics* can be altered by our environment. That statement would have seemed very strange, if not flat out wrong, just fifteen years ago. The evidence indicates that the expression of our DNA can be *permanently* changed by the environment, as these changes were passed on to their children. This is a remarkable discovery!

Epigenetics, at the molecular level, is really an alteration of the control mechanisms of genes. Expressing or not expressing a gene causes the same effect as having or not having that gene. Major trauma seems to affect the expression of genes, and these changes are seemingly passed on to the offspring of those who experienced the trauma!

A separate study with mice also showed that behavioral changes due to environment could be genetically passed on to the next generation. In one experiment, mouse parents were given a shock in the presence of almond scent; the offspring of those parents avoided almond scent for generations.

The more we learn, the more entangled nature and nurture seem to be.

CHAPTER 19

Some Metacognition about My Personal Beliefs

In October of 2023, my wife and I attended a bigfoot conference in the town of Grand Rapids, Minnesota. It was our first bigfoot conference, so we did not know what to expect on that cold and cloudy day.

Upon arrival, it mostly felt like any hotel conference. The lobby smelled like any hotel lobby—cleaning supplies and a hint of chlorine from the pool mixed with the faint odor of a make-your-own-waffle station. The temporary dividers were pulled back in the main room, creating space for at least one hundred guests. The front of the room contained risers to make a stage, with a lectern at the center framed by large pull-down projector screens. Tables loaded with merch and rimmed with the obligatory black fabric skirts bookended the sides of the stage. One table displayed some plaster casts of footprints and even one handprint, while others showcased bigfoot books and even some bigfoot jewelry. About a hundred chairs were arranged in semi-circles facing the risers. I would estimate between sixty and eighty people occupied those chairs.

My wife and I goofing around during a break at the bigfoot symposium in Grand Rapids, MN. I am up on the risers pretending to present behind the lectern. (Photo by Suellen Swain)

I found this conference to be engaging and meaningful in many ways. We heard interesting information from the viewpoint of both bigfoot believers and from bigfoot skeptics. Somewhat surprisingly, the skeptics were as warmly received as the other speakers. The skeptics did harass the other speakers a little, mostly in good fun. I thought, "Wouldn't it be great if political rallies worked like that?" You could go to a rally of any political party, and at that rally hear non-staged, contrasting viewpoints from the opposing party. It is somewhat telling of the state of our union when a bigfoot conference seems like a better blueprint for an exchange of ideas than our current political system.

Audience members' bigfoot sightings were interesting, but my reactions to their stories intrigued me even more than the stories themselves.

Here is one example:

A man, I'd guess in his mid to late sixties, reported, "Now this is gonna sound crazy, but I was standing in a utility line cut between some thicker spruce and brush when this portal opened up . . . the way I can best describe it is that it was a hole, shimmering like an aurora, about seven feet tall off of the ground, and then bigfoot stepped through it. The bigfoot looked at me and told me, using some kind of mind-speak, not to take his photo, and I respected that . . . and then he walked into the forest and the portal closed-up as he left."

My wife and I knowingly glanced at each other, but we politely said nothing until we were out of earshot of everyone. Then I blurted, "Holy crap! That guy was batshit crazy!" On the way back from the conference, we stopped in the twin cities to see our friends, the Gapinskis. They coined a new term for super odd beliefs, "Portal nuts!" There are the run-of-the-mill odd beliefs, and then there is "Portal nuts!"

As I enjoyed making light of this man's beliefs, I remembered a conversation with my father-in-law, Mike, about my interview with Larry Wilson. Mike commented, "Well, he is crazy."

I asked him, "Why?" (Because I had found Larry to be very credible.)

My father-in-law retorted, "Well, he is crazy because he thinks he saw bigfoot."

At the time, I thought that was a very close-minded and circular argument. Years later, *my reaction* to the "portal nuts" guy revealed that I too had limits for open-mindedness. Once I heard "portal," I was mostly done. When I heard "mind-speak," my mind was made up.

The assumption that the "portal guy" was affected by some diagnosable mental illness—or perhaps just a small lesion in his dorsolateral prefrontal cortex, which made him more open to mystical experiences—is a real possibility. On the other hand, he saw what he saw, and he summoned the courage to report it.

To be clear, in my belief system, portals are not real. (I don't even like them in college football.) I am begrudgingly aware that when I dismiss portals and mind-speak as hogwash, that is merely my belief. And my beliefs are not facts!

On the other hand, if I ever saw a portal glowing in the woods, then I would be justified to have a belief that portals do exist. Acknowledging that my beliefs are not facts enables me to appreciate how my belief systems shape my perceptions. A little metacognition also helps me to see how my beliefs can snowball on themselves, and soon my belief about the nonexistence of portals can *masquerade in my mind* as a fact. So much so that I can label someone with a different belief system as "batshit crazy."

CHAPTER 20

Umwelt

Ed Young wrote a fascinating book called *Immense World* about how different animals perceive the world differently, due to their unique sensory apparatuses. For example, many insects see UV light; we cannot. How can an owl hear a mouse moving under a blanket of snow with pinpoint accuracy from a perch atop a mighty oak? It is hard to imagine a world where we can see UV light or hear like an owl because that world is hidden from us. We also experience pain differently than other animals. My dog, a lab named Lola, loves swimming in ice water. Her temperature sensory neurons are calibrated differently than ours. Lola also seems to enjoy the scent of Raccoon poop. She rolls in it whenever she gets the chance. (Using mind-speak, she once told me that she wants to be a dog fragrance model for L'Oréal. She reports that the tagline in her imaginary commercial is, "Ode de la Raccoon poo—because I'm worth it!")

Some fish generate an electromagnetic field that surrounds them. When things, such as other fish or the side of the aquarium, disturb this field, then those disturbances alert the fish to that presence. So even though their eyes are on the sides of their heads, they swim up to, but don't bonk into, the clear glass sides of the aquarium.

In his book, Ed Young uses the old German word, *umwelt*—pronounced ŏŏm-velt—to describe the part of the environment that particular animals can perceive. The word was coined by Jakob von Uexküll in 1909 from the German word for environment. Different animals have different sensory apparatuses on board, and thus they will have different sensory realities. Their umwelt is their perceptual reality.

I started thinking about the umwelt in the context of our belief systems. Even with basically the same sensory systems, two humans can stand in the exact place, experience the same thing, and yet interpret this reality completely differently. Political scientists call this "perception screening." What we view (perception) is affected (screened) by our individual worldview, or our belief systems.

Let me give you an example of how differing umwelts can alter perception: During a postgame interview, a devout Christian from the Ohio State football team thanks Jesus for the game-winning catch in a game vs. Michigan. This warms the hearts of some of the fans watching. They think, "What a nice humble young man giving all the glory to God."

Whereas another group of fans, usually from Michigan, thinks, "But Jesus hates Ohio State. Everyone knows Jesus is a Michigan fan!"

Yet other groups might think, "On what planet does God care about football? The kid caught the pass because he trained hard, and he has good reflexes. He is trying to seem humble in this interview, but he doesn't even believe what he is saying."

Of course, there are lots of various other interpretations of this hypothetical postgame interview. The point is, our *sense perceptions* present us with the exact same data, but the "reality" of what we see is different, depending on *our* belief systems. Our umwelt (or our perceptual reality) is formed, in part, by our beliefs.

As far as I know, nonhuman animals do not have elaborate belief systems. (It will not surprise me if someday we learn that other animals do hold some belief systems, but currently, that does not *seem* to be the case.) For humans, complex belief systems seem to be a new evolutionary layer caused by an enhanced frontal cortex capable of complex abstract thought. Because of our differing beliefs, we can be on the same planet as other people, and yet we can seemingly live in different worlds.

In my view, the term "personal umwelt" is more concise and preferable to "the distortion of beliefs through perception screening." "Distortion of beliefs" seems to imply more judgement than the simpler term of "umwelt." So I will use the term umwelt going forward.

At this the point, I want to make the subtle shift from talking rather broadly about beliefs, to discussing religious faith. Of all the belief topics out there, I find religious faith to be the most interesting. Religious faith often dramatically affects our umwelt.

God and Religion

CHAPTER 21

My View of God and Religion

While writing this book, my instincts were to avoid telling you, the reading audience, what I believe about God and religion. Years of teaching in public schools has conditioned me to obscure my personal beliefs. In the classroom, I would step back and attempt to discuss things as third-party narrator. I would say to my students, "If it is clear to you what I believe, then I am doing something wrong." Also, it is against the law for a teacher to impose their religious beliefs on their students. Teachers, as authority figures, can be seen as imposing their beliefs by merely sharing them.

So when I Initially wrote a draft of this section, I intended to present myself from an impartial perspective, striving to conceal my personal beliefs. My editor did not like this approach. She explained, "Writing a book is different than teaching a class. The reader will want to know what you believe. In the absence of you directly telling them, readers will jump to conclusions about your beliefs. Many of these conclusions might be incorrect. Most readers would prefer not to play a guessing game. Just be upfront and tell them."

So here is me being upfront about my religious beliefs.

My beliefs about God and religion are best articulated by the band *Modest Mouse* in the song "Missed the Boat": "I'm certainly uncertain, at least I'm pretty sure I am." So, I guess that makes me an agnostic, someone who does not believe or disbelieve in God.

I was brought up in the Episcopal Church, and many of my positive views about religions are associated with Episcopal theology. Most of my life, I would have called myself a Christian, and most of that time I was closely aligned with the theology of the Episcopal Church. Of all the world religions, Christianity is my favorite. I have not always been agnostic and I'm not sure I will always be. If I were to step back from agnosticism, I would likely return to the Episcopal Church, or at least their version of Christianity.

Episcopal churches are not big in Iowa. They exist, but they are far outnumbered by Methodist, Catholic, and what are now called "Bible churches."

As a quick little aside, during the Revolutionary War against England, the Anglican Church, at least in America, was renamed to the Episcopal Church. The reason is obvious if you know that Anglican means "of England." Episcopal simply means "ruled by bishops."

But I digress. Back to me. More recently, I have found the arguments presented by atheists to be compelling. People like Sam Harris make wonderful arguments for the rejection of all religion. I am not sure he is wrong. But I find his arguments against *all* religion less airtight. His arguments rely on an absolute *faith* in *logic* and *science*. As we previously discussed, science and logic alone are not well suited for addressing big spiritual "why" questions.

I realize some may say that my position of agnosticism is a cop out. They could argue that my fence straddling simply covers an opinion that I'm unwilling to share. But I am not hiding anything; I have simply made my peace with uncertainty.

To some, uncertainty feels the same way that a fork in the garbage disposable sounds. They just want it to stop. I admit that I also find comfort in certainty. But for me, certainty is more of a want than a need. I am reluctant to invent certainty when I don't believe that it exists.

Enough about me, let's get back to the questions. I can't provide many answers. I find the *questions* more interesting anyway.

CHAPTER 22

Religion and God

Most, a smidge under 80 percent, of the world's population identifies with a religion. Often, the core belief of religion anchors many people's umwelt.

(If you skipped ahead to this section about God and religion because you don't give a rat's behind about ways of knowing, belief, and bigfoot, I would suggest that you back up and read the bigfoot and epistemology chapters first. Understanding ways of knowing and understanding belief and faith are pretty darn important before we tackle a discussion of God and religion.)

Brother-in-Law Conversation

This seems like an appropriate moment to share a little conversation with my brother-in-law, Jeff. Several months ago, he asked me how my book was coming along. I told him that the God section is proving to be harder for me to write than the bigfoot stuff, because frankly, God is a more complex topic. I said, "I am starting with some basic overview stuff on different notions about the very nature of God. Like monotheistic or polytheistic, or some religions that have no deities . . ."

Then Jeff interjected, "Sounds like you are talking more about religion than about God." An interesting distinction. He then suggested it would be interesting to write about the origins of religion itself. This was a nice enough suggestion.

I told him that I did not plan on doing that because . . . I stammered and stalled, I tried to explain, inarticulately, why I felt that I should not write about the origins of religion. "There is no agreement on religion's origins . . . it all is just faith so the discussions cannot even begin . . ."

Jeff pressed his point, "Sure, there is no proof of an agreed upon origin of religion, but there is historical data, there are studies in the field of brain science. You can offer plausible hypotheses about how religion came to be."

I interrupted, "Science can't really study that question."

"Sure it can!" he retorted. "You can formulate a hypothesis and see if it fits the available data. . . . That's what *science* is!"

I fumbled around trying to explain my thought process but failed. I then got in the car and drove home.

What occasionally happens to me, and I am pretty sure other people, is that my best thoughts on the subject happen *after* the discussion. I live about twenty minutes from my brother-in-law's house, so when I got home, I quickly called him. Being a good sport, he stopped what he was doing to talk more about the difficulty of finding origins of religion using science.

I continued, "When the question is framed as 'Where did religion come from?' there are lots of possible answers. But one of those answers—and it is an important one to consider—is that the origins of religion have nothing to do with man. For example, when God sent Jesus Christ to die on the cross for our sins, God invented Christianity, thus, religion is supernatural in origin. This is a possibility!"

Jeff correctly countered, "If you are doing a scientific study, you would not focus on the supernatural explanations, you would focus on the plausible natural evolutionary explanations."

I gloated, "*Exactly!* The thing that separates science from other ways of knowing is the attempt to eliminate bias. Bias is defined as a presupposition that influences how we view the data." I continued, "The very assumption of 'no supernatural explanations,' eliminates a possible hypothesis. How can you eliminate the competing hypothesis before you begin and then still claim you are attempting to eliminate bias?" I smiled smugly, even though it was a phone conversation.

Our discussion points out how difficult it is to have discussion about complex topics which involve different ways of knowing and even different areas of knowledge. Religion is an epistemological nightmare. It blends historical knowledge, with many ways of knowing like logic, sensory, intuition, and most important of all, faith. Some even use science and math to deepen, or question, their faith.

So even though I argued about this point with my brother-in-law, I have decided that it is interesting to discuss something as inconclusive as the origin of religion. The story of the origin of religions could really be the story of God gradually revealing to humanity the correct belief system. It is a possibility which I will mention, even though it is a hypothesis that is impossible to test. And just for the record, being impossible to test doesn't make it wrong.

Religion and Its *Possible* Origin(s)

The extreme complexity of talking about religion is likely in part why some people avoid the topic. Some people prefer not to discuss religion with other people. Especially those with a differing umwelt. For them, religious faith is a very private matter. I get that.

The upside to this outlook is that it avoids the stress of any potential disagreement. Silence avoids any challenges to your lifelong umwelt.

The drawback is that you end up living in your own echo chamber, constantly having your beliefs confirmed without ever facing opposing views.

In a book, an author can just prod us to quietly think about our thinking without confrontation. The author can't judge us, and we don't need to judge the author, at least to his face.

Personally, I love a good, in person, discussion about religion. If you never allow your ideas to be challenged, it is difficult to grow. Bad ideas can flourish without challenge. I personally like polite challenges to my thinking.

One of my big, unanswered, questions is, "Did we humans invent religion, or did the creator of the universe make us and give the information that allowed us to worship the proper deity?"

The archeological evidence implies that the first hunter gatherer societies believed in some form of an afterlife. This, in turn, implies some kind of religion has always been with our species. But complex organized religions did not seem to exist until approximately 1500 BC, and those religions were initially polytheistic. The world's first monotheistic religions appeared on the planet around 1200 BC.

Robin Dunbar, a British anthropologist and evolutionary psychologist, has done some interesting studies on different types of societies. In hunter gatherer societies, which still exist today, he found that incidences of death caused by homicide—as a percentage of total death in the population—in particular groups tend to be very low when group size is small, and quite high when the groups are large.

He looked at data from fifteen different current hunter gather clans over the course of several years, the smallest clans being ten members and the largest being approximately eighty members. Since he was using different sizes of populations, he used multipliers so that all the homicide deaths rates could be given at standard rate of homicides per 100,000 individuals. In the six smallest clan sizes, all below twenty-five members, homicides per 100,000 individuals were between ten and one hundred, whereas in the two largest groups with seventy or eighty individuals, homicides per 100,000 individuals were over 800. The middle six clan sizes homicide rates ranged between 150 and 750. When these rates were plotted on a graph, it did not result in a straight line, but the correlation was clear. The data seems to show that being in larger social settings is contrary to our basic nature.

Humans only *recently* became highly social creatures (around 9,000 to 8,000 years ago). The birth of agriculture changed our social structure from small bands of hunter gatherers into larger groups living in more permanent agricultural villages.

In our development as a species, humans had to transition from small fighting clans into larger social communities. It has not been a smooth transition. One thing that really seems to help us stay civil in a larger group is a common organized umwelt. Finding those with common shared beliefs systems reduces stress. Dunbar speculates that social rituals began to alleviate the stress caused by the gatherings of us humans. As societies transitioned from dispersed small clans to more cohesive, church-sized communities, the adoption of a shared belief system may have contributed to a reduction in homicide rates. This hypothesis states that the societal transition to organized religion happened when and where communities were "forced" to gather. This hypothesis is consistent with the data.

Here, some caution is warranted. It is important to remember that correlation is not causation, so it is hard to imagine this idea ever getting beyond the hypothesis stage. Still, it is interesting to ponder.

"Closer to Truth"

There was a good series on PBS called *Closer to Truth* that ran for twenty-two seasons. It had the subtitle *Consciousness, Mind, Cosmos, Meaning*. The narrator, Dr. Robert Lawrence Kuhn, often tried to use science and logic to get answers to life's big questions. Many episodes focused on the existence of God. Dr. Kuhn interviewed theologians, cognitive scientists, and philosophers. Using logic and reason, he tried to answer life's big spiritual questions (or at the very least, get "closer to the truth").

I thought that the show was mistitled. It more accurately should have been called, *Circling, but Not Getting Any Closer to Truth*. Just like the *Finding Bigfoot* show should have been called *Not Finding Bigfoot*, as literally every episode featured Rene, Cliff, Matt, and Bobo walking around in the woods at night, not finding bigfoot.

"Does God exist?" Logic, reason, and evidence cannot definitively answer this question. God's existence, or God's nonexistence, is a matter of faith. If you were hoping I could shed some light on this mystery, you will once again be disappointed. So far, I have not helped you discern whether bigfoot or God is real or not. Sorry, no refunds.

In the case of God, a definitive answer is not possible. (I guess you could argue that we will know upon death, but obviously that is in the category of personal knowledge.) In the case of bigfoot, it might exist; we just don't know yet.

Because God is purported to be supernatural, we should not expect physical evidence. Some might point to the Shroud of Turin or the Dead Sea Scrolls as physical evidence. And yes, there is *historical* evidence that Jesus, Muhammad, and Siddhartha, existed, along with some other historical religious figures. Some events within the Bible are consistent with archeological evidence, but that should not be mistaken for evidence of the divine. Further, because no *physical* evidence of the *divine* exists, there is nothing to test. It should be noted that an absence of physical evidence, should not be taken as evidence of the lack of the supernatural divine.

Bigfoot and God

The stakes of believing or not believing are *potentially* so much higher with God than they are with bigfoot. I don't think anyone is spending eternity by a lake of fire because they did not accept the reality of the sasquatch. (I don't *believe* that anyone is spending time in Hell for not believing in God either, but of course, I don't *know* that.)

Another huge difference between these two beliefs is the public's perception. Roughly 80 percent of the world's populations report a belief in God, or gods, or "chosen ones." Compare that to only 21 percent of people in the United States that believe in bigfoot. Just as being impossible to test doesn't make it wrong, being a more popular belief doesn't make it more justified.

I think it's appropriate to use logic, historical context, reason, etc., to attempt to explore questions regarding the supernatural. Logic and reason are important tools for the formation of our own personal belief systems. But when it comes to questions of God's existence, *faith* is the key "way of knowing"—and faith doesn't use physical evidence.

Whether or not God exists is less interesting to me than this question: "If God exists, what is God?" I find the impacts that religious beliefs have on their followers to be the most fascinating questions of all.

How we interpret God's existence has implications for our personal belief systems, personal behavior, and perhaps our very souls. So, the nature of God in various religions is obviously worth exploring!

CHAPTER 23

The Nature of God/ Types of Belief Systems

I will begin by categorizing the religions of the world by the number of deities worshiped. Monotheists worship one deity. Polytheists worship many deities. And nontheistic religions have leaders that are not supernatural deities.

Nontheists

Nontheists are not the same as atheists or agnostics.

Nontheists often worship a chosen one, as opposed to a deity. A classic example is the worship of the Buddha in Buddhism. By some definitions, the lack of deity worship precludes Buddhism as a religion. I'm choosing to embrace a more inclusive definition.

Confucianism is another example of a nontheistic religion. People follow the philosophy of Confucius, but they do not regard him as a God. Some tribal religions fall under the nontheistic umbrella, while others acknowledge a single Creator who is in charge. Like most attempts to categorize anything complex, we often find things sitting atop those very lines that we draw to separate categories.

Polytheistic Religions

A classic example of a polytheistic religion is Hinduism. Hinduism has thousands of Gods. Buddhism could also be considered polytheistic due to the presence of minor spiritual entities alongside Buddha. Similarly, Shinto and many tribal or folk religions often worship multiple spirits from nature.

Monotheism

The major monotheistic religions include Christianity, Judaism, and Islam. (Sometimes, these three are referred to as the Abrahamic religions.) Added together, they account for the religious beliefs of approximately 55 percent of the world's population. These monotheistic traditions arose from polytheist groups, specifically the Bedouin tribes. These tribes existed (and still exist) in the geographical area that would become the birthplace of Judaism.

This quick overview of world religions points us to at least two, diametrically opposed, worldviews:

Worldview One: The fact that nearly all cultures worship God shows that God created us in his image, and we are therefore hardwired to believe in him. I have heard pastors say we are all born with a God-shaped hole in our hearts that only God can fill.

Worldview Two: *We humans created* God in different cultures. If one religion is correct, and it came from the divine, then all religions should be more uniform in beliefs. At the very least, the notion of God should be consistent.

I know we are talking about faith here, but there is some science to support Worldview One. Our brain is in fact predisposed to have animistic notions about the world. Watch children play or recall your own childhood; we gave agency to inanimate objects without a second thought. Dolls and stuffed animals had feelings when we were children. (My kids used to have kung fu tournaments with their stuffed turtles, it was hilarious and adorable.) A mountain or volcano possessing a spirit is like stuffed turtles having personalities. Our brains are wired to think about everything as having agency, including inanimate objects. The wiring to see outside agency predisposes us to see the world through a supernatural lens.

Volcanos did not erupt because of some understandable geologic process; they blew up out of anger. Our brains are predisposed to believe that something beyond ourselves oversees cause and effect. We do have "God-shaped holes" in our brains, and they're ready to be filled by whatever version of God is present within our culture. This view is echoed by Ara Norenzayan, a psychologist at the University of British Columbia. I recently heard Ara interviewed by Shankar Vedantam on the podcast *Hidden Brain*. Ara explains, "Our mental architecture plays a really big role in the way that we entertain religious beliefs and practices around the world in predictable ways."

Additionally, I would also put forward this hypothesis. Our very prolonged childhood also predisposes us to believe in God. At birth, our parents are our world. All-knowing, ever-present, loving, caring and providing for us. As we age, we want there to be a bigger version of this for the world at large. It is the only world order we know. All living things seem to have a father and or mother. By extension, all of living creation should have a creator.

When we look at the language of religion, it seems that this supernatural parental role is part of the all the Abrahamic religions. We are "created in his image"; he is "God the father." God seems modeled after a father figure. Of course, not all dads are the same, so God is not uniform in description. Sometimes, he is described as a comforter—all knowing and loving. Other times, he has a temper, and he can be quick to wield punishments for those that disobey. He is even described as jealous at times.

Often, in more matriarchal societies, deities are modeled on mothers. In many folk religions, the language of "Mother Earth" is common. Many Hindu Gods are mother-like. The Greek Goddess "Giai" is the mother creator. Mother Mary holds a significant place as a religious figure within Catholicism. Mothers and fathers seem to be templates for many religious figures or deities.

It is possible that God designed our brains to be receptive to belief in a higher power. This hypothesis is difficult to test, but it interesting to consider. Our brains seem predisposed to believe in some agent beyond ourselves in the universe.

Naturally, one could also suggest that humanity created the concept of God—or gods—precisely because of our brain's particular architecture.

CHAPTER 24

Overview of World Religions

At this point I want to switch gears slightly from talking about different conceptions of God to exploring some basic information about different religions.

What seems like several lifetimes ago, during my freshman year in college, I took a course called Living Religions of the East. I found it fascinating. I later spent some time working with many First Nations people. Through that experience, I learned a bit about different Native American spiritual traditions. That history, coupled with some friendships with people from a variety of world religions, laid a basic framework for my understanding of religious traditions. While researching material for this book, my interest in world religions became reignited. I believe that understanding another person's umwelt often involves understanding a religious belief system other than your own.

I'll roughly organize these religions or categories of religions by order of appearance on Earth.

Folk Religions

Due to the oral transmission of folk religions, accurately determining their origins presents challenges. Folk religions are very likely the first religions on Earth. The earliest versions of religion predate the invention of agriculture. At one time, they were the only form of religion. As of 2010, approximately 6 percent of the world's belief systems involved a folk religion of some kind. They include various Chinese folk religions, aboriginal Australian religions, Native American religions, many of the various African tribal religions, and many others.

Hinduism

Scholars estimate that Hinduism began approximately 1500 BCE. That date is not universally accepted. (That is why I say approximately in front of it, it absolves me of any responsibility.) As of 2010, about 15 percent of the world's population practiced Hinduism.

I am reminded of a *The Simpsons* episode, where the Christian character, Reverend Lovejoy, talks about world religions with Homer, Abu, and Moe. Lovejoy begins with " . . . be they Christian, Jew, Muslim . . ." and then he looks at Abu and says, "or miscellaneous other."

Abu, a Hindu, objects, "Hey, there are over one billion of us!"

What a great show, with such a fantastic jab at how most Westerners know so little about non-Christian religions.

Hinduism, as I already mentioned, is polytheistic. No central God. Everything belongs to a single, central soul, called Brahman. Hinduism has four main sects, each containing numerous subsects. One could choose from thousands of different gods to worship in Hinduism. In addition to the god of your sect, you might also worship a particular god or gods.

To say there are many Hindu texts, is an understatement. There are four Vedas and hundreds of Upanishads, and that is just the tip of the iceberg. The Abrahamic texts (old and new Testaments combined) are tiny compared to ancient Hindu texts.

Judaism

Judaism is the world's first monotheistic religion, and the religion from which Christianity and Islam arose. Judaism got a strong foothold in the Middle East around 1200 BC. About *two tenths of a percent* of the world's population identifies as followers of the Jewish faith. This number surprised me. I think of Judaism as a major world religion, so I assumed it would be a bigger piece of the pie than just 0.2 percent.

This monotheistic way of thinking was introduced to the world through the prophet Abraham. Moses also holds a significant role as a prophet within this religious tradition. The way that Judaism views God can be complicated. He is depicted either as vengeful and judgmental or as fair and loving.

Buddhism

Buddhism has its roots in Hinduism, but it didn't become established as a separate entity until 563 BC. Not everyone categorizes Buddhism as a religion because it has no deity to worship. Siddhartha—who would later be referred to as Buddha by those who follow his philosophy—was a wealthy man with no special powers. He became interested in suffering and created a philosophical way to live on this planet that would help to minimize suffering. His goal was to get to an inner peace or Nirvana. As of 2010 about 7 percent of the world's population were Buddhists.

Christianity

Christianity is an extension of Judaism. This Abrahamic religion includes the teachings of Jesus Christ, the Messiah. The New Testament contains Christ's teaching and the interpretations of the life and death of Christ.

Christ was crucified in the year 33 AD, and the New Testament of the Bible, which includes several books by sixteen different authors, was completed between 70 and 120 AD. Christianity began as an organized religion approximately 100 AD.

Judaism views Jesus as a prophet, while Christianity sees him as the Messiah. The idea of this monotheistic God became more complicated by having a Messiah. This gave rise to the uniquely Christian idea of the Trinity. The Trinity concept defines God as the Father, the Son, and the Holy Ghost. Still a single God, but in three forms.

The idea of the Trinity came about as an effort to understand the crucifixion, death, and ascension of Jesus, as well as the relationship of Jesus and God. If Jesus is the son of God and divine, then God is the Father. "God the Father" serves as the creator of everything. This "God the father" is the complex God of the Old Testament, who made people in his image and made the entire universe. If Jesus is divine, then Jesus is God in human form—also known as "God the Son." A third form is "God the Spirit" or "God the Holy Ghost." Here, God is in the form of comforter. The totality of these three forms of God is referred to as the Trinity—one God, three forms.

As of 2010, about 31.5 percent of the world's population is Christian. Like all the major world religions, the Christian faith has many denominations. Worldwide, Christians are represented by four major denominations by the percentages shown.

Catholic: ~50%   Protestant: ~37%
Orthodox: ~11%   Other: ~2%

Calling "Protestants" a denomination is a bit misleading. There are hundreds of different protestant denominations; their religious views can be quite different from each other.

I grew up in the town of Cherokee, Iowa. It had a population of 8,000. My cohort of high school friends was composed of some Catholics and at least eight different protestant denominations. There were Baptists, Evangelicals, Episcopalian, Lutheran, and Methodist. I even knew a few Presbyterians, a Mormon, and a Jehovah's Witness. Of course, I did not know a soul from any other world religion. I had the false belief at the time, as *The Simpsons* would later articulate, that there were Christians, Jews, and a few miscellaneous other religions in the world.

The reason for such a high density and diversity of Protestants in the USA is complex. In the last section of this book, I will expound on America's religious history, which is quite unique, and I find it interesting.

Prior to writing this book I admit that I thought that Protestants, were the dominant Christian denomination. The data shows that, globally, Catholics account for approximately 50 percent of all Christians, while Orthodox Christians account for 11 percent, and the Anglican Church represents the largest Protestant group at around 15 percent.

When these groups are added together, they constituted 75 percent of all Christians. The remaining Christians are hundreds of Protestant groups, that when combined, make up less than one-quarter of all Christians. That surprised me.

In the US, non-Episcopal Protestants make up a larger slice of the pie. Approximately 38 percent of adults in the US are non-Episcopal Protestants. Catholics comprise approximately 19 percent of adults, whereas Episcopalians total a little less than 2 percent of the population. In the US, the other world religions are all the low single digits, with the remainder of the US population identifying as agnostic or atheist.

Islam

Islam, like Christianity, arose from Judaism. This split of Islam from Judaism occurred about 500 years after the Christian split from Judaism, around 600 AD. In 2010, twenty-three percent of the world's population were Muslims, but a whopping 90 percent of Muslims were Sunni, and only 10 percent were Shia. By doing a little math, you can see this makes Sunni Muslims the largest single religious denomination in the world.

In the Islamic tradition, Allah felt that Judaism (and Christianity) had corrupted his message. So through the prophet Muhammad, he sent a clarified version of the Old Testament called the Quran. The Quran and the Old Testament are similar because it is the same God talking about the same stuff, but they are different because it is a new, uncorrupted, clearer message (according to Muslim teachings).

Muslims worship Muhammad, but they do not view him as divine. They view Allah as the one God, whereas Muhammad is viewed as a very special prophet. Muslims also regard Jesus as a significant prophet, and they refer to him as the Messiah in the Quran.

Nonbelievers

Nonbelievers have long existed, but their numbers have recently increased. The current size of this group varies depending on how the poll is taken. Atheists (people who do not believe in any god) and agnostics (people who think the existence of God and the nature of God is unknowable) are sometimes separated as distinct groups in some religious surveys. In most surveys, they get lumped together as nonbelievers. Sometimes, nonbelievers can be even broader, such as "anyone who does not belong to a church, temple, or synagogue." Qualifiers aside, nonbelievers are in the ballpark of 20 percent of the world's population.

Miscellaneous Other

For the last category, I will take Reverend Lovejoy's quote and rudely call this group "miscellaneous other." Some, I include here because they are relatively new religions, others simply don't belong in any other category. Still, others are here because they are cults and not really religions, an admittedly complex distinction to make. All that reside in this category only make up a small percentage of the world's population. Whatever the reason, I have lumped "religions" like Shinto, Confucianism, Scientology, etc., together as "other." When we group these together, they account for the remaining approximately 1 percent of the world's population.

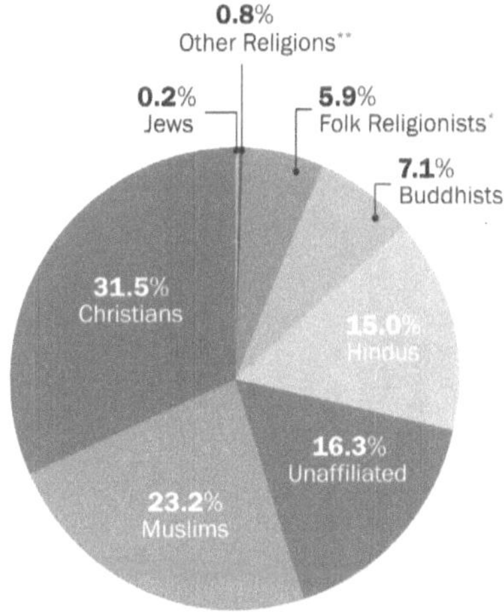

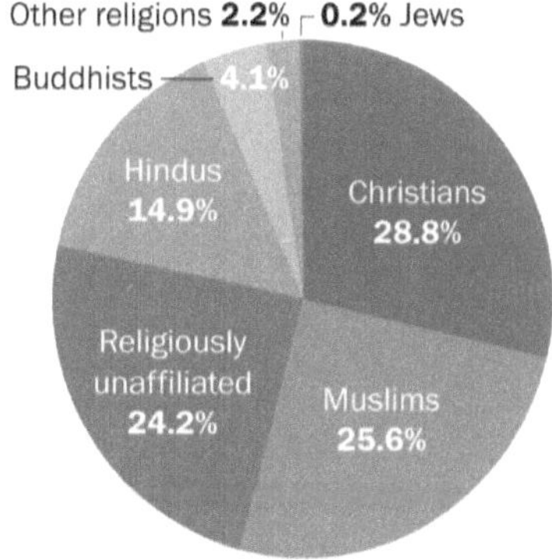

When I initially wrote this section, I used data from the 2010 Global Religious Landscape surveys. In June of 2025, the new 2020 Global Religious Landscape surveys became available. I include the new pie chart here because data is fun. Many, but not all, world religion affiliations ticked slightly downward. Significant gains occurred in the category of "Religiously unaffiliated." (Courtesy of PEW Research Center, copyright@pewtrusts.org)

CHAPTER 25

Who Is Right about Religion and God?

Obviously, this little book will not even pretend to answer the question, "Who is right about God?" I learned my lesson from sitting through the *Closer to Truth* series. Some questions are too big, too complex for a simple answer key. Even if there is an answer key, I certainly don't have it.

So what to do? One could assert that all religions are just slight variations on a theme. Unfortunately, this approach doesn't really work. Sure, there are similarities, but the differences are stark. Some religions describe the afterlife as "eternal life" (if you make the cut), others describe it as "an escape from the cycle of death and rebirth" (again, if you make the cut). Some religions insist on one only God, in others, multiple gods, and in still others there are no gods. These ideas do not blend well.

Some religions focus on the individual's well-being, happiness, or prosperity, while others focus on the individual's relationship with God. Still, others focus on the elimination of suffering. Given these differences, we cannot assert that that religions are basically the same, just viewed from different cultural vantage points.

I will, however, take a moment to lend a bit of support for looking for commonalities. The Christian Golden Rule, "Do unto others as you would have done unto you," has striking similarities to the Buddhist rule, "Hurt not others with what pains yourself." The sentiment is the same: treat others how you want to be treated. That sentiment is broadly expressed among many world religions.

These broadly expressed sentiments are often referred to as "spiritual truths." These "truths" are ideas we seem to all know, but maybe we did not know we knew them until we heard them articulated. We can all get behind these "truths" in a cooperative living situation. Religious leaders throughout history, and across religions, have attempted to communicate these "spiritual truths."

The problem with the use of intuition to claim "We just know they are true" is that intuition is quite low on the veracity scale. This partly explains why religions (and their denominations) are such a complex collection of differing "truths." When intuition, emotion, and faith are the primary guiding forces for identifying spiritual truths, we should not expect complete alignment of all the differing umwelts.

I'm going to just ignore the argument over "which is correct" because all religions are based on faith. Reaching a definitive conclusion without any physical evidence, seems futile. Instead, in the next chapter, I will explore a more interesting question.

CHAPTER 26

Evaluating the Health of Your Religious Beliefs

I nstead of asking, "Are our beliefs true?" perhaps we should be asking, "Are our beliefs healthy?" The hardest part of this second question resides in trying to define healthy.

Are Religious Beliefs Healthy for Individuals?

This question is *orders of magnitude* more interesting than the question of correctness, at least to me. Here, I'm biased toward my dad's umwelt. As I have previously stated, our own belief systems are greatly impacted by our parent's belief systems, and I am no exception.

My dad was the chief psychologist at the Mental Health Institute (MHI) in Cherokee, Iowa. The Cherokee MHI was one of three mental health institutions in the state of Iowa. Prior to his career as a psychologist, my dad received his Masters of Divinity degree at the Virginia Theological Seminary in Alexandria, Virginia, in 1970. He never had any intention of getting ordained and entering the clergy. His interest was the psychologically healthy and unhealthy relationships with God. In other words, he was concerned with theological relationships of individuals with God and their effect on mental and spiritual health.

My dad explained to me that some variations of Christianity are very psychologically healthy, while others are very damaging to people.

My dad was a lifelong member of the Episcopal Church. His dad, spent most of his life as an Episcopal priest on the Rosebud Indian reservation near Winner, SD. I never met my grandpa; he passed away three years before I was born.

My dad summarized healthy and unhealthy Christian faith this way: "Theology that focuses on sin, salvation, judgment, and the end times tends to be unhealthy. Theology that focuses on love, forgiveness, and God's grace tends to be more psychologically healthy." He would say, "Everyone worships, it is hard to avoid. Some people worship money, power, or fame. God as love, is a healthier thing to worship. Focusing on God's judgement, literal Scripture, or your own salvation is generally unhealthy."

As a psychologist, my father often worked with adolescents, several of whom had been diagnosed with schizophrenia. People with this disorder often have religious delusions. My dad told me that it was rare to find a mental health institution without someone who claims that they were being talked to by God or demons. Slightly less common were people that were convinced they were a prophet or the Messiah. Teaching these individuals how to have a healthier relationship with God helped them with their therapy and healing.

"Unconditional love is a powerful healer," he would say. "Not everyone gets to feel unconditional love on Earth." He felt that God's grace was the offer of unconditional love. According to my dad, grace was the most important part of the message of Christ.

Mental illness can force people to deal with real despair and often guilt. Bad theology that focuses on God's punishment often makes this situation worse. When we fixate on God's judgment, and ignore God's grace, we do psychological damage to those who are already struggling. My dad would say, "Judgment and punishment theology is manipulative; these ideas have little to do with the teachings of Christ."

I always felt lucky to gain my dad's perspectives as I navigated my own journey in faith. (I felt lucky he was my dad in lots of ways, but in this chapter, I'm just going to focus on his spiritual guidance.)

I recently saw a study on the health benefits of religions. It basically compared the health of those who attended a church with those who did not. In my opinion, that is akin to asking the question, "Are drugs good or bad for you?" The answer, of course, depends on the drug and the medical situation. Insulin is not helpful when you have strep throat, but penicillin works pretty darn well. Penicillin is worthless for diabetes. In the same way, religion can be healthy or unhealthy depending on how a specific theology affects a particular person. Individuals should ask themselves if *their* theology is helping them or manipulating them. If your religion is isolating you or asking you to deny empirical facts, then these are some big red flags telling you this is likely not healthy.

Other red flags might include a church that encourages you to withdraw from society or relationships with certain friends or family members. Another warning sign might be a focus solely on an interpretation of "God's word," while neglecting any negative impact on others. (Some, of course, would reject that red flag and label it as humanist. I guess I can just reject their rejection. Rejection can go both ways. ☺)

If your religion, or your God, does not focus on your relationship with mankind and the creation, then what's the point? It seems to me that if your goal is solely *your* salvation, then your religion is encouraging you to be self-absorbed.

My dad acknowledged that evangelism was part of the mission of the Church. But his idea of evangelism was different than that of other churches I have attended. To him, evangelism was about spreading the good news of God's grace through the sacrifice of Christ. It was spreading a healthy view of man's relationship to God. He was not one bit interested in saving souls. In his view, everyone was saved. Christ died to save the world. There were no strings attached. Christ's death was an act of God's grace. Christ didn't just die for the thirty-ish percent of the world who are Christian, and certainly not just for the tiny slice of the protestant pie that think they must utter the magic phrase, "I have accepted Jesus as my personal savior." In his view, Christ died for everyone. No one goes to hell. Christ killed that concept. (Again, I know that this is not the view of all Christians, but it was my dad's view.) Damnation for those that did not develop the "proper" belief system—due to parenting, geography, genetic wiring, culture, etc.— seemed absurd to my father.

My dad was a devout Christian, and I respected his beliefs. He always said he wanted to write a book about theology. Unfortunately, he never got around to it. His several strokes, heart attacks, and finally Parkinson's disease got in his way. He passed away four years ago. As a tribute to him, I would love to get some of his thoughts out into the world. I believe that his ideas are too important and too relevant to simply be buried in the ground with him.

Those last few paragraphs were for my dad. My eyes are welling up a little . . .

Are Religions Helpful to Communities?

I grew up in the Church. I saw firsthand that religion can be healthy for a community of people. Shared rituals and stories unite us. As I mentioned at the start of this section, Robin Dunbar's research indicates that without bonding rituals, communities of greater than twenty struggle to hang together. I concede that these bonding rituals do not *need* to be religious in nature, but historically, churches acted as unifying forces within communities.

When I was in my twenties, I told my dad that I didn't like to go to church. I said, "I don't feel like I get anything out of it."

He smiled and said, "You don't go to church to *get*, you go to church to *give*." Even if you set aside for the moment the spiritual benefits churches might provide to individuals, there are pragmatic reasons to support these institutions. Churches, synagogues, or temples are where we celebrate important human rites of passage, such as baptisms, confirmations, bar mitzvahs, bat mitzvahs, weddings, and funerals. These places of worship provide both a structured ritual and a venue for life's big rites of passage.

In addition, many churches provide social services to not only their parish, but also to their communities. Food pantries, services for refugees, coat drives, soup kitchens, all serve to lessen some suffering in vulnerable populations. Of course, these services are not solely the domain of churches. Public libraries, government agencies, local schools, and other secular institutions do this work as well, but much of it is often done by pastors, priests, rabbis, and congregations.

Are Religions Helpful to Countries?

When considering religions impact on entire countries, the arguments for the positive impacts of religions become much less compelling. Historically, the merging of religions and countries or empires ends badly. At this scale, the problem becomes the entanglement of religion with power. For personal gain, those in power often use religion to manipulate their subjects or constituents.

A reoccurring theme in Christianity is victory through submission. The crucifixion of Christ, God as man, is a submission, a surrender. The submission allows for Christ's victory over death. Even his father sacrificing his only son for humanity, is an act of unfathomable love. This sacrifice is the demonstration of God's grace. Submission to accomplish a greater good is also a common theme in many other religions, mythology, and quite frankly, as well as in many good movies. Some social movements, which did not have power in the traditional sense, adopted the "victory through submission" approach with a good deal of success. One good example comes from Ghandi's peaceful/passive resistance to the British empire. Another example was Martin Luther King's campaign of passive civil disobedience to gain civil rights. My favorite cinematic example is in *Star Wars*, when Obi-Wan Kenobi sacrifices himself. As he explains to Mr. Vader, "If you strike me down, I will become more powerful than you can possibly imagine." And he simply willingly dies. This theme of "victory through submission" seems to be a spiritual truth, which is precisely why it resonates with us.

Whereas religion is often about *submission*, politics are often about *gaining power*, which is why these two—politics and religion—make for such strange bedfellows. When Jesus is in the desert and is tempted by the devil who offers him unlimited *power* to do good. Jesus rejects this offer, because he realizes the "doing good" part is merely the bait. Satan is really offering him *power*. Jesus rejects the temptation because he understands God's message is unrelated to power. An old Charlie Chaplin quote seems fitting here, "You need power only when you want to do something harmful; otherwise, love is enough to get everything done."

My goal with this section was to shine a light on the formation of our own belief systems. Understanding our own thinking can potentially help us prune destructive beliefs and reinforce healthy ones.

Our different belief systems stem from our different personalities, learning styles, strengths, talents, genetics, experiences, cultures, as well as which religion or denomination we happen to choose. True empathy becomes possible only when we try to grasp another's umwelt. Religious beliefs are a significant part of the umwelt of many people.

Evolution

At first glance, a sudden transition to the topic of evolution may seem jarring. For many, evolution seems unrelated to religion. But for some, the topics of religion and the theory of evolution have become oddly intertwined. As a biology teacher, I can tell you that every part of the study of biological sciences is tied directly to the topic of evolution. However, many people harbor misconceptions regarding the theory of evolution, the scientific process, and the theology of creation. So deep are these issues that I have first-hand experience seeing parents telling their kids not to not accept this scientific theory. That never happens with gravitational or heliocentric theory, but the theory of evolution gets different treatment. The source of that different treatment usually involves a specific type of religious theology.

Understanding the theology and the scientific misconceptions around the topic of evolution can help sort out this epistemological mess. The upside of this mess is that it makes evolution a fantastic subject for examining the processes by which knowledge is acquired, how our beliefs interact with that knowledge, and how knowledge can interact with belief.

CHAPTER 27

Evolution and Theology

R on Reagan, son of former president Ronald Reagan, once said, "One of the most important questions that should be asked of any potential presidential candidate is this: Do you accept the theory of evolution as a scientific fact?" He pointed out that someone in charge of the country should have a basic grasp of scientific facts. For him, evolution was a basic litmus test. It should be noted that his father did not share this view.

I want to start my discussion about evolution with the elephants in some rooms. I use "rooms" in the plural because it turns out that there are a lot of umwelt rooms. In many rooms, there is no elephant: religion and evolutionary theory are not in conflict. In other rooms, there is a huge elephant, because there is a perceived conflict between the theory of evolution and their faith.

The Perceived Theological Problem of Evolution

God and bigfoot are interesting case studies pertaining to "how we know" because they lack an agreed upon empirical "truth." Evolution is interesting for the opposite reason. The theory of evolution *is* an empirical "truth" that many people think is a poorly justified belief. These people tend to hold the view that science is just another belief system— an "alternative to religion," as my student stated way back in Chapter 8.

During my years of teaching, students would often ask me if I "believed in the theory of evolution." That very question points out that my students thought of this established scientific theory as a belief. Yet I have never been asked if I *believed* in the theory of gravity or the theory of relativity. Or even the seemingly more absurd question, "Do you *believe* in Newton's laws?" I say "seemingly more absurd" because laws do not hold a higher status than theories. Theories actually explain laws.

Part of the problem lies in the terminology. "Theory" is a problematic term. The layperson's understanding of the term is the opposite of its meaning in a scientific context. As I previously mentioned in the "language of science" section of this book, a theory *is not* a hunch or an educated guess. Instead, in the scientific context, a theory is a grand unifying idea that explains many concepts within a field. To be a theory (again, in the context of science) it must be *"yet to be refuted"* (I know that sounds a bit awkward but that is the proper language of science), and it must explain a wide range of phenomena. "Theory" is the pinnacle of scientific thought. "Theory" is the polar opposite of a hunch. Theories are not possible beliefs; they are established, *yet to be refuted*, scientific explanations.

There are not many scientific theories. Here is a list of them: germ theory, the theory of evolution, gravitational theory, theory of relativity, heliocentric theory, big bang theory, cell theory—but not many more. It would be very radical to not accept a theory in your current field without evidence to do so. "Do you believe in germ theory?" or "Do you believe in the heliocentric theory?" are odd questions indeed.

If you met an astronomer who did not embrace the heliocentric theory or a microbiologist who did not embrace germ theory, then you would be justified to question their expertise in their field. If you had a physics teacher who taught "alternatives" to the theory of gravity or alternatives to Newton's laws of motion, you would be justified in complaining that this person is not qualified to teach physics. If the astronomer, microbiologist, and physics teacher rejected these scientific theories based on their *faith* or gut *intuition*, it would not strengthen their case, it would weaken it! We never use intuition or faith to challenge established scientific theories. That would be considered, well, absurd.

But can't scientific theories be overturned? Yes, this is the nature of science. All knowledge is tentative. A theory can be overturned if evidence—gathered through processes that eliminates all personal bias—shows that the theory or model is incorrect. But it is extremely unlikely that we will find out that: 1) pathogens don't cause infectious diseases (germ theory), 2) masses do not attract each other through a field force (gravitational theory), 3) that the Earth does not revolve around the Sun (heliocentric theory), or 4) populations do not change over time because of artificial or natural selection (theory of evolution). The amount of evidence for each of these (and all theories) is quite overwhelming, and that's part of the reason we call them theories!

The other reason they are called theories is that these particular ideas *are grand unifying concepts* that explain many different phenomena or even scientific laws.

So why don't some people accept the evidence for the theory of evolution? Many academics think that people simply don't understand the concepts. I have watched biologists engage in debates with creationists, armed with mountains of evidence for evolution. This approach doesn't seem to work.

Last summer, I spoke with a faculty member in the Department of Philosophy at The University of Iowa. He suspects that people conflate biological evolution with social Darwinism. He explained that people then equate evolution with a loss of morality. There may be something to his explanation, particularly the part about the "loss of morality."

I subscribe to a simpler hypothesis. People reject evolutionary theory because of a specific theological belief system. Some individuals were raised within a *theological* system that rejects science when it *seems* to oppose Scripture. Most of those with this theological view don't reject science outright; they reject it only in the cases where they *feel* the "evidence" conflicts with their theology.

When people who subscribe to this theology are unable to square scientific evidence with their personal religious beliefs, they deal with this cognitive dissonance by simply rejecting the evidence, as if that evidence came from a competing belief system. Thus, to them, the question, "Do you *BELIEVE* in evolution?" does not even seem like an odd question.

When I was teaching, I spoke to parents, or in one case a grandparent, who held anti-evolution/creationists belief systems. Very few of these parents told their children that all science should be rejected. Most rejected science *only* when it came to specific *theories*. They even attempted to use information that was "scientific" to validate creationism. (For example, finding coral fossils in Iowa was proof of the flood story found in Genesis.) I put "scientific" in quotes because creationists are not really doing science. They are not trying to *refute* their creationist hypothesis, instead, they are gathering evidence to prove their hypothesis. In addition, there is no mechanism to eliminate *their* bias. It looks like science to the untrained eye, but there are really no similarities to the actual process of science.

When teaching my anti-evolution students, I empathized with their plight. They were forced to make a difficult choice. They could either rewire their brains and modify their central belief system (not an easy task), or they could reject obvious evidence (which also made them feel uneasy). Many students developed a work-around that made the rejection of evidence seem like the smart or logical choice. By viewing science as a biased belief system that was an alternative to religion, their problem could be solved. They simply ignored science if it conflicted with their entrenched belief system. This selective rejection of science and scientific findings has been normalized within fundamentalism.

If their denomination frames the choice as one between "faith in the divine Scripture" versus "faith in secular science," then the student's choice becomes easy. Who do you *believe*, God or your science teacher?

Theological Problems with Evolution

Science teachers really don't stand a chance when the choice is framed as such. When I tried to combat this problem with more scientific evidence, it didn't work. Within this belief system, scientific evidence is the enemy. Science represents the "so-called experts" attacking the students belief systems. If I provided more evidence, some students would view this as simply more attacks.

I believe that the rejection of the theory of evolution stems from a problem of theology. The data seems to support this hypothesis.

Belief in evolution highest among atheists and agnostics, lower among evangelicals

% of U.S. adults who say humans have ...

	Evolved over time	Due to natural processes	Guided by supreme being	DK / ref.	Existed in present form	DK/ref.
	%	%	%	%	%	%
Christian	53	21	29	4	42	5=100
Protestant	48	17	28	3	47	5
Evangelical	38	11	25	2	57	5
Mainline	65	28	31	5	30	5
Historically black	50	16	31	3	45	5
Catholic	66	31	31	4	29	5
Orthodox Christian	59	29	25	5	36	5
Mormon	42	11	29	2	52	7
Jehovah's Witness	20	6	15	0	74	5
Non-Christian faiths	78	55	18	5	18	4
Jewish	81	58	18	5	16	3
Muslim	53	25	25	3	41	6
Buddhist	86	67	13	6	13	1
Hindu	80	62	14	3	17	3
Unaffiliated	82	63	14	4	15	3
Atheist	95	91	2	1	5	<1
Agnostic	96	83	8	4	3	2
Nothing in particular	76	53	19	5	20	4
Men	65	36	25	4	31	4
Women	58	29	25	4	37	5
Ages 18-29	72	44	25	3	26	2
30-49	63	35	25	4	34	3
50-64	58	27	27	4	38	4
65+	52	25	22	5	39	9
College grad.	73	44	25	5	24	3
Some college	62	31	27	4	35	3
H.S. or less	53	27	23	4	40	6

Note: Figures may not add to 100% or to subtotals indicated due to rounding.
Source: U.S. Religious Landscape Study, conducted June 4-Sept. 30, 2014.
"The Evolution of Pew Research Center's Survey Questions About the Origins and Development of Life on Earth"

PEW RESEARCH CENTER

(Courtesy of the PEW Research Center, copyright@pewtrusts.org.)

This data is very interesting. I like data! Let's break this data down by theological groups. I suppose I need to define "fundamentalism" before diving too deeply into the data. Fundamentalism is a form of a religion, especially Islam or Protestant Christianity, which upholds belief in the strict, *literal* interpretation of a *Scripture they believe is a sacred text.*

Now I want to divide the data between the primarily fundamentalist Christian denominations and those that are primarily non-fundamentalist. The lowest acceptance of the idea that "life evolved over time" belongs to two groups: Evangelical Protestants (38 percent) and Jehovah's Witnesses and (20 percent). Those two denominations have little in common except that their parishioners often hold fundamentalist views of the Scriptures. Together, they accept evolution at an average rate of 29 percent.

The two largest remaining groups, Catholic and Mainline[6] Protestant, accept the Theory of Evolution by an average of 65.5 percent. That difference of acceptance, 65.5 percent to 29 percent between these theological groups is striking!

Remember, this difference of acceptance is not a difference between Christian and non-Christian. This difference is between a fundamentalist theology and a non-fundamentalist theology. Many Mormans are also theologically fundamentalist, though they use a slightly different Scripture. Only 42 percent of Mormons accept evolution.

Many of us who understand that evolution is an empirical truth are often tempted to jump to the conclusion that fundamentalists are dumber than people in other groups. I think that it is important to stress that this is not the case. Some of my best students have been fundamentalist. Let me tell you about one of them, who I will call "Trent."

---

6.   Mainline simply means those churches with a long history in US. The Mainline Church is the "original version" if you will. It is primarily a term used to differentiate the protestant churches from their breakaway churches. American Baptist is Mainline Protestant for example, whereas the Southern Baptist is not. Lutheran is Mainline, whereas Missouri Synod Lutheran is not. The term "Mainline" is specific to the protestant denominations of the US. In general, the newer Evangelical churches are the breakaway churches, and they tend to be more conservative than their parent churches. Usually, Mainline churches are far less fundamentalist in their theology then the newer evangelical churches. Mainline does not mean more popular or mainstream.

Trent was one of my top students. He was a great kid, super bright, and we got along very well. He simply held a theological viewpoint that got in his way when it came to learning about evolution, or any topic where there was an *apparent* rift between science and his sacred text. (He also had some trouble with the Big Bang theory.) "Trent" took an F on my evolution test out of protest. He knew the material, but to him, he felt that if he answered the questions correctly it would be an acknowledgement of the reality of evolution. So he left them blank.

I had a different experience with another student, who I will call "Garett." At parent teacher conferences, I talked with Garett's grandpa, who told me that he and Garett had gone to the creationist "museum" in Kentucky as part of their summer vacation. When his grandpa described the museum to me, he was clearly awestruck with the facility. His grandpa was very kind to me. He gently explained that his philosophy was that Garett should learn the concepts taught in school, but he obviously did not have to *believe* those concepts. Garett earned the highest score of any student on my evolution test that year. I was sure Garett understood the material, but it was unclear to me if he ever believed that which he understood.

When people are called stupid or uneducated because of their different umwelt, it only serves to widen the rift between science and those with a fundamentalist theology. It is important to keep in mind that there is also a cultural and geographic aspect to belief systems. In geographic areas where many fundamentalists live (primarily rural areas or in some urban areas in the South), you have many parents and even other teachers who reinforce those beliefs.

When I was telling my friend Dave about my book, he wondered if this section of the book was even needed. In his experience, adults and high school kids don't really think about this stuff, he viewed it as a non-issue. Dave went to a Jesuit high school, and from his viewpoint, the conflict between evolution and religion was pretty fringe. I disagree. In the US, members of the evangelical denominations are close in number to all the parishioners of all Mainline Protestants put together. The majority of Protestant Christians in the US are not fundamentalists, but the percentage of Protestants who hold fundamentalist views is certainly significant.

Another interesting piece of data from the PEW Research Center survey, is that *only* 66 percent of Catholics say they believe life gradually evolved over time. I say "only" because it should be much closer to 100 percent, given that the last several Popes have publicly stated that they believe life gradually evolved over time. The Catholic Church has renounced young Earth creationism—the view the Earth is between 6,000 and 10,000 years old—as bad theology and bad science. As early as 1950, Pope Pius XII stated that there is no inherent conflict between evolution and the doctrine of faith concerning humanity. In 1996, Pope John Paul II reiterated this view, saying the evidence for evolution had increased and now it was much "more than a hypothesis." In 2014, Pope Francis stated that "evolution in nature is not inconsistent with the notion of creation." He also added that the Big Bang theory does not contradict a divine act of creation.

It turns out that some Catholics hold fundamentalist belief systems even though these views are not the position of their church.

In Mainline Protestant denominations, the data is similar. In Lutheran, Presbyterian, Methodist, and Episcopal, 65 percent of individuals agree with the concept that life evolved gradually over time. This number is also lower than expected, given that the official stance of their churches is pro-evolution and anti-creationism. It appears that not all the parishioners of these respective churches received that memo.

Am I surprised? Not really. Evolution is rarely a topic that is ever mentioned in non-fundamentalist churches. Most churches largely ignore science and instead focus on other important ways of knowing. These churches usually stay in their epistemological lanes, so to speak.

Churches Teaching Science

I want to insert a quick little story here, mostly for entertainment purposes. Shortly after I got married, my wife and I went to California for Christmas to visit her parents who had recently moved there from Michigan. On Christmas Eve, my wife, her brothers (Joe and Andy), her parents, and I went to a Presbyterian church. It was a warm evening, with palm and orange trees around the parking lot. Very different from the frigid, snow-covered Christmas Eve services of my youth in northwest Iowa. The service was normal enough, until the sermon. The pastor started talking about science. He began talking about all of things that science did not understand. He listed several concepts that were in fact well-known to science that he insisted were wonderful examples of "natures unexplained miracles." "Why are the colors of the sunset beautiful hues of orange and red? How does water move from the ground to the very top leaves of the tallest trees?" I raised my hand behind the pew so only my new brothers-in-law could see, and I whispered to Andy, "Pick me, I know that one." Andy, Joe, and my wife, Suellen, began to giggle. The sermon dragged on for a while. Toward the end, I whispered to Joe, "I knew 80 percent of those." We all, unsuccessfully, attempted to suppress our church giggles. I am pretty sure my father-in-law caught a case of the contagious church giggles. I think my mother-in-law was a little embarrassed by our behavior. We all agreed that we would not attend that particular church again.

Maybe it is best that churches don't double as science education centers.

Theological Problems Continued

So, churches don't teach science, and in science class, we often pretend that theological issues have nothing to do with science. In the absence of a school or a church providing information, people just pick up beliefs from the culture in which they live.

The belief that evolution refutes the Scripture is strong in many parts of the country. For some, to be pro-evolution is to be anti-God. Culture is so important to our beliefs that if rejection of evolution is a strong belief where you live, then you might feel compelled to reject the theory of evolution on religious grounds, even if it is not the official stance of your church. Most Christian denominations do not oppose evolutionary science or the theory of evolution. The parishioners often just don't know that about their faith.

Back to the Data

Moving on to other data, the non-Christian faiths are also interesting. In the Jewish faith, which uses the exact same sacred text of creation that the Christians use, 81 percent accept that life on Earth evolves. This is even higher than Mainline Protestant. I'm only speculating here, but I think this might have as much to do with geography as theology. Not a lot of rural or southern Jews in the US.

Buddhists and Hindus also accept the empirical truth of evolution at a high rate, at 86 percent and 80 percent respectively. Buddhist and Hindus don't tend to have much fundamentalism with these religions.

Muslim is more complex. At 53 percent acceptance of evolution, this rate is close to the average of Protestant Christian (48 percent). It is harder in the Muslim faith to break down the prevalence of fundamentalism by denomination. There are two major denominations, Shia and Suni—and the variation even within those large groups is substantial. The anti-evolution—and the radical groups—tend to be composed of the fundamentalist individuals. Some Suni and some Shia.

In conclusion, it is *incorrect* to frame evolution as an argument between science and religion. It is also incorrect to frame it as a debate between science vs. Christianity. There is a *theological* debate in America as to whether *fundamentalism* is an appropriate way of knowing when it comes to physical and testable questions. (Islam has the same debate between its fundamentalist and non-fundamentalist factions.)

I thought it necessary to spend several pages addressing those epistemological elephants before I set out to discuss science of evolution. It's important for science teachers to know how to teach students struggling with science and faith issues. I decided that a section titled "How to Teach Evolution" was likely too large, and too specific for this book's ill-defined target audience. Maybe I'll write a book specifically for teachers another year. For now, I simply added a section of "Frequently Asked Questions" about evolution in Appendix D. This can serve as a guide for science teachers, and maybe it will also address some specific questions that other readers might have about evolution not covered in this chapter.

But for now, let's talk a little about the actual science behind the theory of evolution and the theology of creation itself.

CHAPTER 28

Science of Evolution

Think of evolution as two related topics: the *process of evolution* and the *theory of evolution*. Let's begin with the process of evolution. To understand the theory of evolution, you first need to understand the process of evolution.

Six Core Ideas Needed to Understand the Process of Evolution

1. Within almost all populations of living things, there are variations in traits among the individuals within that population. Most of these traits are associated with proteins that are controlled by genes. (Genes are sections of DNA that code for proteins.) This difference in genes within a population is broadly called "genetic variation." Different genes, different traits.

2. Those genetic variations might be deemed useful and be preferred, or selected for, by a farmer or plant breeder, or even a beekeeper. This is called artificial selection. (For example, selecting for the cows that give the most milk and using those individual to breed to create a herd that gives more milk.)

3. Artificial selection is a subset of natural selection. Artificial selection is what occurs when people are the ones

doing the selecting. With natural selection, nature itself, without the help of people, does the selecting. Those traits that help an organism survive and mate are chosen. Conversely, the traits that hinder the ability of an individual to survive or mate are not chosen, or they are selected against. Many traits have little to no effect on survival or reproductive success.

4. There are various pressures in the environment that affect survival and reproductive success. These factors are called "selection pressures." There can be either natural or artificial selection pressures.

5. Traits that are more helpful than harmful are more likely to be passed on to the next generation. Traits that are harmful to reproductive success are not passed on because, as you might expect, the animal with those traits did not survive and/or mate.

6. As a result of these facts, over time the genetics of a population will often change due to artificial or natural selection pressures.

We call this genetic change over time "biological evolution." Evolution is a word in the English language that means change. Biological evolution is the term given to the idea that the genetics of populations change over time due to selection pressures. This "idea" is not simply an idea; it's an empirical truth, an observed fact. It is also some bulletproof logic. We can observe the results of the genetics of populations changing over time due to selection pressures, be they natural or artificial.

When I was teaching, getting students to understand and accept these six core ideas was the easy lifting. Most students would accept them without batting an eye. Sometimes, they found it so obvious that the concept was boring to them. Even my students with a fundamentalist background and a strong predisposition against all things evolution, would accept this process. (But they would sometimes squirm when I used the words "evolution" and "fact" in the same sentence.)

The difficulty arose for some students, when I began to talk about the *theory of evolution*. Even though the *theory of evolution* is only *slightly* different from the *process* of evolution.

The *theory* of evolution states that life on Earth came about gradually through the *process* of biological evolution. One might think that the adoption of the "theory" would logically follow the understanding of the process. But this is not always the case.

The theory of evolution is a grand unifying idea which explains a lot about the life we see on Earth. For example, the theory of evolution explains how life, in all its forms, came to be on Earth! If you are a believer in a religious creator, it is important to remember that the theory of evolution does not need to be an alternative to a religious creation. Evolution could simply be the elegant mechanism used by the creator.

Evolution, as a mechanism, also explains why whales and pythons have hip bones. It explains why we find the skeletons of animals that no longer exist buried all over the Earth. It explains why during development, humans have tails (and even gill slits). It's why the mechanisms used to turn DNA into specific proteins is the same in Plantae, Fungi, Monera, Protista, and in all animals. It explains why the organelles chlorophyll and mitochondria have their own DNA. It explains why the wide variety of finch species on the Galapagos Islands look very different from each other, and yet have very, very, similar DNA—thus pointing to a single common ancestor. The same principle occurs in the marsupials of Australia. The theory of evolution explains why Native American mitochondrial DNA is very similar to mitochondrial DNA in East Asians, but dissimilar to those with Northern European or Jewish ancestry. It explains how resistance to antibiotics in bacteria develops and how pesticide resistance develops in insects. It explains how domesticated dogs evolved from wolves. It explains how the wings of populations of peppered moths changed to a black color after the Industrial Revolution. And it explains how, years later, the genes for the color of those populations, were selected back to the original genes that coded for their original colors in the mid-twentieth century. Evolution explains the appearance and disappearance of the dinosaurs. The theory of evolution is a grand unifying concept that explains an awful lot.

Ideas That Competed with, and Lost to, the Theory of Evolution for Acceptance

The theory of evolution used to have some competition. If you lived back, say, in the 1200s, in a land before science, your belief as to how life appeared on the Earth varied depending on your geographical birthplace. Different world religions had, and still have, different creation stories. There are almost as many stories as there are cultures. In 1200, in North America for example, a variety of creation stories were mostly passed down from generation to generation through oral traditions. There is one from the Tule River Tribe, located in Central California amongst what is now called the Giant Sequoia National Monument, that explains why eagles, coyotes, bears—and the hairy man (aka bigfoot)—behave the way that they do. Another creation story from the Lakota Sioux explains how Mother Earth gave birth to all living things through an opening in Earth that we now call Wind Cave in South Dakota. I really like that account because I have spent time in and around Wind Cave. It seems so natural to think that this cave—which seems supernatural because of the way it "breaths"—could have given birth to the bison and all life. Accepting any creation story as literal truth suggests that all other stories, from all the other cultures and religions, are incorrect. Which, if you stop to think about it, is rather rude.

From a scientific perspective, the only real competition to Darwin's Theory, came from Jean-Baptiste Lamark, in the 1700's (a half century before Charles Darwin and Alfred Wallace were born). Lamarck recognized the obvious evidence for various life-forms changing over time. Lamarck proposed a mechanism for how these changes in life-forms took place. His explanation had to do with what he called "acquired traits."

Lamarck had reasoned that because giraffes, for example, spend their lives stretching their necks to reach leaves near the tops of trees, their necks lengthened a bit. These slightly longer necks were passed on to their offspring. Over time, the species got longer necks. Now biologists understand that "acquired traits" are different from genetic traits. Weightlifters, for example, don't have naturally stronger babies.

People who spend time in tanning booths don't have children who have a darker complexion.

Sometimes those who understand evolution laugh when they hear Lamark's ideas, but I cut him a lot of slack. Remember, we are talking about the 1700s. Gregor Mendel, who is considered the "father of genetics," was not even born until 1822. I think Lamarck gave a reasonable hypothesis given our lack of understanding of genetics at the time.

A little over one hundred years after Lamark put forward his hypothesis, a different hypothesis was put forward by two different men at roughly the same time. Almost everyone has heard of Charles Darwin, but fewer people have heard of Alfred Wallace. In the1830s, Darwin had his epiphany while looking at the variety of life in the Galapagos Islands. Wallace was struck with the exact same idea while studying life on some islands in Malaysia. Wallace likely had the idea first. The two men both wrote papers on evolution that were both read at the London Linnean Society Meeting in 1858. Darwin was surprised that someone else was working on the same idea. This competition lit a fire under him. His famous book, *Origin of the Species* was published the following year. Wallace graciously allowed Darwin to take all the credit for the idea because he conceded that Darwin was further along in his thinking about evolution.

CHAPTER 29

Evidence for the Theory of Evolution

Darwin's evidence drew mostly from observations of living creatures and some fossils. The evidence for evolution is overwhelming, but other than logic, I have not offered any evidence yet.

The easiest way to break down the discussion of evidence is to put all of it into some categories. I will try to keep my summary brief by exploring only five of the many intertwined types of evidence for the theory of evolution.

1. Fossils

When I was in graduate school in the late 1980s, I met a girl from Minnesota's Twin Cities. I will call her "Linda." She was a friend of a friend. I think I only talked to her twice in my life. I am including her in my book for the two amazing lines of dialogue she said. I don't remember the location or anything else about that rather uneventful day, I only remember the dialogue.

She said, "I do not believe in evolution."

I went into biology-guy mode and tried the gotcha question of, "So, what do you think about all the dinosaurs?"

She stated flatly, "I don't believe in dinosaurs."

I thought, but did not say, "Well okay then, I think we are done here." Had I already invented the term "portal nuts," I think I may have used it here. Instead, I kept my mouth shut.

We know dinosaurs existed. We know this empirical fact through the fossil record. The fossil record also tells us humans and T-Rex did *not* overlap. We were not even close to overlapping. The interval between these two species spans approximately *fifty-three million* years. When we speak of the fossil record, we are not talking about a few fossils here and there. Over *forty million* fossils have been found and catalogued.

We find fossils all over the Earth. Some of these fossilized remains come from things that still exist on the Earth, but because fossils are so old, most of these remains are from species that are no longer here. For example, many fossils come from various species of a group of animals that we call dinosaurs. (If you *believe* in dinosaurs.)

We find fossils for ground sloths larger than bears, mastodons, mammoths, saber-toothed tigers, and many types of extinct bacteria. In addition, a multitude of plants, insects, even footprints are preserved in the fossil record. We can, and do, also find fossils of a few species that still exist, but have simply been here for a very long time. (Examples include many still common species of trees, now petrified; fossilized shark teeth; many still-living mollusks; crocodiles; and ancient bacteria and blue-green algae that still live today!)

The actual number of fossils is astounding. And it grows every year as more and more are discovered. I saw close to thirty fossils this morning as I walked my dog along the Coralville reservoir near my home in Iowa. Many of the fossils I saw were corals, thus the name Coralville. If I had taken time to actually hunt for fossils, I could have found hundreds.

The number of species that have existed on the Earth, based on simply counting fossilized species, is a much higher number than the number of species that are currently known to exist on the Earth today! This not only implies that current life on Earth is different from the original life on Earth, but it also empirically proves that life on Earth has changed over time. Life has evolved. It is an undisputed fact that many life-forms are different today than they were in the past.

(top) A large, fossilized dinosaur bone and many other smaller bones embedded in the rock at Dinosaur National Park in Colorado. (My wife, Suellen, provides scale.) (bottom) Allosaurus skull. On the next page (top) More dinosaur bones, including part of a backbone, some ribs, and what looks to be a femur. (bottom) Fossilized dinosaur vertebra. (My ChapStick for scale.)

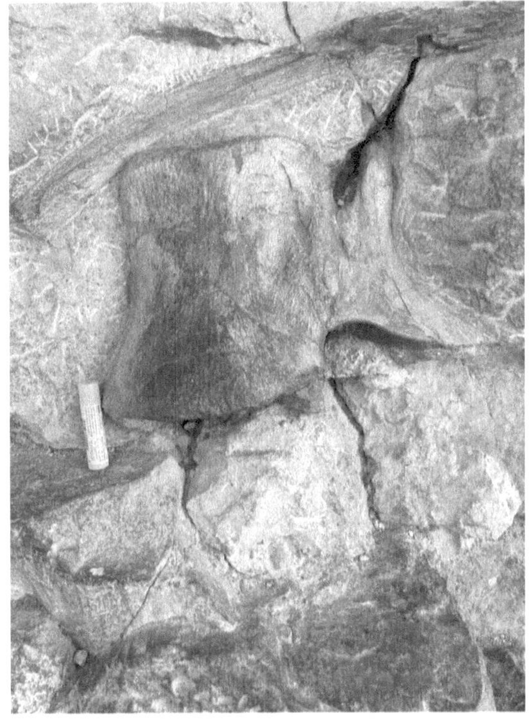

(top) Various skeletons of dinosaurs reassembled using fossilized remains. (My son, Max, provides scale.) (bottom) A skull of a Tyrannosaurus rex skull found in the Badlands of South Dakota, nicknamed Duffy. (My son, Henry, provides scale.)

(top) A reconstructed mammoth skeleton on display at The Mammoth Site in Hot Springs, South Dakota. (My son, Henry, once again provides scale.) (bottom) A dig in process at The Mammoth Site, showing many random mammoth bones. (My somewhat blurry son, Max, once again provides scale.)

Life has changed over time. Toy Poodles did not run across the plains of North America prior to the Ice Age. The T-Rex and the myriads of other dinosaurs are clearly not around anymore. Dinosaurs did exist. That is an empirical fact.

The age of these fossils tells an important part of their story. At the time that Darwin wrote the *Origin of the Species*, modern fossil dating techniques were not known. Despite this limitation, one could get at least a *relative* age, and therefore a *relative* chronology of some of the fossils that had been found at the time using a "layer method."

Let me explain the logic behind the layer method. If you are digging in a hole and you find fossil A, then in a deeper layer of soil you find fossil B, then it would be logical to think B was there first. Further, if you *never* find B with A, and B is *always* deeper than A, it becomes logical to assume B was here before A. So if Fossil B existed before fossil A, it is safe to assume species B existed before species A. For over one hundred years, using this simple logic, we have known that the dinosaurs existed long before the large mammals. The layer method, though not full-proof, yielded no evidence that would refute the idea of evolution.

In the 1940s, science entered the atomic age. Building on the work of Marie Curie, newly discovered understandings about radiation and the nuclei of atoms lead to the development of radiometric dating. Some elements convert part of their nucleus to a different isotope or even a different element as they undergo radioactive decay. By understanding this decay, we can use isotope ratios to determine the age of rocks, sediments, or fossilized material. This is called radiometric dating. There are different methods of radiometric dating that can be used. If the sample in question is really, really old—say it was found in a very deep layer of rock, such as Canadian Shield rock—one could use uranium series dating. If the sample is in sediment that is just moderately old, or if the sample is in volcanic ash, then potassium-argon dating works quite well. If the sample is relatively young—say less than 30,000 years—the *actual age* of the fossil itself can be determined within a margin of error of only tens of years through radiocarbon dating. There are also newer non-radiometric dating methods, such as bioluminescence dating, thermoluminescence dating, and biostratigraphy.

Using these various methods of dating fossils, we get a good idea of the sequence and some of the approximate time spans that different species have spent on Earth. I use the word approximate because we cannot know the exact month or year that some species appeared, or the year something died. But based on fossil evidence, we can make reasonable estimates. These methods have more veracity then simply using the layer method to determine relative age. We have pieced together the puzzle of when life came to appear and disappear. It is not complete, we still find new puzzle pieces, but the picture is mostly clear—even if it still needs to be tweaked from time to time.

People from around the world, and from various belief systems, have looked at this data and concluded the exact same thing: We have all the evidence we need to see that species appeared and changed gradually or in many cases a species ceased to exist. This timeline of when different forms of life seemed to appear and disappear is well documented with physical evidence. None of this data refutes the theory of evolution. I could "drop the mic" after just presenting fossil data, but of course, we have quite a bit more evidence.

If species arose from common ancestors through the process of evolution, we would expect to see closely related groups within closely related groups across the vast array of life on Earth. For example, within all animals we find all birds, within all birds we find all raptors, within all raptors we find all hawks or all owls. All life seems to exist in these nested hierarchies.

2. Nested Hierarchies

A nested hierarchy is a system where things are ordered into nested sets, like Russian dolls. Each level of organization contains a sub level, which creates a structure of relationships.

Long before Lamark was looking at mechanisms for change over time in living things, Carl Linnaeus took on the complex task of the classification of living things. He was not thinking about evolution; the idea of evolution did not exist yet.

In the early to mid-1700s, Linnaeus began to develop the nomenclature to classify living things. He began with plants and then moved on to the classification of animals.

Linnaeus used the idea of nested hierarchies to organize all living things. He grouped living things based on their morphology (physical traits). Plants are green and have roots, let's put those together. Nested within the plant group we have trees; they are all tall and made of wood, let's put those together. Nested within that group, there are kinds of trees that all make acorns, let's put the oaks all together. He did this with all the plants. And later he did this with all animals, and then the rest of living things.

One way to look at nested hierarchies is to treat these groups as if they were more closely related. Of course, he had no evidence that they were related, but when you look at life on Earth, it sure *seems* like there were groups that were related in a nested hierarchical way.

This type of classification based on similarities and relatedness can also be done with a gathering of your relatives, at say a Thanksgiving dinner. In a typical family, we have a mom, dad, and kids. Going out from this core group, you have aunts, uncles, and grandparents. Going further, there are cousins, nieces and nephews, and further still, second cousins. You can see physical similarities between closely related people. As people get less related, there are fewer similarities. Though not perfect, you can often guess relationships based on similarities. This extends beyond the obvious relatives. We can often ascertain as to whether someone's ancestors came from Japan, Europe, Mexico, or Africa just by appearance.

Between different species, we still see relatedness. But instead of siblings, first cousins, and second cousins, Linnaeus used categories like Genus, Family, Order, and Classes. The further out you go, the less related to that species you are. Carl Linnaeus saw the biological relatedness of all species before Darwin or Wallace were even born. According to Linnaeus's system, all living things seemed to belong within these nested hierarchies.

To understand how nested hierarchies provide evidence for evolution, it is somewhat important that we understand his system. Here are two examples to hammer home this concept. Since I'm a beekeeper, I'll start with a honeybee example, specifically the European honeybee.

Linnaeus used "classification types," each of which had Latin names. These "types" were nested within each other. They moved from least related to more related types, with each type dividing critters into increasingly smaller, and more related, groups.

Classification Type	Latin Name	Common Name/ Examples
Kingdom	Animalia	All animals (including honeybees)
Phylum	Arthropoda	Arthropods/ crabs, spiders, insects
Class	Insecta	Insects/ moths, beetles, (and bees)
Order	Hymenoptera	Hymenoptera/ ants, wasps, bees
Family	*Apidae*	Bees/ bumble, sweat, and honeybees
Genus	Apis	Honeybees/ approx. 11 different species
Species	*mellifera*	The European honeybee

European honeybees, Apis *mellifera,* are most closely related to the bees in their own hives. They are also very closely related to *mellifera* honeybees in other hives. Just as we are related most closely to our families, but we are very closely related to other humans in the world. More so than any other species.

In terms of other species, the honeybees, Apis *mellifera, are* most closely related to groups in their Genus, after that, their Families. As relatedness decreases, we move up the nested hierarchy. After Families, honeybees are next most closely related to animals in their order, Hymenoptera—the ants, other bees, and various wasps, hornets, and yellow jackets. From there, we move up to all the other insects in their Class.

The largest category in the honeybee's nested hierarchy is the animals. Honeybees are Animalia, or animals—as they are not Plantae, Fungi, Protista, or Monera.

Here is a second example: The only thing I have been longer than a beekeeper is a human.

Classification type	Latin name	Common name/ Examples
Kingdom	Animalia	Animal/ honeybee, humans
Phylum	Chordata	Has spinal cord/ deer, salmon, frogs, humans
Class	Mammalia	Mammals/ dogs, cats, deer, humans
Order	Primates	Primates /monkeys, apes, chimps, humans
Family	*Hominidae*	Hominids/ Australo-pithecus, Homo
Genus	*Homo*	erectus, habilis, modern humans
Species	*sapien*	Modern human being

We are not very closely related to the honeybees. We are not even in their Phylum. We are more closely related to frogs, which are in our Phylum, but not in our Class. We are closer still to dogs, cats, and deer; they are all in our Class (mammal), but we are in a different Order. Monkeys and apes are in our Class and Order, but still, it's a distant relationship. By the time we get to our Genus, now we have critters that are close enough in relationship to us be invited to our Thanksgiving dinner, evolutionarily speaking.

Seeing life through the lens of nested hierarchies helps us understand how all life is related. Even fossils can be placed on this nested hierarchy system.

Isn't it amazing that one hundred years before Darwin—and just a hundred years after Galileo—Linnaeus looked at the big picture of life on Earth and saw the relatedness of all living things? Linnaeus saw this empirical truth with clarity. He knew nothing about the process of evolution, but when a mechanism became clear, one hundred years later, his nested hierarchies and the process of evolution would completely complement each other. That is so cool! Truth is often simple and elegant when people observe it with an open mind.

3. Anatomy

What Linnaeus did was no small task. It is tricky to determine where a critter fits within a hierarchy by just looking at it. Consider bats. Are they flying rats or furry birds? Are dolphins air-breathing tuna, or really fast small whales? If you rely solely on how things look or act, you might not have enough information. Sometimes you need to dig deep into the anatomy—literally go beneath the skin.

The bone structure of dolphins is more like walruses and whales than it is like tuna. Bat wings, at the level of skeletal anatomy, are like big mammal hands, less like the structure of bird wings. Skeletal anatomy helped Linnaeus use his nested hierarchies to create a system of classification. Darwin would later see the origin stories of those species within their anatomies.

Why would a whale have hip bones? Perhaps it is a leftover from the species from which whales evolved. Why do large snakes like pythons have hips bones? Again, if their ancestral species had legs, then of course this would make sense. All hominids have tailbones, including us, yet no hominids have a tail. Therefore, it makes sense hominids evolved from populations of their ancestors—tree-dwelling primates. Turns out, this hypothesis not only makes sense, but it is consistent with the timeline in the fossil record for whales and dolphins, as well as primates and hominids.

As Darwin, and Wallace, were beginning to explore the idea of evolution, it looked as though life on Earth had gradually changed over time, revealing more and more species.

4. Genetics and DNA evidence

Long after Darwin had died, evidence continued to pour in. The evidence continued to support, and importantly, *not refute*, the theory of evolution. In 1953, James Watson and Francis Crick, with help from Maurice Wilkens and Rosalind Franklin, discovered the structure of DNA. This discovery has transformed agricultural science, medicine, forensic science, economics, and of course, our understanding of basic biological evolution.

The study of DNA has afforded us a new tool to enhance or even challenge our understanding of evolution. Some of what we thought we knew needed to be revised. Yet, as it turns out, most of what we *thought* we knew from just using morphology was spot on! DNA evidence has clarified our understanding of the details of evolution.

We don't usually use the word proof in science, but sequenced DNA provides proof of relatedness. It is robust enough to prove who the father was in a paternity lawsuit. It can be submitted in a court of law to prove that someone should be imprisoned for the rest of their life. In some states, the DNA proof can even land someone in the electric chair. It is also true that old court cases have been overturned based on new DNA evidence: DNA evidence has a very high level of veracity.

We no longer just use external morphology to classify living things. Now we classify life using DNA. It turns out, relatedness was not just imagined by Linnaeus, Wallace, and Darwin. Honeybees *are* more closely related to the other insects than to spiders. Bees *are* more closely related to lobsters than, say, to hummingbirds. Their DNA *proves* this.

In the early 1990s, humans undertook a seemingly impossible task. We set out to sequence all the base pairs of DNA in all the chromosomes of a human. (They also started to sequence some nonhuman genomes, including a bacterium (E. Coli), some nonhuman animals (a nematode, a mouse, a fruit fly), and a fungus (baker's yeast)). The project, called the Human Genome Project, was one of the most ambitious scientific endeavors ever undertaken. The order of every base pair of every chromosome was revealed. The specific order of these bases dictates individual characteristics as well as species identity. For the human being genome, our sequenced DNA turned out to be thirty *billion* base pairs long! Each pair was labeled with one of four letters—A, T, C, or G—corresponding to the name of one of the bases. I believe this accomplishment was greater than—or at least on par with—putting a person on the Moon and bringing them home. Like the Moon shot, when the Human Genome Project began, the technology to accomplish the goal was nonexistent. Sure, we could sequence, but it was very slow going. New technological inventions sped the process along. Even with these advances, the project still took thirteen years.

In addition to spawning a biotech revolution, adding billions of dollars to the economy, this project gave biologists new tools for understanding evolution. What we learned supported, and in no way *refuted*, the theory of evolution.

5. Junk DNA

As we sequenced more and more genomes, we learned some odd things that we were not expecting.

We learned, for example, that the majority of human DNA was "junk." By junk, scientists mean that most of the DNA in each of our cells does not code for any proteins. Or it could be that some proteins are not made. In biology jargon, we say these proteins are not expressed. For example, if the protein lactase is expressed, then you will be able to make lactase, and therefore be able to digest lactose—the sugar found in dairy products. If it is not expressed, or if you lack the code for lactase, you will be lactose intolerant.

In our DNA, for example, we have DNA for the precursors of gills. This is the same DNA that we find in fish. These proteins are only briefly expressed during embryo development, when humans briefly have "gill slits"—technically pharyngeal arches. To be clear, we do not have the DNA for making gills, but we do, for some unknown reason, have the DNA for their developmental precursors.

Even this "gill slit" DNA doesn't really qualify as junk because our DNA does code for pharyngeal arches proteins, albeit briefly. Junk DNA, on the other hand has no known function. And we have a lot of that. When we look at all this *unexpressed* DNA, there is still variation between species. The more closely related the species the more closely the junk DNA aligns. That is a remarkable fact. Even our useless, or junk, DNA still fits within the same nested hierarchies as our functional DNA. Even though these new facts were unexpected, they certainly made sense within the context of the theory of evolution.

These related nested hierarchies—where one life-form comes from a related ancestor—are now undeniable. The fossil record shows this clearly. The morphologies and the anatomies seem to show this as well. The DNA sequences of the expressed DNA *prove* relatedness in these nested hierarchies.

If that wasn't enough, even the sequences of the *non-coding* or *junk* DNA also prove the relatedness and common ancestry of all living things on Earth. DNA evidence doesn't *seem* to show that evolution happened, it shows *well beyond any reasonable doubt* that evolution did happen. No other hypothesis competes with this explanation. No other hypothesis fits all of this data.

CHAPTER 30

Human Evolution

For some people, the idea that humans evolved from animals—or are even classified as animals—is very upsetting. I have heard students say, "Sure, evolution explains nonhuman life, but scientists take it too far when they suggest that we came from monkeys!!"

Calling humans a "type of animal" conflicts with some belief systems. In fairness, we are different from the other animals. We lift weights in front of mirrors, we smoke cigarettes, we spend hours staring at TVs and phones. Clearly, we are the pinnacle of creation. (Textbooks like to talk about the human virtues that separate us from the animals, virtues like compassion, language, and art. I find the not-so-flattering traits to be more amusing.) But seriously, many of these so-called "human virtues" are not unique to our species. It turns out that many nonhuman animals have complex languages, play, and even use tools. Many animals even seem to show compassion and have emotions. Some have even been shown to be capable of abstract thought.

Our social structure is not unique either. Ants, some bees, and termites all have developed complex societies. We can also add elephants, crows, wolves, and even two species of naked mole-rats to that list.

The desire to be different from other animals seems to run deep in many human belief systems. This desire often stems from religious traditions. But even many nonreligious people want to live in a world where we are special, different from the nonhuman animals. The mere desire for something to be true, does not make it true. We are in a nested hierarchy just like all animals. We are in the animal-chordate-mammals-primate-hominid-homo hierarchy.

Missing Link

Occasionally, over the course of my teaching career, a student would ask about the "missing link"—the mythical species that came between the apes (or "cavemen") and modern humans. I would explain that there is no "missing link." We have discovered fossils of many different species of upright walking apes going back twelve million years. There are at least ten different species within the *Homo* genus (*Homo* is Greek for same. *Homo* is also the Latin name for the "human-like" genus.) In this context, *Homo* refers to species that closely resemble modern humans. The differences between a Neanderthal man (*Homo sapiens neanderthalensis*) and a modern human (*Homo sapiens sapiens*), for example, are not even large enough to technically consider these two different species. My genetic profile from 23andMe shows that I have DNA that is unique to Neanderthals in my personal genome. I wasn't surprised, as my ancestors are of Northern European heritage. Neanderthals (*Homo sapiens neanderthalensis*) and modern humans (*Homo sapiens sapiens*) overlapped in both geography and time. Recent DNA evidence also shows that *Denisovans* also interbreed with *Homo sapiens*. As we previously discussed, the lines that separate one species from another can be pretty fuzzy.

Neanderthals are not the so called "missing link." There is no single connecting link, because human evolution is no longer thought of as a straight line from chimps and apes to modern humans. We now know that human evolution was more complex. Our "evolutionary family tree" has many branches, which branch from other branches. It doesn't move toward a pinnacle in some straight line. Human evolution is not a line. It is not even like a tree—more like a bush. Many different human-like species clearly inhabited the Earth at the same time we did. One of these species, Homo *floresiensis*, is particularly interesting.

While we now know this is not an accurate view of human evolution, images like this still permeate a few textbooks and pop culture. As a result, many laypeople still think of human evolution as a linear progression. ("Designed by macrovector / Freepik.")

Nova's documentary *Alien on Earth* first brought this 2003 archeological finding of *Homo floresiensis* to my attention. *Homo floresiensis*, nicknamed "the Hobbit" was an odd geological find. The fossils indicated it stood upright; adults were about three feet tall, the bones initially dated to around 20,000 years old. Their antimony suggested they were a close relative of *Australopithecus africanus*, (nicknamed "Lucy"[7]). Unfortunately, the jungle conditions where these fossils were found made the sequencing of DNA impossible—at least for now—so the anatomy is our only clue. To me, the anatomy suggests that it may be misnamed. I think it is an *Australopithecine*, an ape like Lucy, not in the genus *Homo*. The skull size, the trapezius (a bone in the wrist), and the stature are all dead ringers for a Lucy-like species.

Two things are odd about those observations: 1) "Lucy" had only been found in Africa, the Hobbits (*Homo floresiensis*) remains were found only in Indonesia; and 2) "Lucy," as a species, was thought to have gone extincted three *million* years prior, whereas the last Hobbits were estimated to still be alive between 100,000 and 50,000 years ago. The more you learn about this little relative, the more questions you

---

7. Lucy was found in 1974 in the badlands of Hadar, Ethiopia. During the initial find, The Beatles hit song "Lucy in the Sky with Diamonds" was playing on the Radio at the dig site. The team of paleoanthropologists started referring to the skeleton as "Lucy," and the nick-name stuck.

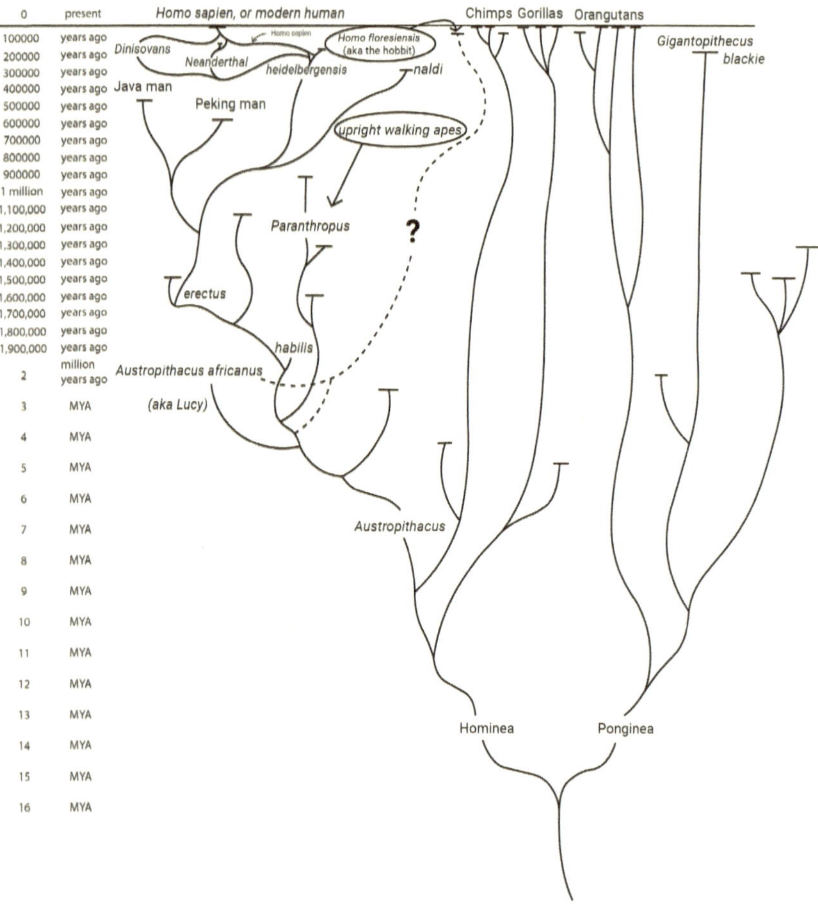

The modern view is that human evolution (and all evolution) is less linear and more closely resembles a bush. Side note: Since we don't have DNA for *floresiensis*, we don't really know exactly where it diverged from our family tree. Personally, I am with the camp that thinks *floresiensis* diverged long before *Homo habilis*. This claim is based in part on the anatomy of its wrist—which is *identical* to Lucy's wrist. We won't *know for sure* until we find a fossil that yields high quality DNA—I'm okay with some uncertainty, mystery is fun! (Chart drawn by Will Swain, with graphic design by Henry Swain.)

have. We know it used complex tools, but yet its brain was far smaller than anything else in the *Homo* genus. Interestingly, it did have an abnormally large prefrontal cortex given its small brain size, which may account its ability to craft complex stone tools.

My take home point with this aside is simply that evolution does not progress in a straight line toward some final species. The history of evolution is a multibranched bush that grows in multiple directions. The finding of *Homo floresiensis*, along with several other finds within the last thirty years, put an end to the old notion that human evolution was linear.

Human Evolution Paradigm Shifts and Bigfoot

Whereas I spent my life figuring out laypeople's misconceptions about evolution, Dr. Meldrum spent his time exploring why academic misconceptions about evolution lead to rejection of the idea that bigfoot—or relict hominoids[8]—might exist.

There are really two big academic misconceptions about human evolution which hindered acceptance of the possibility of bigfoot's existence: 1) the "linear nature of human evolution," and 2) the related but different, the "one species, one niche hypothesis."

The narrative for the first idea went, "Bigfoot did not fit nicely on the line of evolution that yielded humans, so it could not exist." Back in 1967, when the notion of bigfoot first became popularized with *Patterson-Gimlin film*, the understanding of human evolution was still in its infancy. Lucy had not even been discovered yet. The paradigm of linear evolution was entrenched.

The second idea was also problematic. "Since we replaced previous hominoids, there could not still be one present." This latter point was sometimes called the "one species per niche hypothesis." In 1967, the one species per niche hypothesis regarding hominoid evolution

---

8. Meldrum found that giving serious academic consideration to an animal often featured in tabloids can be problematic. Meldrum understood that messaging is important. He found the term "relict hominoids" came with less baggage than the term "sasquatch," and a far lower cheesy/campy factor then the term "bigfoot."

was also firmly entrenched. These old paradigms die slowly. In some corners of academia, they still guide people's thought processes. The process of science always moves toward truth, but individual scientists can cling to older paradigms tightly.

Even In 2003, when *Homo floresiensis* fossils were first discovered, some paleontologists were doing mental gymnastics to get these hominoids to fit into some old narrative. They desperately avoided the paradigm shift that was needed to incorporate this new information. Science always works, but on the frontiers of science, scientists themselves can be very wrong and stubborn.

The data showed these old ideas to be in error. And in science, data is king.

Much of the resistance to the *Patterson-Gimlin film* can be traced to these early paradigms, which are gradually being replaced by explanations that better incorporate the new discoveries.

It is now crystal clear that many hominoids were all walking around at the same time as modern humans. In 1967, this was not known, or at very least not accepted. (Remember: Lucy's fossils were not found until 1974, *Denisovans* fossils were not found until the 1980s—and they were not found in large numbers until this millennia—and *floresiensis* wasn't discovered until in 2003.)

These arguments in science are not arguments that threaten the theory of evolution. They are arguments about little details.

A football analogy could be that occasionally fans get bent out of shape about a particular call on the field. Was it pass interference or not? Was it a fair catch signal or not, etc.? Arguments about some calls in the game do not imply that fans question whether a football game took place. We argue about details, but no one—who has given the matter any serious consideration—thinks that evolution did not take place.

I believe that it is likely that more branches will be added to this bush of human evolution as more fossils are found. But these new branches will not overturn the big picture of human evolution, or the bigger picture of the theory of evolution.

Anthropologists dated fossil evidence for *Homo floresiensis* to around 70,000 years ago. It's likely that the last remaining *floresiensis* did not die at that time, unless we just happened to have unearthed the last one. In fact, it is even possible that they are not extinct at all! They may still be here. Small bipeds roaming the forests are certainly part of the indigenous folklore on the island of Flores. Locals call it "ebu gogo." In 2022, a retired archeologist, Gregory Forth, claimed there were several current sightings of small bipedal ape men that matched the description of *floresiensis* or "ebu gogo." Others believe that these sightings are highly unlikely.

All of this should sound a little familiar from the first section of this book. Indigenous populations report it as a real animal, they are dismissed, and current sightings from non-natives are also dismissed. Is "ebu gogo" real? Are bigfoot or relict hominoids real?

Seems like the better questions might be, are populations of animals that match the description of "ebu gogo" still around? Are populations of animals that match the description of *Gigantopithecus* or one of our many hominid relatives still around? We have recently shared the Earth with a variety of apelike and humanlike bipedal ancestors. "Are they still here?" is the correct question. Their reality is not in doubt.

CHAPTER 31

The Book of Genesis

Time for a dramatic topic switch from evolution to the topic of biblical scholarship. Because the topic of evolution is viewed by many to be at odds with the Bible, if I ignore what the Bible says, this discussion will be incomplete. We can't just speak of evolution without addressing the concerns of those who feel that evolution is at odds with creation, as described in the book of Genesis. All three of the Abrahamic religions, which are followed by about 55 percent of the world's population, have Genesis as their go-to creation story.

I know several intelligent people (former students as well as some current friends) who take the following position: "Genesis describes exactly what happened at creation, and therefore the science doesn't matter. You have your secular evidence, but I have the ultimate answer key, the word of God. God made humans and all the living things as described in Genesis, case closed."

So let's forget science for a bit. What does the "answer key" in the book of Genesis really say? It might surprise you.

The Biblical Story of Creation

The statement "I believe in the biblical account of creation" is akin to the statement "I think the Moon landing was faked." They are alike because the follow-up question, regarding both *the Moon landing* and *the Bible's creation story*, is exactly the same:

"Which one?"

The "fake-Moon-landing people" often don't grasp that there were seven attempted Moon landings, and six of them were successful. So the task before them is to explain seven major conspiracies, not just one.

In the case of people who are adamant they believe in *the literal biblical account of creation*, my question is, "Which one?" There are two accounts found in the Abrahamic religions.

Finding out there are two biblical accounts of creation can be disorienting to those who claim to believe in the literal translation of the Bible. They must get their heads around two stories, not just one. Growing up in Iowa, a state where Christianity is by far the most common religion, I find it fascinating how many people don't know that the book of Genesis has two accounts of creation. In many biblical translations, they are even labeled as "account one" and "account two."

I keep saying this is a fact, but I'm not providing any evidence. All the evidence comes from the book of Genesis itself. If you don't quite trust me, go get your Bible and read along with me. While you are getting your Bible, I am gonna go make some nachos . . .

Creation Story Number One

Ok, I have my nachos. Are we ready?

Genesis, chapter one, verse one . . . Before I proceed, I want to embarrass one of my sisters by telling a story that I find amusing.

When my sister was getting married, she and her husband-to-be met with a pastor to pick Bible verses for the readings at their wedding. The pastor asked them to "turn to Genesis . . ." whatever verse it was. Her husband and the pastor were waiting for her to find it. After thumbing through the Bible for a while, she finally looked up and asked, "Where is Genesis?"

That will be funnier to some of you than to others. (It is funny because Genesis is the first book in the Bible—super easy to find.) I include this story because it highlights the differences in people's general familiarity with the Bible. In my family, we went to church every Sunday, and my dad was a trained theologian. By the time I was a junior in high school, I had read the Bible cover to cover. I regularly went to Bible study. My sister, on the other hand, could not find the book of Genesis in the Bible.

I also include the story to help some of you find Genesis in your Bible.

Okay, quick heads up, your Bible will read slightly differently depending on whether you are reading from *King James, Good News,* or from whatever version you happen to have laying around. I am reading from *The Jerusalem Bible, Reader's Edition.* I received this Bible from my dad on my confirmation day in the fall of my freshman year of high school.

FYI: I will put actual quotes from my Bible in quotations. If it is not in quotes, I'm paraphrasing. Instead of using verses, I will number each day.

"First Account"

Genesis 1:1 begins with, "In the beginning God created the heaven and the earth." "The earth was a formless void . . . God's spirit hovered over the water."

1. "God said, let there be light." "God divided light from dark." He then named day and night. "Evening came, morning came: the first day."
2. "God said, let there be a vault." (In many versions, the word "vault" is replaced with the word "firmament.") He divided the waters. (Heaven is in the vault between the waters.) "Evening came, morning came: the second day."
3. "God said, let the waters under heaven come into a single mass . . . allowing dry land to appear." He named land "earth" named water "seas." Then God made plants and trees. "Evening came, morning came: the third day."
4. "God said, let there be lights in the vault of heaven to divide day from night." These lights were to indicate festivals, days, and years. He describes the lights of the Sun and Moon and stars to govern day and night. (Though described, the names of the Sun and the Moon are not used here.) "God saw that it was good. Evening came, morning came: the fourth day."

5. "God said, let the waters teem with living creatures and let the birds fly above the earth within the vault of heaven." "Evening came, morning came: the fifth day."
6. "God said, let the land be teeming with living creatures." God then makes cattle, reptiles, and "every kind of wild beast." And then "God said, let us make man, in our own image, in the likeness of ourselves . . ." He goes on to give man dominion over all the various living things. "God created man in the image of himself. In the image of God . . ." He tells mankind "to be fruitful, multiply, fill the earth and conquer it." and to be the masters of all living things and to eat the plants. "Evening came, morning came: the sixth day."
7. "He rested on the seventh day . . ." "God blessed the seventh day and made it holy."

"Such were the origins of heaven and earth when they were created"

If you went to Sunday school those words should be somewhat familiar. The second account of creation begins in Genesis 2:5. It is another familiar story, but different to be sure.

"Second Account"

Genesis 2:5

"At the time when Yahweh God made earth and heaven there was no wild bush nor had any wild plant yet sprung up, for Yahweh God had not sent rain on the earth, nor was there any man to till the soil. However, a flood was rising from the earth and watering the surface of the soil. Yahweh God fashioned Man of dust from the soil. He breathed into his nostrils the breath of life, and thus, man became a living thing."

So far, four sentences in, this is a different story. We start with land, not water. That is a big difference. Also, it states that Man was created before plants and animals. If you are reading from the Quran, God fashioned man from *clay* not *dust*; I would call that a tiny difference. Land before water, man before any living thing, those are big differences.

The story continues to have Yahweh "plant a garden in Eden," and then to "place man in the garden." He makes the tree of life and "the tree of knowledge of good and evil. A river flows into Eden, and it is divided into four rivers" (including the real rivers of Tigris and the Euphrates). Then, a bit of important foreshadowing, God gives man a tour and tells him, "You may eat of any tree in the garden but . . . of the tree of the knowledge of good and evil you are not to eat."

After that, "man is alone in the garden." Feeling bad for him, God decides "to make him animals and birds. But man is still lonely." So taking a rib from man, he uses it to fashion a woman.

"Yahweh God built the rib he had taken from the man into a woman and brought her to the man. The man exclaimed: 'This, at last, is a bone from my bones, and flesh from my flesh, this is to be called woman, for this was taken from man.'"

When I first read this, I thought, *Well that seems like kind of a weird thing for Man to exclaim.* I later learned that in Hebrew, woman translates to *ishshah* and man translates to *ish*. So the verse really breaks down the etiology of the word *ishshah*. If it is read in Hebrew, it is not only less weird, but it is quite interesting and poetic.

The story continues and gets more and more interesting. But I'm going to stop here because I want to put my focus solely on these two accounts of creation.

Let's begin with the order of events. Side by side in two different columns:

Order of Events

In the first account	In the second account
Water is present in the beginning	Only land, specifically states "no water no plants"
Light	
Water divided by vaults (or firmament)	Waters rise from the land

Water under the vault is divided	(no mention of Sun, Moon, or seas)
Seas created	*Man is created* from dust while the life is given to man with god's breath.
Sun and Moon are created	God makes plants, makes a garden
Vegetation is created	God puts Man in the garden.
Fish and birds are created	Man seems lonely sitting amongst the plants
Land animals are created	God creates land animals
Then mankind is created	After a while, it's clear that the animals are not helping man with loneliness so God makes women from man's rib.
Rest day. Story ends.	No rest day, and the story goes on to get even more interesting . . .

Some people maintain that the second story recaps the first story but as you can see, it doesn't. That is clear, based on the order of events alone. In the first account, mankind is the crown jewel of creation after everything else was completed. In the second account, Man is created *literally before* plants and animals.

Water's appearance is also literally different. In the first account, water and God are present before the story even begins. Land is not created until day three. In the second account, land is literally there before water. The water emerges from the earth. There is also no vault (or firmament). These are literal, easy-to-spot differences.

I'm not suggesting that a literal reading of these creation accounts is a theologically appropriate way to read the Bible. I am pointing out that those who oppose a scientific view of creation because it conflicts with the literal biblical account have a literal problem with the order of events of the two biblical accounts being literally different.

Many people have no idea that these are two different accounts of creation, which is understandable. After all, we were told these stories when we were small children, in some cases before we could read. We likely conflated these two stories together in our minds. Most of us don't revisit them later in life after we have become good readers with mature adult brains. If we do revisit the stories, we skim over them and assume the second is a recap of the first.

The name ascribed to the Creator is also different in the two accounts. This is most apparent in the Hebrew texts, which give us the Torah and the rest of the Old Testament. In the original Hebrew, the name "Elohim" is only used in the first account of creation. (Elohim is often translated to "Lord God," but many Bibles simply translate Elohim as "God.") In the second account, the name YHWH is used. (Some Bibles translated YHWH to "Yahweh," and others just say "God.")

YHWH was originally supposed to be unpronounceable because to name something is to give you power over it. Evidence of the significance of the act of naming is shown by God giving man the power over the animals by letting him name them. Ironically, translators translated YHWH to Yahweh in many accounts, making it pronounceable.[9]

Pronoun use is also interesting and easy to miss on a casual read. In Genesis 1:26, "God said, let *us* make man, in *our* own image." Why is a singular God using plural pronouns? (There could be some fun jokes here, but I don't want to digress.)

In Hebrew, the word Elohim can be, and often is, a plural noun. It is a difficult word to translate into English. Sometimes Elohim refers to the heavenly beings: God(s), angels, and spirits. Other times, Elohim refers to just God, the singular. In the first creation story, the name Elohim is particularly troublesome because this is also the story

---

9.   That explanation is not universally accepted. Another explanation for Yahweh being written as YWHW is because, in that dialect of Hebrew, it was a common practice to occasionally remove vowels when writing. Thus, YHWH instead of Yahweh. This explanation is less popular, but I thought it was worth mentioning.

of a new *monotheistic* religion. Elohim, in the singular form, was replacing the polytheistic deities from the neighboring Bedouin tribes.

Elohim is used exclusively in the first account, and YWHW is used exclusively in the second account. But only occasionally, in the first account, Elohim is translated as a plural noun, thus the plural pronouns.

Implications of Two Accounts

So what? Does having two different versions prove that these creation stories are wrong? My simple answer is again, no.

Pointing out that there are two accounts is not some secular "Gotcha!" I am not trying to undermine the significance of these stories.

Sometimes when devout Christians, particularly fundamentalists, hear that there are two versions of the of creation story, they can feel as though they, and the Bible itself, are under attack. I think this reaction is unfortunate, and in my opinion, unwarranted. The fact that there are two different creation accounts does not in any way challenge the divinity of the Bible.

There are multiple times in the Bible where more than one author recounts the same story with differing details. Christians who have read the Bible are familiar with Mathew, Mark, Luke, and John for example. Within these Gospels are four versions of the same basic story that is told by different authors. One story does not simply recap the other. No one freaks out about that. Mathew, Mark, Luke, and John are all canonized books because they all have something to say about the teachings of Christ.

The creation accounts should, in my opinion, be viewed in the same way. The two stories say slightly different things about mankind's relationship to God, mankind's relationship to creation, and man's relationship with women. And most importantly, later in the second account, the story explains the philosophical problem that arises from consciousness, or self-awareness. This is theologically important stuff!

When people of faith use their interpretation of Scripture as the "key" to answer testable, non-supernatural questions—they get themselves into trouble. Not understanding which type of knowing is the most appropriate for which kind of question is a problem of epistemology—how we come to know what we know.

It is not just the fundamentalists who have misunderstandings about epistemology. I'd also like to point out that this misunderstanding can also come from scientists. When *some* scientists assert that because Scripture got the details of creation wrong that the Bible itself is flawed, then they, too, are treating the biblical accounts of creation as if it is a flawed key to a testable question, which it is not.

In my opinion, these Bible passages are in the context of relationships. They are not intended to be an answer key to physical, testable, hypotheses.

There are reasons for science and religion to stay in their epistemological lanes. For religious questions, faith, logic, intuition, language, and emotional knowledge all play an important role. But in the domain of testable physical phenomena, science, as a type of knowing, is more reliable than faith.

As I learned in eighth-grade shop class, "Use the right tool for the job you are doing!"

Science, logic, and history are the proper tools to answer the important question: "How did we get here?" But science is horrible tool for spiritual questions.

Religion, faith and art are some very good tools to explore the spiritual, the why questions: "Why are we here?" But religion is a horrible tool for testable, physical questions.

It is not healthy for a religious faith to deny a scientific empirical truth based on Scripture. Back in 1633, when Pope Urban VIII declared that it was heretical to claim that the Earth goes around the Sun, his wrongness did far more damage to faith in the Church than it did to show its infallibility. Fast forward about four hundred years and now Christian and Islamic fundamentalists damage the credibility of Scripture when they use it to challenge the established canon of scientific knowledge.

CHAPTER 32

Importance of Evolution in the Political Culture Wars

I was purposeful when I picked the theory of evolution as my second-to-last topic in this book. The misunderstanding of evolution and the Bible result from people not thinking about the veracity of the different ways and types of knowing. These misunderstandings have actual real-world consequences. Again, this is not just an academic discussion about epistemology.

Further, evolution-denial can be like a gateway drug. It is a precursor to denial of many known empirical facts. For example, there is considerable overlap between those who do not accept evolution and those who don't trust vaccines, don't accept climate science, or believe that the Earth is flat. When intuition and faith guide our thinking, even in the face of objective empirical evidence, there are real-world consequences. Denial of climate science has stopped our species from fighting climate change. Mistrust of vaccines has recently led to the reemergence of measles. These are serious consequences.

In addition to these specific issues, a large section of the US population now holds an altered umwelt about how we understand reality itself. Some of these belief systems threaten our very democracy.

What caused roughly 30 percent of America to have a falling out with science? What caused half the country to dismiss the scientific theory of evolution? I would argue that the earliest shots, in what pundits now call the "culture wars," were fired, during a hot and humid Tennessee summer.

CHAPTER 33

Scopes "Monkey Trial"

On July 10, 1925, the Scopes "Monkey Trial" began in Dayton, Tennessee. The case centered on a substitute teacher who taught from a textbook that supported the theory of evolution.

For two weeks, a circus like atmosphere developed around the "Monkey Trial" in Dayton, Tennessee. A huge crowd gathered inside and outside the courthouse during this trial. Anti-evolution merchandise was sold by the Anti-Evolution League. (For example, monkey dolls in human clothes and books by T.T. Martin such as *The Conflict, Hell and the High Schools*, and *Evolution or Christ*.) People carried picket signs that read, "We didn't come from monkeys!" Hundreds of people drove to Dayton from around the country. It was dubbed the trial of the century.

In 1960, thirty-five years after the trial, MGM Studios released the movie *Inherit the Wind* about the Scopes trial. *Inherit the Wind* received four Oscar nominations. (It's an okay movie; I'm not sure I'd recommend it. I reference this movie only to highlight the significant role that the Scopes trial played in American culture.)

The "Monkey Trial" was a big deal. To put this spectacle into perspective, this case got even more public attention than the 1995 O.J. Simpson trial. Some of you who are reading this might remember who the lawyers were in the O.J. trial, but by the mid-summer of 1925, *everyone* knew the lawyers in the Scopes trial. William Jennings Bryan for the prosecution and Clarence Darrow for the defense.

Anti-evolution books for sale in Dayton, Tennessee, where Professor John T. Scopes is on trial for teaching the theory of evolution in public schools. (Photo by © Hulton-Deutsch Collection/CORBIS/Corbis via Getty Images.)

Prior to the "Monkey Trial," Bryan had won the Democratic nomination *for* President of the US *three times*, and he had also been the forty-first US Secretary of State. Bryan often fought for prohibition and was adamantly anti-evolution. He was also very involved in an—albeit lower profile—internal theological debate between the modernists and the fundamentalists within his own Presbyterian church.

Clarence Darrow, though not as well-known, was a worthy adversary. Darrow was involved in the labor movement and had won many high-profile cases. He was an advocate for child labor laws, and he was against capital punishment and prohibition. Widely regarded as a brilliant lawyer, Darrow was a master debater.

So why were such heavyweights brought in for a trial of a science teacher who had received only a one hundred dollar fine? The Scopes "Monkey Trial" was about "ways of knowing" and what we believe. (I hope that you have come to realize, as I have, that "how we know" and "what we believe" are the most interesting and important topics that there are!)

William Jennings Bryan (seated left) being interrogated by Clarence Seward Darrow during the trial of the State of Tennessee v. John Thomas Scopes, July 20, 1925. That Monday afternoon, because of the extreme heat, Judge Raulston moved court proceedings outdoors. The session was held on a platform that had been erected at the front of the Rhea County Courthouse to accommodate ministers who wanted to preach during the time of the trial. Defense lawyers for Scopes are visible seated to the extreme right. One of the men, left, with his back to the photographer, appears to be Scopes. (Courtesy of Smithsonian Institution Archives via Wikimedia Commons.)

To the press, and those watching the story, the spectacle was framed as a showdown between science vs. religion. As I already attempted to demonstrate, this was just theater. The theater of this nonsensical debate became embedded as permanent fixture on the American cultural landscape.

The trial's impact on the relationship between religion and science cannot be overstated. In many ways, the Scopes trial laid the groundwork for religious dysfunction in America. The divisions between the theological modernists and the fundamentalists were both illuminated, and deepened, by the Scopes trial.

During the sweltering summer of 1925, Bryan tried to cast evolution as "Evil-lution." Bryan argued that teaching evolution was a departure from the word of God. You will still hear the echoes of religious rhetoric from the Scopes trial used to this day.

In 2020, while I was teaching evolution, I heard one of my students mutter under his breath. "We didn't come from monkeys!"

I thought to myself, but did not say, *Wow, that ridiculous slogan has been around for nearly one hundred years!*

The public saw the Scopes trial less as a court case and more as a debate: evolution vs anti-evolution. Bryan appealed to the fundamentalists' usual arguments, thereby popularizing those arguments to a good chunk of 1925 America. Contrastingly, Darrow appealed to intellect. He left theology mostly out of his arguments. In the end, Darrow lost, not the argument—most thought he out-debated Bryan—but he lost the legal case.

Legally, Darrow had no hope of winning. His client did, in fact, break the law. The Butler Act in the state of Tennessee made it illegal to teach evolution, and John Scopes did, in fact, use a textbook that taught the theory of evolution. Darrow had no chance of winning.

When the verdict was announced, many in the public saw Bryan's legal victory as a vindication of their faith. Bryan's personal victory celebration would be short-lived. He died in his sleep, likely of brain aneurism, just days after the verdict was announced. The heat and stress of the trial may have contributed to his death.

Darrow, on the other hand, went on to appeal the decision to the Tennessee Supreme Court. Of course, he lost again.

He also lost on a much more important issue, the legality of the ban on the teaching of evolution. The court reaffirmed that the ban in Tennessee was, in fact, perfectly legal!

Science, as a "type of knowing," was declared inferior to Scripture. This view had the blessing of the courts. From that time on, states were free to construct their own "faith-based" reality disregarding evidence. Many other states, particularly in the South, did just that.

Sometimes, if people are open-minded, a good argument can convince them that a belief system they hold is inconsistent or flawed. But this rarely happens. Instead, arguments tend to awaken people's competitive nature and compel them to fight harder to win the argument.

In 1925, the debate regarding evolution led many individuals to adopt, or more firmly reinforce, their anti-evolution position.

Participation in the argument served to galvanize people's beliefs rather than prompting them to question them.

Contrastingly, during this same period, the theory of evolution seemed very compelling to those with a background in science. The theory of evolution fit all the old and new data, so it was increasingly accepted.

In the spring of 1925, before the Scopes trial, most people didn't much talk about evolution. But, by the end of 1925, many people had strongly held negative opinions about not only evolution, but about science itself. Science shifted, in their minds, from being a process to get to truth into a belief system that was in opposition to Scripture.

I believe the origin of the anti-science narrative begins with the Scopes trial. In this faith vs. science debate, the jury said, "Faith wins!" (At least that is the way some in the public saw it.)

The verdict in the Scope's Trial, and later in the Tennessee Supreme Court trial, were not successfully challenged again until 1968, when the US Supreme Court heard the evolution case of Epperson v. Arkansas. This time, the US Supreme Court struck down an Arkansas law that had banned the teaching of evolution.

Let those dates sink in for a moment. From 1925 to 1968, faith was often considered superior to science for answering testable questions. Faith was said to be *superior* to empirical data gathered through a systematic process that attempts to eliminate bias.

The lawyers for Epperson, in Epperson v. Arkansas, argued that the State of Arkansas was promoting a specific theology and that this was a clear violation of the separation of church and state as outlined in the US Constitution. When this challenge was successful, it came as a blow to those who subscribed to that theology. They believed that Scripture, or I should say "their interpretation of Scripture," should drive the law of the land.

In my umwelt, I think the courts finally got it right with Epperson v. Arkansas. However, in the umwelt of fundamentalists, the courts let them down.

Most Christians are not fundamentalists.[10] Asserting that their interpretations of Scripture are authoritative, this minority group has taken it upon themselves to represent all Christians.

The culture wars are, in a sense, epistemology wars. When people argue about culture, deep down, the real argument is about how we come "to know." Another way to view the current culture wars are as theological disagreements within the Christian faith.

Political pundits tend to talk more about economics, about education levels, and race relations. These pundits often ignore the theological underpinnings of these different umwelts. The theological rift which drives some of today's culture wars had its genesis—pun intended—with the Scopes "Monkey Trial."

---

10. Protestants make up about 37 percent of Christians worldwide, and about 50 percent of Protestants are Anglican, the remaining group is roughly split between other Mainline and Evangelical denominations. Some quick math shows that fundamentalist Christians make up less than 7 percent of the Christian population worldwide. In America, the Christians in churches with fundamentalist views make up a much larger piece of the pie at nearly 23 percent. The numbers of people with fundamentalists views are likely a bit higher, as some people in non-fundamentalist churches can hold some fundamentalist views. Though difficult to precisely measure, I think it is safe to say those with fundamentalists views don't represent the majority of Christians, even in the US.

Beliefs, Repercussions, Free Will, Christian Nationalism, and Birds

In this final section of the book, I want to explore the idea of people "being entitled to their own beliefs." Is everyone entitled to their own beliefs? Even if the justification for those beliefs is weak? What if the justification is strong, does that change the answer? Are some beliefs unethical? When we combine the topics of belief with responsibility, the discussion gets complicated very quickly. We are now entering the fascinating discipline of epistemic responsibility.

CHAPTER 34

Responsibility and Free Will

Before we can delve into the question of responsibility, we must first ask: "Do we control our own beliefs?" This is not a silly, hypothetical question. If we are in control, then yes, we are responsible for the consequences of those beliefs. If we are not in control of what we believe, then the discussion gets messy very quickly. Any talk of responsibility requires that we first tackle the daunting topic of free will.

Free Will

Do we choose our beliefs? Or are our beliefs imposed upon us by circumstance, genetics, and/or geography? How much of our belief system comes from our mind, and how much is simply a product of our brains?

The mind/brain distinction is admittedly confusing. I'll try my best to clarify.

"Mind" is an entity that is separate from the brain and body. Mind is the essence of who you are. It is like your soul. Your mind is you, apart from the flesh and blood you. Your mind directs your decisions.

Put a slightly different way, if your body was a car, your mind would be the driver. The driver is not part of the car, but the driver controls the car. Your mind is firmly in the driver's seat, and your mind is in control of your thoughts and your beliefs. This is the free will version of our life.

There is an alternative. There might not be a mind. My car analogy here works like this. Imagine you get into an AI self-driving Uber. You still experience the driving, you still get to your destination, but you are not in control—the car is. That is the version of "driving"—or living—without free will. The mind is not in control; the mind, or the essence of self, is just along for the ride.

Based on prearranged programming and environmental inputs, the car goes through its route, *as if* a "mind" is in charge. But it's not. There is no mind! In this "no free will" version, the brain is the preset software.

In this "no free will" version of the car analogy, it seems like conscious decisions are being made, but this is an illusion. The AI Uber's sensors react to stimuli from the environment. The car's environment provides inputs to the car's computer, using the car's sensors, GPS, and traffic patterns, the computer—analogous to our brain—makes decisions. There is no separate driver—analogous to the mind. For example, the computer will direct the car to slam on the antilock brakes if a kid runs out in front of it. You, the passenger (the identity of self), is just along for the ride. Even when the ride is not completely predictable, the AI car's computer (the brain) will make decisions for you based on its wiring. If the mind exists at all, it is not in charge.

When I first heard this "no free will" explanation, my *intuition* rejected it. I thought, *Clearly that is false. I know I make decisions.*

To be clear, even people in the "no free will" camp would say, "Of course we make decisions." But (and it is an important but) those decisions are the only decisions that we could have made—given the environmental inputs we received and how our brains were wired when we received those inputs. It might feel like (our mind) is making decisions, but from this no free will perspective, we did not have a choice but to choose what we chose.

A third possibility is partial free will. Here a driver (the mind) drives a car (the body) with lots of AI features and sensors (the brain), but, the driver can override some of these AI features if he or she wants too.

In this version, "the mind" thinks it is in complete control, but the driver couldn't lock up the brakes if they wanted to. The computers in a modern car would simply override this instinct. Here, the car's computer (brain and sensors) is partly in control, but the driver (mind) can override some things.

So in which of these three situations—no free will, partial free will, or total free will—do we find ourselves? Before you answer this question, let's listen to what some cognitive scientists and philosophers have to say.

Dr. Sapolsky's Answer

Do we have free will? Dr. Robert Sapolsky, who teaches neurology and neurosurgery at Stanford University, says, "No!" In his latest book, *Determined: A Science of Life Without Free Will*, Robert makes a compelling case that humans do *not* have free will.

Let me summarize Robert's case to the best of my ability. He says that our beliefs and decisions are products of many things, all of which are outside of our control. Dr. Sapolsky explains that our neural networks determine our core values and belief systems. We are driven by both our environmental inputs and these well-entrenched neural networks to such a degree, that our reactions to stimuli are preordained. The brain is a machine, and by its very design, it will turn certain inputs into certain outputs. Mind, the entity outside of our brain, is an illusion.

Max Story

I'm going to tell a little story about my son Max that is related to free will.

When Max was in sixth grade, I found myself getting increasingly annoyed with his lack of academic motivation. Some of his teachers suspected he might have ADHD. I pooh-poohed this idea because, having taught many students with ADHD, he did not seem very ADHD to me. We finally brought him to a specialist for some testing to see what was going on. When we got the results, we learned that one doctor thought he had ADHD while a different doctor on the team did not. I chose to interpret that data with the conclusion that Max did not have ADHD. (I'm not immune to biased interpretation of data.) We also learned that his intelligence was very high, and his processing speed was very low.

After gathering all that information, my wife and I were still not sure how to proceed. Whenever Max worked on homework, he would struggle to do anything at an appropriate speed. A small assignment would take him forever to complete. We finally decided he should work at the kitchen table so we could try to keep him working along at a reasonable clip.

We watched him constantly space off. He repeatedly dropped his pencil. In one incident, that I'm sure cost me the dad-of-the-year award, I barked, "Just hold on to the frickin' pencil and do your work!"

By the time he was in eighth grade, we noticed that sometimes he would space off in the middle of his own sentences. We asked his doctor about this, and she suggested that maybe he should see a neurologist. She thought he might be having seizures. I was sure that they were not seizures. With seizures, one flops around or goes catatonic. Max's eyelids just sometimes barely flickered a little, but he was not going catatonic. In spite of my qualms, we did take him to the neurologist, and it turns out, for the second time in my life, I was wrong. First the gas line, now this.

The doctors called Max's form of epilepsy, "absence epilepsy." The neurologist estimated that Max was having about eighty seizures a day. I quickly apologized to Max for the pencil incident. "Sorry for yelling at you because you had epilepsy," I said sheepishly.

I tell this story to highlight a truth about behavioral control. We often assume those exhibiting certain behaviors have the power to change those behaviors, when, in fact, they do not. Max could not have held on to his pencil for all the tea in China. Yelling at him did not help.

The fact that personal control of our thoughts or beliefs is often an illusion, becomes even more apparent when we study disorders of the brain. "The mind" is not always in the driver's seat.

Toward the end of my dad's life, he was prescribed a medication which was supposed to help with his Parkinson's-induced drooling. This drug, in his specific case, caused hallucinations. His particular hallucinations were heartbreaking to watch. He was convinced he had just murdered someone. "Take me to the police station," he pleaded. "I killed them, there is blood all over the walls." His eyes darting back and forth over his little nursing home room. He was in a state of panic and fear. I was able to talk him down from that, and he appeared to calm down. But the cruel irony of this was not lost on me. Here was someone who once had intellectually understood hallucinations, and spent his life helping those with schizophrenia, now being sabotaged by his own declining brain. It was truly painful to watch.

We obviously discontinued the drooling medications, and thankfully he was back to his almost normal self within a day or two. As I reflect on this tragic chapter near the end of my dad's life, I can see Sapolsky's point. Perhaps we are *not* always in the driver's seat after all.

These incidents from the lives of my son and my dad are both stories of some disorder or malfunction. You might wonder, but how about in "normal" brains, don't "normal people" make their own decisions? I have come to believe that normal people are pretty rare. At the very least, there are a lot of different kinds of "normal."

Back to Sapolsky

Dr. Sapolsky asserts that there is no mechanism for something outside of the brain to tell synapses how to fire. Now, I think it is important to qualify that just because "the mind" has not been physically identified, doesn't mean it's not there. That said, the idea of a "mind" doesn't fit in with what we know about the brain.

Our neural networks, those connections that allow us to make decisions, were developed precisely the same way that our beliefs formed. Our brains are shaped by genes, upbringing, culture, peers, and other influences from both nature and nurture.

The notion of a "lack of a mind" makes me a little uneasy. This notion forces me to ask myself about choices I thought I made. Did I choose to write this book? Or was I compelled to write it due to certain motivations caused by the interaction of the wiring in my brain and my environment? Did I simply possess a set of character flaws—and strengths—that compelled me to spend years of my life on this project?

Writing this book seems like a choice I made. It seems like I could have chosen *not* to write it. It seems that I could have found something else to do with my time in retirement. Now, I'm starting to question it all.

I enjoy fishing. Why didn't I do that? As I edit this book repeatedly, the thought of grabbing the fly rod is very appealing to me. Why is my butt parked in front of a computer on this beautiful day? I'm not getting paid; I have no boss. And yet here I sit, as if I don't have a choice. Fishing does sound nice.

When I stop to ponder it, a world without free will leads me down quite the rabbit hole. For example, should anyone get credit for their accomplishments? If I win the Pulitzer Prize for this book, should I even accept it? Were all the events in the writing process just environmental inputs causing neuronal outputs, while I was just along for the ride? I must admit, the concept that I am without agency over my choices doesn't sit well with me, even if it might be true.

Daniel Dennett

The lack of free will did not sit well with Daniel Dennett either. Daniel Dennett (March 28, 1942–April 19, 2024) was a cognitive scientist and philosopher who spent much of his career at Tufts University. His studies focused on the philosophy of science and biology. Dennett believed that as our brain evolved, we developed the ability to make choices that could override our neuronal wiring. He made the case that, as a species, we evolved a new synaptic layer within our brain that allows us to be self-aware, to have consciousness, and control our primitive urges. He also thinks that in a world without free will, motivation for improvement is removed. The lack of free will absolves everyone of personal responsibility.

He argued that the *mere presumption* of a lack of free will is harmful. Whether we do or do not have free will was less of a concern to him. If people merely *believe* there is no free will, then there will be problematic behavioral consequences.

He cites a 2008 study by Dr. Kathleen Vohs of the University of Minnesota and Jonathan Schooler of the University of California at

Santa Barbara. In their study, two groups of college students were given two paragraphs from a book written by Francis Crick. One group read a paragraph that explained why personal free will is an illusion, while the other group read a different paragraph about consciousness.

The two groups were then given a computerized math test that was intentionally glitchy. When a student hit the space bar, it "accidentally" showed the answer on the screen briefly. The students in the study were told in advance about this glitch, but they were also told explicitly that they should not cheat by hitting the space bar.

The students who read the passage about how "free will is an illusion" cheated significantly more than the control group who simply read about consciousness.

Participants were clearly influenced by the subtle rewiring of their brains that occurred when they read the passage that made the case for the absence of free will. They seemed to lose their moral impulse that kept them from cheating. Their inclination to cheat was measurably heightened.

Interestingly, this study supports the idea that we don't have free will—their moral compass had been subtly shifted by an environmental input—while simultaneously condemning the notion that we should spread the "no freewill hypothesis," precisely because of its impact. When people believe they are not in the driver's seat, they rationalize their bad behaviors.

Robert Sapolsky has a solid counter argument. He claims that there is a moral upside to embracing a lack of free will. He believes that if we treat others as if they do not have control over their own brain, this could lead to less judgment. Perhaps fewer dads would yell at their sons for accidentally dropping pencils.

I think the most appropriate course of action might be to embrace a double standard. Normally, a double standard is viewed as a bad thing, but in this case, I believe that if we think of *ourselves* as *having* free will, and think of *others* as *not* having free will, we could get the benefits of both philosophical viewpoints.

It is inappropriate to justify our shortcomings solely by attributing them to inherent traits or environmental circumstances. We should not just say to ourselves "I am not a good speller" or "I'm bad at math."

Instead, we should work to improve. We should also continually question what we think. We should not act as though our own beliefs are outside of our control. I would like to encourage people to embrace the idea that beliefs can and should change with new information.

On the other hand, we should not be so judgy of the choices that *others* make. We should understand that when that annoying student asks ten thousand clarifying questions and asks for constant reassurance, it might not really be a choice for them. They may suffer from anxiety. Their need for certainty may just be overwhelming. I must remind myself that other people's beliefs and belief systems, though foreign to me, are rooted in their own personal natures and experiences. I believe we can affect the beliefs of others, but a judgmental attitude toward their beliefs is not helpful as we attempt to gain an understanding of their perspectives.

I want to be clear, the following section on epistemic responsibility is *not* about getting others to take responsibility for *their* beliefs, it is about *us* taking responsibility for *our* beliefs. I realize this may seem somewhat inconsistent, but I think this approach offers the most constructive path forward.

CHAPTER 35

Epistemic Responsibility

So, assuming we have some control over *our* beliefs, how do we evaluate them? Unlike facts, beliefs are not verifiable. What do philosophers, other than me, have to say about responsibility for our own beliefs?

Way back in the 1850s, philosopher William Clifford wrote, "It is wrong, always and everywhere, for anyone to believe in things upon insufficient evidence." Clifford asserted that we have a moral obligation to consider the impacts of our beliefs on ourselves and others. Clifford argued that we cannot hide behind the defense of "I am entitled to my own beliefs."

William James, a prominent philosopher, founder of the Psychology Department at Harvard, and a leading thinker of the late nineteenth century, held the view that there are certain conditions when a person might be justified in having beliefs without evidence. While he agreed with Clifford about the moral indefensibility of having beliefs that go against known evidence, in cases where there was no evidence, James felt that one could still hold a justified belief.

James felt that three conditions needed to met to hold a belief without evidence:

1. The belief must be a live option. "Live option" just means that it is possible for you to have that belief.
2. It must be forced. "Forced" simply means you must adopt a belief. Not choosing can be considered a choice in some

circumstances. Do you want to go somewhere or sit on the couch? By not deciding, you just decided to sit on the couch.

3. It must be momentous. "Momentous" means believing or not believing must have a major consequence.

James would say, for example, that belief in God is morally defensible even if you do not have evidence because belief in God fits these criteria.

So, who wins this battle? William Clifford, who thinks all beliefs must be grounded in evidence, or William James, who thinks we can, in certain circumstances be justified to hold beliefs which are not grounded in evidence?

Perhaps it is a good time for another William to chime in. Philosopher William Swain—a.k.a. me—asserts, "The key criteria for evaluating our beliefs are the *implications* of those beliefs, *implications* are more important than the justification. It is essential to closely examine your beliefs to ensure that your beliefs are not causing harm to yourselves or others."

Beliefs without evidence are inevitable, but beliefs should be justified in some way. Sometimes, such as in the case of belief or disbelief in God, there is no way to gather physical evidence, so the *consequences* of the belief become far more important than its *justification*. What are the implications of your beliefs? Are your beliefs, or even your larger belief system, harmful to you or anyone else? Is your belief helpful to you or anyone else?

Are Your Beliefs Harmful to Yourself or to Others?

All of us have beliefs that some people disagree with; that is the nature of beliefs. I believe—in the specific case of religious belief—our beliefs should be evaluated, not as to whether they are correct, but rather, through the lens of consequences.

Are your beliefs helping you to be the best version of yourself? If so, great! Is the belief in God helping someone beat addiction—awesome! Does the belief in the teachings of Buddha, or God, inspire you to help alleviate the suffering of the downtrodden? If yes, fantastic. Does your religion help you find hope or inspire you? More of that please. Does your belief system call on you to right social ills, such as calling for the emancipation of the slaves? Again, this seems like a positive belief system.

On the other hand, if you are burning witches because of your belief in God, please stop. Are your beliefs asking you to marginalize kids who have gay parents because you believe God wants you to fix America? That is not okay. Do your beliefs make you feel like you should be punished, or cause you debilitating anxiety about hell? Less of that please. Do your beliefs cause you to feel hate and anger? Probably not a healthy system. Does your belief in God ask you to deny scientific facts, logic, and your own sense perceptions? That should be a warning sign that maybe those beliefs are not coming from the divine. Does your belief system ask you to sacrifice your own life and/or the lives of others by, say, flying planes into buildings? Well, that seems like an obvious hard no! Does your belief system justify genocide? Then for God's sake abandon that horrible belief system.

Most Muslims and Christians do *not* have those negative beliefs incorporated into their faiths, but those negative beliefs involving religion have historically existed, and unfortunately, some still exist.

Of course, both the positives and negatives of these belief systems can be found within various interpretations of the Torah, Quran, the Bible, and other sacred texts. Having a belief simply because it is "the literal word of God," generally does not hold up to scrutiny. This literal approach is often riddled with internal inconsistencies. People's belief systems are often impacted, particularly in the Abrahamic religions, by the way particular groups view the Bible or Quran.

Peter Gomes, professor of Christian morals at Harvard Divinity School, and author of *The Good Book: Reading the Bible with Mind and Heart*, says there is an inherent challenge in interpretating Scripture due to the dichotomy between the "spirit of the word" and the "literal word." Gomes refers to those big take-home messages in the Bible as "the spirit of the word." He goes on to say that unfortunately, within the collection of books that make up the Bible, there are many passages which, in isolation, seem to conflict with the spirt of the word. The apparent discord between the spiritual truths and specific Scripture passages can be very perplexing, especially if we blindly assume every word is from God himself and meant to be taken literally. Let me offer some specific examples.

In Exodus 21: 20–21, it says, "If a man beats his slave, male or female, and the slave dies at his hands, he must pay the penalty. But should the slave survive for one or two days, he should pay no penalty because the slave is his by right of purchase." In Exodus, it also goes on to say that when you beat your slaves, you should not break their teeth or cause them to go blind. Leviticus 27: 1–8 offers price lists for men and women slaves and at different ages.

The not-so-subtle implication is that it is certainly okay to own and beat slaves. However, the owners must make sure not to knock their teeth out or make them go blind, and don't kill them right away. Scripture passages that give outright or tacit support for slavery are common in the Old Testament. Similar support can be found in the New Testament as well. Ephesians 6:5 states: "Slaves, be obedient to the men who are called your masters in this world, treat them with deep respect and loyalty . . ."

These proslavery passages are an obvious contradiction with the teachings of Christ. "Love your neighbor as yourself" and "Do unto others as you would have done unto you" are words attributed to Christ. Christ's compassion for all the downtrodden and the underdogs, is on constant display in all the Gospels. How do you reconcile those disparate words attributed to God the Son with those purported words of God the Father?

I, thankfully, don't personally know any fundamentalists that defend slavery. Yet many people have no problem taking other passages in isolation and using them to defend other agendas. Gomes argues that picking specific pieces of Scripture is less instructive than understanding the broader themes.

Are You Certain about Your Beliefs?

I think there is a distinction between believing with some justification and believing with absolute certainty. Clifford said the that "belief without evidence is a sin against Mankind!" The kinder, gentler Mr.

Swain says, "Holding a personal belief with absolute certainty—as if it were a collective empirical truth—has historically caused human misery." (I like quoting myself in my own book ☺.)

If someone believes the fundamentalist interpretation of the Quran or the Bible, that, in and of itself, is not necessarily a destructive thing—I have fundamentalist Christians friends who are kind and caring people.

But when anyone becomes so certain, so unquestioning of *their interpretation*, that they fly airline jets into buildings, or shoot abortion providers, that is when their belief becomes morally indefensible. If you are *pretty sure* your belief is correct, you might write an angry letter to the editor. But being certain, puts you at risk of causing misery to others and yourself.

Are Your Beliefs in Conflict with Empirical Evidence?

It is quite common these days for people to hold beliefs that oppose current empirical evidence. These are beliefs which deny that which is known. I highlighted the belief systems involved in creationism earlier in this book, but there are many examples of this phenomenon. Examples include: climate science deniers, flat-earthers, Holocaust deniers, Moon landing deniers, and election result deniers. All these groups employ basic denial of scientific, historical, or numerical facts.

Although admittedly a slightly more nuanced topic, the views of the anti-vaccine movement can be considered another example of science denial. I say nuanced because early in the COVID vaccine story, it was not ridiculous to consider mRNA vaccines as "frontier science." The discussion about the safety of mRNA vaccines was a reasonable discussion about risk assessment. What is not debatable is that established vaccines work. Vaccines developed and tested using the process of science nearly eradicated smallpox, rubella, measles, and polio. We know this as an empirical and historical truth. We also know that vaccines do not cause autism. The hypothesis claiming otherwise has been soundly refuted with data and evidence gathered and analyzed through the bias-reducing methods of science.

Clifford, James, and well, everyone who has given the matter any thought, finds the rejection of established scientific or historical truths undefendable.

So what? What is the big deal if people think the Earth is flat? On one hand, whether the Earth is flat or spherical will not change most people's daily life. In addition, one could argue that being skeptical of authority can be a useful intellectual skill.

Here is the subtle, but very important, point. The attempt to foster a questioning, skeptical intellect by rejecting science or history ends with people questioning the wrong things and the wrong people. Ironically, in the conspiracy theorist's quest to become skeptical intelligent humans, they become pawns of nefarious individuals who feed them falsehoods to feed their manipulative agendas. This is a dangerous road. Rejection of scientific and historical facts can unravel the fabric of reality. Scientists and historians are not the villains; they are guardians of reality. In a world where it is hard to know what is real and what is fake, using processes which are built to remove bias is our best hope.

Once you go down this path of rejection of science and history, anything can become a conspiracy. A couple of years ago while I was teaching, I had a student tell me that the story of Hellen Keller was a complete fabrication. (This student was also anti-vaccines, anti-evolution, and a climate change denier.) Fact denial gets woven into people's thinking. Fact denial had become part of this student's personal identity.

John Oliver, a comedian/journalist did a great bit on his show *Last Week Tonight* where he talked about a poll regarding climate change. He started with a news story which stated, "A new poll finds one in four Americans are skeptical about (or don't believe in) climate change."

To which Oliver responds, "Who gives a fuck! We don't need a poll to tell us people's opinions on a fact. You might as well conduct a poll on: Which number is bigger, five or twenty-five? Do owls exist? Or are there hats?" I loved this bit.

Facts are not opinions.

If one's beliefs are not consistent with facts, then those beliefs need to be reexamined. Stubbornly refusing to accept a fact, is not the same thing as holding a contrary belief. When someone holds belief contrary to a fact, we are no longer talking about a belief. The person is simply wrong about a fact.

In conclusion, I believe that when we evaluate our belief systems, we should try to ensure that they 1) do not cause harm to oneself or others, 2) are internally consistent, and 3) align with known facts.

CHAPTER 36

Political Beliefs

Once we get to political beliefs, the process of examining our beliefs becomes even more complicated. Sometimes we operate with the same facts, but our opinions merely differ. We simply have different umwelts that leads us in different directions. Abortion is an issue that demonstrates this kind of complication. There is, in fact, a rock-solid, simple, internally consistent, logical argument to be made against abortion. There is also a rock-solid, simple, internally consistent, logical argument to be on the pro-choice side of that debate. The facts in this case are not really in dispute. This an argument of ethics. When does human life begin? Is it at conception, at first heartbeat, first brain activity? There are good arguments to make for any of these options. Are the rights of the embryo more important than the rights of the mother? Who should answer these questions?

The argument is difficult to mediate because the moral high ground is elusive. Here, my only plea, is to dial back our certainty when an issue has some inherent uncertainty. As I write this paragraph, a man just shot some representatives in the Minnesota legislature because they supported reproductive rights. Being so convinced of your "pro-life" beliefs that you are willing to kill people is more than a little ironic. Beliefs, by their very nature, are inherently uncertain. Certainty in the uncertain often causes the trouble.

There are other political issues which can be evaluated based on facts, internal consistency, and amount of harm done to others.

In my home state of Iowa, members of the LGBTQ community find themselves as collateral damage in an unnecessary culture war. Fundamentalism is a driving force in these culture wars. Fundamentalists, and politicians attempting to curry their favor, often quote passages of Scripture—sometimes called "proof texts"—to rationalize their attacks. At least that is how I see this playing out through my particular umwelt.

Just like support for slavery, if you want to find anti-homosexual "proof texts" in the Bible, you are in luck. They exist. Some people I know, who belong to fundamentalist churches, use these biblical passages to justify their resistance to, and outright marginalization of, the LGBTQ community. Yet when it comes to treatment of LGBTQ community, those same people can ignore the broader themes of love, acceptance, and defending the marginalized. The "proof texts" about defending immigrants and defending the marginalized are also easy, actually *much* easier to find, throughout the Bible.

To their credit, these fundamentalists are good at ignoring "proof texts" that support slavery. They also ignore the "proof texts" that call for the stoning of people who work on the Sabbath. Despite their claims to the contrary, it seems like fundamentalists *do interpret* the Bible after all. They selectively follow some biblical passages while ignoring others.

I wanted to bring up the LGBTQ example because I have gay and trans friends and family who are hurt by the very policies that my fundamentalist friends support. The harm does not just come from the political policies; my gay and trans friends are also negatively impacted by the intolerant rhetoric that comes from these politicians and pulpits.

Here is the important point. The beliefs of my gay friends do not impact my fundamentalist friends. Not one bit. But the beliefs by those who believe that God does not approve of "the gays" certainly do negatively impact the lives of my gay friends. This is especially true when those beliefs are translated into government policies or hurtful judgmental rhetoric.

In my umwelt, the broader spiritual themes of kindness and supporting the marginalized matters more than some isolated literal passage. Through the lens of consequences, I think it is easy to see which beliefs are most problematic.

Sometimes, the anti-LGBTQ crowd assert the transgender kids are being rescued from parents who are forcing them into gender roles that they were not born with. Or they assert that kids need an adult to force the "proper" gender role on a confused kid for the kid's own good. They think tolerance equates to promoting this gender confusion. They believe that tolerance worsens the plight of those with sexual or gender "confusion."

These beliefs are easy to hold if you have not spoken with those in the LGBTQ community. I believe if they ever spoke with the individuals or their families, and took some time to understand their umwelt, those who are fighting this unnecessary culture war might change their minds.

On March 12, 2025, Larry Jones, an eighty-five-year-old conservative, went to a Wisconsin congressional assembly hearing with the intention of supporting a bill that would ban gender-affirming care for minors. He didn't plan on speaking but went because his grandson invited him and it wasn't far from where he lived in Milwaukee. After listening to both groups testify for hours, he decided he wanted to speak.

"I have very little knowledge of gay people and things like that, so when I came here, my eyes were opened. I was one of the critics (of gender-affirming care) that sat on the side, and I made the decision there was only two genders, so I got an education that was unbelievable. And I don't know just exactly how to say this, but my perspective for people has changed. . . . I'd like to apologize for being here (to initially support this bill), and I learned a lot about this group of people."

Larry Jones is a great example of someone who took some time to listen to the perspective of others and then changed his mind. Unfortunately, most people don't bother hearing perspectives different than their own.

There are some scientific and historical facts that are worth bringing to the trans issue. People are born with different sex chromosomes. On the twenty-third pair of chromosomes, most people are born with XX, some XY. Some are born with XXY, XYY, and even a just X with a missing Y chromosome. Some people are born with both male and female parts. Did God not make them in his image? I find when I talk to fundamentalists about this, they recite a similar response: "You have your proof, all I need is my Bible. If the Bible says literally that God created Man and Women, then that's final. That's all I need to know. No interpretation necessary." This is a similar response you get when you cite evidence for evolution. It is the old "don't try to confuse me with the facts" response.

Fundamentalists interpret the Bible. They pick what issues they choose to fight and then use Scripture to bolster their position. They have chosen to fight the battle against homosexuality, while they choose to ignore the widespread practice of working on the Sabbath. I am very bothered by this inconsistency. (To be fair, it is not just the inconsistency that bothers me. If they were consistent, and stoning people for working on the Sabbath, that would piss me off too.)

I know some fundamentalists will have differing takes on this. I know that what I have written in this paragraph is not a fact but rather *my* beliefs. However, my hope is that everyone will be encouraged to reevaluate their beliefs through the lens of consequences on others, internal consistency, and alignment with known facts. When some fundamentalists use "proof texts" to harm the already marginalized, those actions have two negative consequences: 1) somewhat obviously, it harms the victims of their self-righteous rhetoric; but 2) it also undermines the credibility of God's words. In my view, using "proof texts" to target a group of people has no positive consequences.

CHAPTER 37

Christian Nationalism

For the next several chapters, I want to talk about Christian nationalism. Christian nationalism is more complicated than, say, the beliefs of flat-earthers because it is built on multiple misconceptions, not just one. It is also complicated because Christian nationalism is such an ill-defined belief system.

Most Christian nationalists don't even use the term "Christian nationalist," but it is an accurate term to describe those who feel America's identity is inextricably Christian.

Christian nationalism is a subset of just regular nationalism. Nationalism is found all over the world and has been, and currently is, hotly debated within many nations. It has been in America for a long time. Nationalism's popularity has ebbed and flowed throughout American history.

Most recently, the Christian nationalists received some bad press because some of the January 6 rioters were self-proclaimed Christian nationalists. In the last decade or two, Christian nationalist rhetoric has resurfaced in American politics.

Nationalism is the belief that nations are distinct cultural groups defined by shared traits like language, religion, and ethnicity. Nationalists believe that governments should promote and protect this identity. According to Samuel Huntington, a Havard political scientist who supports some Christian nationalism ideas, "America is defined by its 'Anglo-Protestant' past, and we will lose our identity and our freedom if we don't preserve our cultural inheritance."

Linguistically, Christian nationalism does not sound that bad. *Christian* means following the teachings of Christ, and *nationalism* is often conflated with patriotism. But unlike peanut butter and chocolate—two things that are awesome together—Christian nationalism is more like ice cream and mayonnaise: two things that are nasty if combined.

I want to be clear, nationalism is not the same as patriotism. (Many people have positive feelings about patriotism, but patriotism and nationalism are *not* actually interchangeable terms.) The terms "Christian" and "nationalism" appeal to a large segment of the US population.

Nationalism pretends that the borders of a region have within it a uniform cultural heritage. I say "pretends" because most areas contain many cultural identities. For an area as large and diverse as the USA, a "one cultural heritage" proposition is a false narrative. It's make-believe. Even if one were to pretend that we are only a Christian nation, we would still need to decide which version of Christian. Are we a Mormon nation? Catholic nation? Evangelical? Mainline Protestant? None of these groups represent a majority, and they all hold different theological beliefs.

Christian nationalism is really a political movement masquerading as a Christian movement. It is a bit of a Frankenstein, created from parts of radical right-wing politics that infected an often well-meaning, fundamentalist theology. In the United States, Christian nationalism resides primarily within the dark corners of fundamentalist Christian theology. In Iran and Afghanistan, the nationalistic push toward theocracy is most prominent within fundamentalist Muslim theology.

Fundamentalism is not inherently related to politics. So why have Evangelicals and other fundamentalists been more susceptible to the Christian nationalist movement than other denominations? My hypothesis is that fundamentalist theology is susceptible because it contains the toxic mix of certainty, combined with the normalization of the rejection of scientific or historical facts. (Specifically, if those facts conflict with their interpretation of Scripture.)

Additionally, and importantly, imbedded in both Christian nationalism and fundamentalism exists a kind of persecution theology. Early Christians were, in fact, persecuted. So, one can find lots of "proof texts" about persecution in the Bible. Today, persecution theology is very common in the US. This is a bit ironic because Christianity is a common religion in most areas of this country. Hard to persecute the majority.

Nationalist persecution theology serves as an insurance policy of sorts. It protects Christian nationalism, and fundamentalism, from criticism. By framing any attack on *their interpretation* of their divine text as an attack on Christians—and more importantly, on the *Scripture itself and thus God*—they have put *their* interpretation above criticism. In their umwelt, they are now aligned with God. This is why arguing with fundamentalists often goes nowhere. They are not arguing as "themselves," they are speaking as spokespeople for "God." A line that often ends a logical argument with a fundamentalist is, "This isn't my belief; this is what God tells us in Scripture." This little rhetorical trick makes them believe that you are arguing with God, and their role, is to support God by denying your logic and scientific facts with "proof texts."

The History of Christian Nationalism in Politics

The earliest version of Christian nationalism flourished in the South during the Reconstruction in the late 1800s. This version of Christian nationalism was a secret society called the Ku Klux Klan. The Ku Klux Klan was an effort to protect White rural protestant heritage. Jews, Blacks, and Catholics were all viewed as a threat to rural White protestant culture. The atrocities of the KKK eventually contributed to its demise. However, the Klan, and some of its ideas, are still with us today.

The Scopes "Monkey Trial" began the modern rift between Christian fundamentalism and science, as I explained earlier. Politically, Epperson v. Arkansas also drove some Christians to the conservative side of the political divide. Later Roe v. Wade drove more Christians—initially mostly Catholics—to the conservative side of the political spectrum. In the minds of many Evangelicals, and a few fundamentalist Catholics, "Christian" and "conservative" were gradually becoming synonymous with each other. Conservative politics, and a distrust in science, became entangled identities. In the 1970s, a strange hybrid of evangelical theology and conservative politics emerged.

In the minds of the conservative right, liberals were creating an increasingly more immoral country. Something needed to be done. Conservatives *felt* like they were in the majority, and yet their voices were not being heard. Many of the progressive changes, such as civil rights, forced integration through busing, abortion rights, teaching of evolution in schools, the women's rights movement (specifically the Equal Rights Amendment) were seized upon by this movement.

In 1979, Jerry Falwell and the political action group known as the Moral Majority stepped into this large groundswell of social change. Falwell energized fights against the ERA, gay rights, abortion, pornography, and the teaching of evolution. Unlike the KKK, some Catholics and Mormons were welcomed into this new group. The conservative Catholic stance on abortion added much needed numbers to the group. As a result, the Moral Majority turned into a political force. The inclusion of the Mormon fundamentalists made strategic sense because they were one of the fastest growing denominations. This new "moral majority" group catered to those who opposed all the "social upheaval" that came with change. Politically, the Moral Majority was effective. It was a major part of the coalition that helped propel Reagan and later George Bush Sr. to victories using campaigns of "family values." The group disbanded in 1989, but these "culture wars" persisted across conservative talk radio and Fox News throughout the 1990s. The narrative was simple: progressives were the bad guys. They were taking us away from a better, more moral time. Progressives were taking us away from our cultural heritage. Scientists with their talk of "*evil*ution" and the "big bang" were also on the side of "bad" progressives. In this umwelt, it was a good vs. evil war. The seeds had been sown for the current version of the "Christian nationalist" movement.

But what does it mean to be a Christian nationalist in 2025? In a nutshell, Christian nationalism currently focuses on these ideas:

1. To remain in God's favor, Americans must behave and adhere to a biblical moral code. God judges not only individuals, but countries. God punishes us, as a country, when our fellow countrymen misbehave.

2. We should roll back the separation of church and state. Christian values are under attack. Let's get back to "one nation under God!" In the 1990s, the so-called "War on Christmas" was a reoccurring "news" story on Fox News, portraying Christians in a War against evil and the Government persecution of Christians is a major part of the messaging for Christian nationalism.

3. We need to fight for our freedoms. Freedom from government, freedom from fear, freedom to bear arms. Freedom is a big part of this theology. Particularly religious freedom—well at least for one set of beliefs. Oddly, even issues such as gun control, taxes, and "onerous" government regulations have been co-opted into the Christian nationalism.

4. We must abandon multiculturalism. It is an evil, failed experiment. (Sometimes Christian nationalism is called White Christian nationalism. Historically, there was a particular emphasis on preservation of White rural culture. However, the racial element was somewhat abandoned in the Moral Majority's version of Christian nationalism. That said, racism is not uncommon in the Christian nationalist movement.

5. We must recognize that this country was founded on Christian principles. The country is in moral decay. Let's return to a time before progressives ruined everything and return to the Christian nation that our Founding Fathers intended. Christian nationalism promotes lots of nostalgia for the good ole days. Principle #5 is very much related to, but slightly different than, principle #1

CHAPTER 38

Theological Origins of Christian Nationalism

Let's start with #1 and #5 on the previous list:

1. "To remain in God's favor, Americans must have and adhere to a biblical moral code. God judges not only individuals but countries."
5. "We must recognize that this country was founded on Christian principles."

The Early History of Religion in Precolonial America

Way back before the United States was born, back in the 1630s, the Puritans[11] arrived in North America to escape religious persecution. Their first winter here was brutal. Hundreds of Puritans died of disease and starvation. In Scripture, particularly in the Old Testament, God is often portrayed as a vindictive punisher.

The Puritans interpreted this Scripture, coupled with their misery, as an indication that God was punishing them because their

---

11. They did not call themselves Puritans, they were a splinter group of Anglicans. The name "Puritan" was a term of derision.

congregation did not meet a sufficient moral standard. So as a group, they decided to refer to the Scriptures and follow them even more rigorously than before, in order to avoid God's wrath. Any deviation from God's word was reason enough for God to harshly punish the entire group. The Puritans did not focus on love, grace, and forgiveness, but rather they fixated on avoidance of group judgment and punishment. As a group, they wanted to gain God's favor.

It did not take long for this thought process to spiral out of control. At the time, no state existed to govern or regulate; the pulpit wielded all the power. Over the next few years, this group placed a higher and higher value on submission and conformity. Any deviation of the norm was viewed as the devil's work, and women were viewed as more susceptible than men to the devil's influence.

This sexist notion came from their very twisted interpretation of the story of Adam and Eve. Eve tempted Adam with the fruit from the forbidden tree. (Of course, even if one believes that the story is literal, Eve had not yet been created when God gave *Adam* the garden tour and told *him* not to eat that fruit. Blaming Eve does not really follow the literal word of the text, but that did not stop the male leadership of the Church from blaming original sin on Eve.)

Back to the Puritans. Their obsession with group salvation, conformity, and moral codes initially led to banishing people from the group—women primarily. (If you are a student of history, you will soon observe that most collective misery begins with banning.) The most famous of these bannings occurred when Anne Hutchinson was banished in 1697. Hutchinson's "trial" featured Puritan clergy as the court and the prosecution; there was no possible defense—much like in Galileo's show "trial."

Anne Hutchinson's crime was that she questioned some of the pastor's interpretations of the Scriptures. She held her own meetings with mostly women to spread her interpretations of the Scriptures. The "official" Puritan ruling in 1637 did not find any crimes against her, but rather they found that she was "a woman not fit for our society." So, they banished her from the community. Anne Hutchinson and her husband moved from the Massachusetts Bay Colony to Rhode Island.

The fear of collective punishment in these early churches only increased over the years, resulting in more forced conformity and forced adherence to strict moral codes. Banning people from your community was bad enough, but what happened a few decades later in Salem, Massachusetts, was the real cautionary tale.

From 1692 into 1693, this Puritan theological idea of group judgment, severe conformity, and fear of God's punishment led to the death by hanging of thirty "witches." Most of the deaths were women and even some children. (An additional man died during torture and several more "witches" died in jail.) Of course, we are not talking about witches. We are talking about the horrendously tragic death of innocent women, young girls, and a few men. Another hundred or so people had to undergo "a trial" to prove they were not witches.

To the Puritans of the day, they were just trying to follow the Word of the Lord to the best of their abilities. To those on the outside looking in, the Puritans had become a religious cult. A mass psychosis phenomenon occurred. This was NOT a, "Well, they are entitled to their beliefs" situation.

With some hindsight, hanging innocent people doesn't seem all that in line with the teachings of Christ.

Hindsight!?

Hindsight should not have been needed! Maybe a smidgen of *foresight* could have prevented this nonsense.

This story is important because it shows the birth of the idea. "To remain in God's favor, Americans must behave and adhere to a biblical moral code. God judges not only individuals but groups or countries."

This cautionary tale is also important because it shows what happens when this bad theology is practiced. We don't need to have a hypothetical discussion of, "What *could* happen if the theology of group punishment got adopted?" The Puritans, the Taliban, and others have done this experiment, and we know the results. Punishment theology, banning, forced adherence to moral codes by some moral authority has *never* ended well, anywhere in the world, at any time in human history.

The Salem witch hunts severely damaged the theological notion of group judgment and punishment.

In the last few decades, Christian nationalists resurrected the theological idea that the *country* is being judged by God. They claim that if *other people* don't follow a particular interpretation of Scripture, or a particular moral code, then we as a *country* will be punished. They believe that our patriotic and religious duty is to hold America to its founding religious ideals so that God will grant us favor *as a nation*. They crave a return to a nostalgic, happy, and idyllic time. They want to make America strong again by strict adherence to Scripture. If they get their way, they believe God will judge us less harshly and that many of the social ills that plague our society will abate.

The notion that Scripture must be enforced—as interpreted by a particular religious theology—is alive and well. Apparently, the death of well over thirty innocent women, children, and men at the hands of a deluded crowd in precolonial America has been forgotten.

Those who don't know their history are condemned to repeat it.

Other experiments in theocracy—from the Holy Roman Empire to the theocracies in Iran and Afghanistan—have also ended in atrocities. Simply more lessons not learned. Apparently, we are to believe that "this time it will be different."

The battle cries from the Christian nationalist call for a return to the "good ole days, when Christians ruled the nation like the Founding Fathers intended." Of course, the Founding Fathers had no such intentions.

CHAPTER 39

George Whitefield

The story of George Whitefield is an important part of American theological history that I don't think most people really know.

My son, Max, and my wife have occasionally given me feedback during the writing process. According to Max, "Sometimes all your digressions into other topics sort of lose me. I think they are interesting, but I think. 'Why are we talking about this?'"

Suellen echoed this general feedback, "I think you should remind the reader why you are even talking about, fill in the blank . . . For example, why are you suddenly talking about George Whitefield?"

I try to defend my choices, "I think the reader will give me the benefit of the doubt, they will see why George is related to my general rambling thesis if they just hang with it."

At this point, I no longer worry about you putting the book down. You made it this far, I think you will continue through the remaining pages. So in this particular instance, feedback ignored.

George Whitefield was an Anglican who left his church in 1739 and traveled to the frontier to hold revival meetings. His big theological contribution focused on the need to be personally "born again" in order to accept the grace of Christ. Whitefield felt that religion was between God and you. You did not need the blessing of ruling-class religion to interpret the Scriptures. At the time, in his home state of Virginia, "ruling class" meant the Episcopalians (or Anglicans as they were called at this point in the colonies' history).

As a result, the Anglican leadership banished Whitefield from teaching in Anglican churches. He was like an Anglican version of Anne Hutchinson. Virginia, the Carolinas, and Georgia were all basically theocracies ruled by the Anglican Church. Meanwhile the "Puritans" were now referred to as "Congregationalists," and their denomination ruled in Massachusetts, Connecticut, and New Hampshire. The other colonies tolerated a variety of denominations. The remaining colonies did not support one denomination over another. So people who were Baptists, Presbyterians, Quakers, or other early American protestant denominations of the day, often decided to migrate to those less-restrictive colonies.

After banishment in 1739, George Whitefield continued his evangelism in other colonies as well as the new frontier. It is not hyperbole to say that he was bigger than Taylor Swift—on a per capita basis. It is estimated that he preached, in person, to one-quarter of the entire population of the colonies. Remember this occurred in the 1740s; he accomplished this feat while walking around on foot. Without a booking agent, or marketing firm, he reached all of those people. His evangelism was incredible.

Rather than deliver boring sermons, Whitefield had a gift for storytelling. He excelled at it. According to Harry Stout, a history professor at Yale, "George Whitefield had the sincerity of a missionary combined with the thrill of a performer." In terms of ways of knowing, George appealed to people's *imaginations* and their *intuition* to engage their *faith*.

Anglican priests did not typically engage with their parishioners in this way. They, like the Catholics, counted on the use of rituals. (Catholics did not arrive in America in large numbers until the mid-1840s, that's another interesting story of American history . . . but heeding Max's advice, I will not digress.)

George Whitfield's style resembled theater that used the Scriptures. He invoked very little appeal to reason or ritual, and emphasized Scripture less than you might think. He employed emotional appeals to engage individuals' desire to participate in a movement dedicated to glorifying God. It was a celebration of Christ. Consequently, Whitefield's audience felt as though they were involved in something spectacular—bigger than themselves, perhaps even divine!

By the mid-1700s, in those colonies without official churches, there existed a free marketplace for any new protestant denomination. This provides part of the explanation as to why America supports such a wide variety of protestant churches. When George Whitfield returned to his very Anglican home state of Virginia, he learned what theocracy really meant. The colony of Virgina imprisoned him for preaching without a license.

Thomas Jefferson advocated for his release. Jefferson was not an Evangelical himself; he was not even a Christian. However, Anglicans dictating that people in their colony could only practice one religion—or in this case, one denomination—bothered him.

As a direct result of how Whitefield, and others, were oppressed by these early theocracies, in 1791, the First Amendment to the Constitution was added. It contained a carefully crafted clause that guaranteed both freedom *from* religion *and* freedom *of* religion.

In 1802, Jefferson reiterated these First Amendment ideals in his letter to the Danbury Baptists:

> Religion is a matter which lies solely between Man & his God, that he owes account to none other for his faith or his worship, that the legitimate powers of government reach actions only, & not opinions. I contemplate with sovereign reverence that act of the whole American people which declared that their legislature should make no law respecting an establishment of religion or prohibiting the free exercise thereof.

The dissolution of the early colonial theocracies coincided with the adoption of the First Amendment to the Constitution in 1791. Separation of church and state allowed Whitefield's evangelical fundamentalism to flourish in any state. Ironically, 230-some years later, the Christian nationalists—a subset of the evangelical fundamentalist movement—now argue *against* separation of church and state. They claim, "We should roll back the separation of church and state. Our Christian values are under attack."

These Christian nationalists seem to be "irony proof." When they say "Christian values," they seem willfully ignorant of the fact that not all Christians share their values.

The Founding Fathers Did *Not* Intend Us to Be a Christian Nation

While we are on this topic, I want to dispel another related myth. Many believe that our Founding Fathers wanted a Christian nation. Some historical facts serve to dispel this myth. As I just described, before our colonies formed a nation in 1776, a few colonies had experimented with the idea of mini-theocracies. But from the beginning of America as a nation, our Founding Fathers opposed a state-sponsored religion or denomination. Two of the most famous Founding Fathers, Benjamin Franklin and Thomas Jefferson, did not even identify as Christian.

Some might ask, "But what about 'In God we trust,' officially printed on our money? Or our 'Pledge of Allegiance,' which clearly states, 'one nation under God'?"

Here are some historical facts.

We added "In God We Trust" to coins in 1864, near the end of the Civil War, during a temporary surge in nationalism.

We added "one nation under God" to the Pledge of Allegiance in the early 1950s, as different threats emerged from within our country called the Red Scare. The Red Scare, also called McCarthyism, was *a reaction* to the external threat of communism. The consequences of this "Red Scare" included the blacklisting of individuals, destroyed careers, and even deportations of suspected "communist sympathizers." Charlie Chaplin was perhaps the most famous deportee. Just like in 1930s Germany, scientists and academics became targets during this heightened nationalism. American hero Robert Oppenheimer (the physicist who invented the atomic bomb, thus ending WWII) was perhaps the most notable academic to be publicly attacked. (He also lost his position on the Atomic Regulatory Commission in the aftermath of the Red Scare.)

In 1953, politicians took many symbolic actions to show their toughness on "Godless communists." In 1954, Congress voted to add the phrase "one nation under God" to the Pledge of Allegiance. Another legislative action, also in 1954, made "In God We Trust" our national motto. In 1957, a third legislative action put the phrase "In God We Trust" on our paper money.

Edward R. Murrow, a distinguished war correspondent, CBS journalist, and documentary filmmaker, was among the select group of individuals who showed the resolve to challenge McCarthy. In 1954, Murrow finally put the final nail in the coffin of Joseph McCarthy's reign of terror by putting together a piece for his show *See It Now*. The episode portrayed McCarthy as a power-hungry bully by using his own, actual, statements. Others tried to stand up to McCarthy, but no one else with Murrow's credibility and popularity did it as well.

Again, there is some irony here when Christian nationalists cite the pledge, the motto, and the inscriptions on our currency to make a case for nationalism. All of these are byproducts of embarrassing times in US history. Times when the heated fervor of the "Red Scare" temporally caused many to embrace nationalism. Back when a relatively small, self-righteous group of misguided folks threw the country into chaos by deporting people and denying many others their basic human rights. And again, let me stress, the phrases "one nation under God" and "In God We Trust" have absolutely nothing to do with the Founding Fathers.

So why the history lesson in the middle of a book about beliefs and knowledge? History, like science, is a process by which we uncover shared, communal facts. The facts we know, or don't know, can affect our beliefs. Certain beliefs lack justification, simply because they do not align with *factual* information. Being willfully ignorant of facts does not entitle people to believe whatever they want. I consider *willful* ignorance to be unethical.

CHAPTER 40

Who Are the Christian Nationalists?

Defining the term "Christian nationalism" presents challenges, as does identifying the characteristics associated with those ill-defined "Christian nationalists." Typically, these nationalists don't even call themselves Christian nationalists. Political opponents or sociologists typically use this term to describe these "Christian nationalists" because they share certain characteristics. In Chapter 37, I outlined five common Christian nationalist ideas. I will summarize the list here as a reminder.

Christian nationalists want the country to:

1. Work to remain in God's favor. Americans must behave and adhere to a biblical moral code.
2. Roll back the separation of church and state.
3. Abandon multiculturalism.
4. Fight for our freedoms. Particularly religious freedom— well at least for one set of beliefs.
5. Recognize that this country was founded on Christian principles—and to return to that heritage.

There is no magic number of how much of this list you need to believe before you get your metaphorical Christian nationalist card. Much like being Republican or a Democrat, Christian nationalists do not necessarily hold identical beliefs. Christian nationalists are even more difficult to describe because they don't belong to some organized party with a written platform. This conundrum reminds me of a quote by Supreme Court Justice Potter Stewart regarding obscenity, "I can't define it, but I know it when I see it."

Some Christian nationalists could be nice people that you might share a pew with at church. While others could be raging white supremist assholes. Some tried to overthrow the government, on January 6, 2021. There might even be overlap between these groups.

Before I studied this topic, my initial impressions of Christian nationalists were that they were people on the fringe—far-right militia survivalist types. I pictured mostly mean losers. I imagined them as unemployed, fanatical white supremacists, primarily from rural areas. Once again, my *imagination/intuition* led me astray.

Robert A. Pape is a political scientist at the Chicago Project on Security and Threats. His research studies international and domestic terrorism. He analyzed the data from the interviews of the 716 people prosecuted for participating in the January 6 attempted coup.

This is what he found:

1. The insurrectionists closely reflected the US electorate on most socio-economic variables and, hence, came from the mainstream, not just the fringe of society.
2. They came from forty-five states plus the District of Columbia, with more coming from counties won by Joe Biden than by Donald Trump. The key county demographic characteristic was that they came from counties which had a recent loss of many White people in their county's population.
3. There were some people from minority populations and some females within the sample, but the makeup was overwhelmingly White (93 percent) and male (85 percent).

The belief most often shared by those prosecuted involved the idea that our heritage was being diluted. Specifically, they believed the rights of minority groups were given preferential treatment. Christian nationalists are very concerned about that. When I hear the term minority, I often think of race, but, in this case, I think the minority umbrella includes LGBTQ folks, as well as any religion, or denomination, that deviates from their Christian theology.

Most Christian nationalists are not insurrectionists. Instead, many people fall into the sort-of-kind-of-Christian nationalist category. They only buy into particular parts of this broad political ideology.

I mentioned my friends Bruce and Blaine earlier in this book. They were my elementary school bigfoot hunting partners from Chapter 1, and my Bible study friends from Chapter 17. They are not at all sympathetic to the insurrectionists. They are most definitely not racists. But they do share overlap with Christian nationalist belief systems within their umwelt. I would put their beliefs in the sort-of-kind-of subgroup of Christian nationalism.

In September of 2024, I took a road trip with these two childhood friends out to their ranch in the Black Hills of South Dakota. I met up with Blaine at his childhood farmhouse home in Cherokee, IA, where he and his family currently live. The door frame to the basement displays a record of the children's heights as they grew serving as a piece of family history. To me, this pencil-marked doorframe serves as a physical reminder of our long friendship history because my childhood heights share marks alongside theirs. I certainly treasure these rare, lifelong friendships.

These two lifelong friends have a very strong Christian faith. Bruce spent eighteen years in Africa as a missionary in both Senegal and Ivory Coast. Blaine spent several years as a missionary in New Guinea. He then taught tribal linguistics classes in Australia for missionaries heading out to remote tribal areas. They are both very smart and very well-read. And they both are also super nice guys.

Bruce has a Master of Divinity degree—the very same degree that my dad held. My Dad and Bruce would not completely see eye to eye in their interpretation of Scripture, but there would certainly be some overlap.

I also do not see eye to eye with Bruce or Blaine on matters of theology. Despite that, we remain friends and have mostly remained civil about our disagreements. (Only once, way back when we were sophomores in high school, did Blaine and I get into a very heated, not so civil, argument about evolution. What began as debate, with some back-and-forth chiding, ended with flared tempers. I think at some point a chair was even tossed.) We are both a little embarrassed by that memory.

This trip was meant for catching up and reconnecting, not for theological or political debates. There would be no chair throwing. That said, I did bring up politics and religion. For one, I am interested in beliefs, religion, and Christian nationalism. And also, the drive across South Dakota is long unless you are having a good conversation.

Somewhere between Chamberlain and the Badlands, I asked Bruce, point blank, "So, what do you think of Christian nationalism?"

He thought for a moment, and then he said, "When I first heard the term, I was bothered by it on a just a gut level. But as I learned more about it, I found that some of it rang true."

The obvious follow-up question should have been, "Which parts?" But alas, my interview skills are not that good, so I did not ask it. I may have been distracted by Blaine's dog Koa, who was trying to decide if my lap would be a trustworthy perch to view the prairie.

A few hours later, we ate a late lunch in a Jimmy John's parking lot outside of Rapid City. We conversed about the general morality of the country and the moral decay (or progress) from past to present. Here, the differences in our respective umwelts became highlighted. Both Bruce and Blaine strongly felt that the country was in steep moral decay. They felt that our country was drifting away from Scripture, and that most aspects of society were crumbling. I told them that I had a contrary view. From a historic point of view, I saw much improvement—except for the extreme partisanship and the decline of civil discourse. I acknowledged that progress wasn't always linear, but it still moved forward—more like "three steps forward, two steps back." I then droned on for a bit about civil rights progress and environmental victories. I said things like, "Bald eagles are back, our rivers aren't catching on fire anymore, Black people can go to White schools, drink from any drinking fountain, and ride in the front of the bus, this progress all happened within our lifetimes."

One of them responded, "But I am specifically talking about the moral character of the country. I feel like there has been an obvious decline. There has been a breakdown of family units, disrespect of teachers in schools . . . Many people just feel spiritually lost and lonely."

I replied that they were looking at the past with some blinders on. I pointed out that, as high school kids in the seventies and eighties, "We didn't know what was going on outside of our own family's idyllic family life." I mentioned some friends of ours who "were putting up with physical abuse and severe alcoholism in their families, that we were blissfully unaware of."

I said "remember (*name withheld*)? He used to sleep in a junk yard in old cars to get away from his dad. There was (*name withheld*), she got pregnant and dropped out and then seemed to just quietly disappear. And she wasn't the only one. Small town Cherokee, Iowa, was not a Norman Rockwell painting of family life for many of our classmates." We didn't belabor this "decline of morality discussion," we simply finished our sandwiches, gave the dogs pee breaks, and then drove through the ponderosa pines toward Custer.

Landmarks along the way triggered happier memories. As we drove past Reptile Gardens, we reminisced about friend our friend Greg who was "attacked" by a small anole or gecko in Reptile Gardens on a trip we took to the Black Hills way back in 1978. An employee told Greg, "Hey! Don't touch the lizards!" Greg responded, without missing a beat, "Tell your lizard not to touch *me!*"

But back to our 2024 trip. The following morning at their ranch, we got into an interesting discussion about multiculturalism. I don't remember how it came up, but I learned that they both had some negative feelings about multiculturalism. I, on the other hand, spent five years of my life working in an office which was called the "Center for Diversity and Enrichment" at the University of Iowa. (As I go back to proofread this section in late 2025, I realize that office—in addition to other offices around the country that work to support and increase diversity and inclusion—have been shut down. They were outlawed by a presidential executive order restricting Diversity, Equity, and Inclusion practices in January of 2025.) Given my educational and work background, talking to anyone who opposes multiculturalism was a foreign experience to me.

On the surface, opposition to multiculturalism sounds racist, and in my opinion, it usually is. But neither Bruce nor Blaine is racist. Blaine explained to me that his opposition to different cultures has nothing to with skin tone, and instead it had to do with various religions. He views some religions as simply culturally incompatible with each other. He is all for the welcoming of different races, he is not for the welcoming of different *incompatible* religions.

He argued, "How can we allow an Islamic sect that makes women wear a bag over their head and tells women to stay at home to flourish in America." (He was not talking about a simple hijab here, but rather the black bag version, the Burka.) "Respecting those extreme beliefs, is not compatible with our values." He sees some non-Judeo-Christian religions at odds with our Judeo-Christian culture.

It is hard to be dismissive of this viewpoint when you understand its origins. Both Bruce and Blaine each spent years embedded in some cultures with wildly different core beliefs and values. Blaine worked in the jungles of New Guinea where head-hunting was still practiced until the early 1930s. Real differences between some religious traditions do in fact exist.

While I—not surprisingly—disagreed with him on this point, I understood his point of view. However, I think using these extreme examples to throw all of multiculturalism under the bus is an overreaction. I do acknowledge that embracing the good, bad, and the ugly of every world culture/religion can be complicated.

As we drove home, back across South Dakota, we continued to talk about a variety of topics. The conversations were not always easy. I'm not sure that I convinced them of any of my opinions, but I think in the end, they understood how I came to believe what I believed. In turn, I understood why they believed what they believed.

One thing that really helps our friendship is trust. We know, and like, each other, despite some different core beliefs and even different umwelts. To their credit (and to mine), we identified our similar values against a backdrop of some different worldviews. We did not ignore the differences—they're very real and important—but we spent more time stressing the values that we share.

Understanding the different ways and types of knowledge and

understanding the difference between facts and beliefs will not settle all the arguments in the world. However, communication and understanding lowers the temperature of the inevitable clashes between different belief umwelts. Some conversations were hard, but no chairs were thrown.

Not All Evangelicals Are Christian Nationalists

In July of 2023, the editor in chief of *Christianity Today*, Russell Moore, released a book entitled, *Losing our Religion: An Altar Call for Evangelical America*. According to his website, Moore "is an ordained Baptist minister, who served previously as president of the Southern Baptist Convention's Ethics and Religious Liberty Commission and, before that, as the chief academic officer and dean of the Southern Baptist Theological Seminary, where he also taught theology and ethics."

In his book, he describes a disturbing trend within the evangelical churches as they participate in the politically motivated culture wars. He writes: "We are becoming the people Jesus warned us about." Years ago, in his role as a pastor, he counseled parents who were distraught that their children were leaving the church. More recently he reports that he sees a trend of having to "council more adult children who are distraught that their parents seem to be leaving reality, swept away in political fever of hatred."

According to the book description on the Random House website:

"Congregations are torn apart over Donald Trump, Christian Nationalism, racial injustice, sexual predation, disgraced leaders, and covered-up scandals. Left behind are millions of believers who counted on the church to be a place of belonging and hope. In *Losing Our Religion*, Russell Moore calls his fellow evangelical Christians to conversion over culture wars . . . to truth over tribalism, to the gospel over politics, to integrity over influence, and to renewal over nostalgia. Believing the gospel is too important to leave it to hucksters and grifters, he shows how a Christian can avoid both cynicism and complicity to imagine a different, hopeful vision for the church."

Moore understands belief and religious faith do not mean that you must reject reality. He has enough foresight to see the damage that

Christian nationalism does to the country. Importantly he also sees how it damages the message of Christ as revealed through the Scripture. He worries that when Christian nationalism cherry-picks and misuses Scriptures in an attempt to "take back America" in order to restore it to "God's good graces," this misuse of the Scriptures does more to discredit than it does to promote the message of Christ.

I bring up Russell Moore because he defies a stereotype. Often, people, including myself, tend to paint religions, or in this case, evangelical denominations, with broad generalizations. Sure, stereotypes save a lot of time, and they can be based on at least some truth, but often they mislead. Russell Moore serves as an example of a very prominent fundamentalist evangelical voice who argues against the promotion of Christian nationalism.

CHAPTER 41

So, Are We Responsible for Our Beliefs?

Now that we have ground rules and some historical context, we can tackle the basic question of the final section of this book: Are we responsible for our beliefs?

If *I* have free will—and that is *my* working assumption here—then my answer is, Yes! *I* am responsible for *my* beliefs, and *I* am *not* entitled to hold any belief I please. Because my beliefs often come with consequences, the responsibility of questioning them falls on me. I believe that belief formations should take time. We must acknowledge that belief formation often requires some *work on our part* to find *credible facts* upon which to base them. I also acknowledge that people are busy and we all don't have the time to educate ourselves on every issue. I recently saw a Facebook meme that said, "Normalize not having an opinion about things you don't know about." I hit the like button. (If I'm suddenly quoting Facebook memes, that should be an indicator that I should probably start wrapping this up!)

As we figure out what we believe, we should be willing to listen to opposing beliefs with an open mind. Since beliefs have inherent uncertainty, this uncertainty should always be acknowledged when we profess our beliefs. (At least I *believe* that is true.) Finally, remember, just because our working assumption declares that we are responsible for our beliefs, that does not necessarily mean that others bear responsibility for their beliefs. We don't know their genetics, backgrounds, experiences, etc.

Our beliefs should align with established mathematical and scientific facts. Denying that pathogens cause disease, claiming the Holocaust did not happen, believing the Earth is flat, believing the Earth was created in seven days just a few thousand years ago, believing the square root of sixteen is three, or believing our Founding Fathers were all Christians who wrote "In God We Trust" into the fabric of America are all likely unethical "beliefs." I use quotes on the word "beliefs" there, because none of the above are beliefs. Instead, these are examples of facts that some people inaccurately view as beliefs.

William Clifford, as I already mentioned back in the beliefs section, would say any belief that opposes known facts is unethical. But is it unethical to simply be wrong about a fact? To me, it depends on three other variables: your intentions, the cause of your error, and its consequences. Is it doing harm? Ignorance itself is not inherently unethical; however, deliberately remaining uninformed might be. When looking at the beliefs of others, and assigning ethical responsibility judgement, it gets complicated. We don't always know the intensions, or why they believe what they believe. That's why we should avoid it. Here is an example. If an oil executive tells people climate science does not prove that global warming is caused by man, he is likely unethical, likely lying, but maybe he believes it. Why does he believe it? Has he been too busy to examine the data? Does he have a brain tumor? Or did he simply adopt that incorrect belief because it was more convenient for his personal interest? If the latter, I'd still say unethical, even if he has come to believe it. It is hard to get into other people's heads and figure out why they do what they do. I'm glad I'm not in charge of judging people.

CHAPTER 42

Birds Aren't Real

As I neared the end of the writing of this book—perhaps due to my previous YouTube searches about bigfoot and philosophy—YouTube's algorithms suggested I watch a TED Talk by Peter McIndoe. Peter was the "brains" behind the "Birds Aren't Real" movement.

I first encountered this "movement" several years ago while driving home after doing some work at my beehives. I saw this guy walking on the shoulder of Highway 6, just outside of Iowa City, wearing a placard with the words "BIRDS AREN'T REAL." I felt a lot of emotions as various hypotheses went through my head. I tried to wrap my brain around what I was seeing. First, I thought, *That is funny. That guy is making fun of conspiracy theorists.* Then I thought, *Or maybe he is really a broken person.* Then I thought, *That guy has way too much free time.* I really wasn't sure what to make of it.

I mentioned the weird placard to one of my high school classes. Much to my surprise, many knew about the movement. (High school kids are good that way; they are hyperaware of whatever is happening in pop culture.) They told me, "The story is that all the birds are automated drones. They act as spies. They charge on the telephone wires." I asked if anyone thought this nonsense was real. Most of my students said no, definitely not, and others said the movement, "actually has some followers." So that was all I knew about "Birds Aren't Real" until this Peter McIndoe TED Talk appeared as "suggested viewing" on YouTube.

Peter McIndoe grew up homeschooled, just outside of Little Rock,

Arkansas. He said while he was growing up, everyone around him believed in some kind of conspiracy theory. Some purported political conspiracies, such as jackbooted thugs are going to come into your homes and take your guns, or Obama works as a foreign agent, or Obama is not even an American citizen. Some conspiracies seemed less political. Such as claims of the government putting microchips in the vaccines to track you, or beliefs about how the Moon landing, and/or 9/11, was staged. Peter even knew some kids who insisted the Earth was flat. The stupidity of all of this interested him.

In the TED Talk, Peter claimed he started the "Birds Aren't Real" movement to see if he could get the media to report on a random, crazy, idea. He viewed it as a farce. He went around the country for four years, preaching that "birds are not real, they are actually government drones." He handed out flyers and held rallies, while in the character of someone who believed that the government uses bird drones to spy on everyone. He purchased space on billboards, and he created an internet presence to promote this "movement."

He accomplished his goal. He received airtime on major news networks claiming to be the recently appointed spokesperson of the "Birds Aren't Real" movement. The networks reported his fabricated background story, including an earlier movement that began in the early 1960s.

McIndoe's TED Talk turned profound when he spoke about how it *felt* to play his invented character. With megaphone in hand, he would lead crowds, chanting, "Birds Aren't Real! Birds Aren't Real! Birds Aren't Real!" He described the experience of addressing the crowds—who were in on the bit—from atop his van, as almost "intoxicating."

However, playing the character did not always feel joyful. During the "Birds Aren't Real" ruse, strangers often verbally attacked Peter. When this happened, he explained that he had expected different emotions than the actual response he felt. He assumed he would feel happy to get people to fall for this farce, but instead, he felt the feelings *of the character* that he played. They called him "stupid." They yelled in his face, "You are the problem with the country today." They expressed anger with him for spreading misinformation. He observed, "They othered me." I like that phrase.

To be othered.

To his surprise, McIndoe suddenly felt empathy for those conspiracy theorists that he initially set out to mock. He realized that people join these groups for one thing: to belong.

He stumbled onto this truth. Everyone wants to belong to a community. And further, when "experts" attack the community of conspiracy theorists, it does nothing to bring them out of the false reality they have created for themselves, no matter how absurd. Instead, he reasoned, the attacks drive them deeper into the arms of their like-minded comrades. (Sociologists call this the *backfire effect*.) Understanding the backfire effect has implications for how we advocate for the truth.

It turns out, experts providing evidence against the nonsense is not *always* the answer. On the other hand, we cannot be so timid about the backfire effect that we don't correct misinformation. Admittedly, finding a balance can be tricky. Sometimes, understanding why someone gravitates toward misinformation matters more than the battle over the "truth." Rather than debating facts, the best approach seems to be to focus on process. Confronting misinformation in a way that does not attack the person or a group. Inquire, in a non-attacking manner, how they came to know their "facts," and have them evaluate why their *process* is better than the *process* you used.

I'm not sure of Peter's initial intent when he started "Birds Aren't Real." But his experience provided a fantastic look into the world of conspiracy theory mindsets. I'm glad Peter decided to reflect on his feelings. He turned his "project" from a farce into a lesson in empathy. I am always on the side of bringing more empathy into the world.

Conclusion

I had many goals when I set out to write this book. When people would ask me to describe my book, I would say something like, "It is about ways of knowing and why we believe what we believe, and how belief and knowing are related and—" Then I would watch their eyes gloss over.

My reasons for writing this book varied quite a bit depending on the section. My approach also varied. In some sections, I felt like a science teacher. In other parts, I was a storyteller. Occasionally, the section called for a philosopher or theologian.

Writing is a very solitary activity. However, as I wrote, certain people from my life figuratively sat in my living room with me, advising me. I imagined former students of mine and replayed classroom conversations in my head. I imagined friends from my high school multi-denominational Bible study at the Mortenson's house, chatting about theology with me.

I imagined my friends from college. I think they are some of the best humans on the planet. I imagined them giving me little pointers here and there. Occasionally, I imagined my teaching colleagues or my in-laws also giving me feedback or just cheering me on.

I did not have to imagine my wife and sons because often they actually were in the room. I would occasionally read bits of the book to them to see what they thought as I wrote, and then we would discuss it together.

As I progressed through the chapters, I knew some of my friends would agree with me on certain points, and other friends would surely disagree with me on those same points. I tried not to offend anyone while still staying true to the facts and true to the concepts that I attempted to explain. When I talked about theology, I tried to write something that my dad would enjoy.

Instead of just recording my thoughts, I wrote this book to encourage us all to think about our own thinking. I hoped that this book would challenge us to think about some of our beliefs in slightly different ways. I wanted to inspire people to explore what we know and what we believe, and to understand the nuanced differences between those two things. I wanted to encourage people to dial back their certainty about those things which are inherently uncertain. Hopefully you, the reader, even learned something about bigfoot, epistemology, science, religion, evolution, or the history of American nationalism along the way.

In the spirit of managing expectations, I don't think that the mere understanding of *how* historical and scientific facts differ from beliefs and personal knowledge will resolve all arguments. But if we distinguish between personal knowledge, beliefs, and collective historical and scientific facts, our inevitable disagreements will, at the very least, be more interesting and civil.

If those goals were even partially met, I'm happy. Thanks for reading my book.

Appendices

Appendix A

Patterson-Gimlin film

On October 20,1967, Bob Gimlin and Roger Patterson either shot some 16mm film of a bigfoot, or they hoaxed a film of a bigfoot along Bluff Creek in Northern California. If you are not sure whether you believe in sasquatch, then watch this film—generally referred to as the *Patterson-Gimlin film*. This is like a Rorschach test for bigfoot belief. If you watch and say, "That's a bigfoot!" then you are a true believer. If, on the other hand, you say, "OMG that's so dumb, it's clearly a guy in a suit!" Then you clearly don't believe.

As a physical film, it contains evidence that can be analyzed. For example, the approximate height of the bigfoot (or the hoaxer) in the film can be estimated. The footage can be and has been scrutinized, checking the suit for seams or zippers. There is no evidence that the *Patterson-Gimlin film* is a hoax. It has not been shown to be a real critter either. It is unambiguously ambiguous, and yet, many people are pretty sure what they are seeing when they look at it.

One thing is clear, "the thing" in the film—nicknamed "Patty"—is tall and has a good deal of girth to her. Her exact size is uncertain, but she is certainly large. (We say "girl" because Patty seems to have breasts.) You will hear different numbers for her height from different people. No one thinks that "Patty" was a small girl.

Within days of hearing about the film, John Green and his friend Jim McClarin went to the film site with Bob Gimlin and Roger Patterson. John shot film standing where Roger stood during the filming while Jim (height six feet five inches) walked where Patty had walked. The tracks were still on the sand bar when they did their recreation. After the film was developed, John Green then overlayed the two films, matching up the backgrounds. From these overlaid films, he could see that "Patty" was larger than Jim, in both height and girth. John made a rough estimate that "Patty" likely stood around six feet seven inches tall.

Peter Byrne also went to the film site, albeit later, and used the same methodology as John Green. Byrne brought a professional forensic examiner along with him as well as six-foot-tall Michael Hodgson. Hodgson stood in for Patty, and they also aligned backgrounds, they decided on a height of six feet eleven inches, give or take a few inches.

Grover Krantz did not go to the film site. Instead, he used Patty's foot as a measuring device. On frame 304, or thereabouts, you can clearly see the back foot vertical, just off the ground. From the casts that were made from the site, we assume this foot was just over fourteen inches in length. Using this fourteen-inch foot for scale, we can now deduce the height of "Patty" from the image. Krantz surmised that the image of the hunched-over "Patty" stood at roughly at six feet. He concluded that "Patty" would stand at six feet three inches or six feet four inches, if standing up straight.

Dr. Jeff Meldrum did digital forensic analysis of the film and got a number originally closest to Peter Byrne's number. He has since revised that estimate, and now he thinks "Patty" is much closer to Green's number of six feet seven inches.

I decided to take my own crack at it. I calculated that Patty was about six feet four inches. I used my own measurements, some basic trigonometry, and my assumptions about the reported distance from Patty when the film was shot, my own big screen TV, and my replica of a track cast at the film site to make that estimate. Of all these estimates, I trust mine the least—but I did land near the lower edge of the average of the estimates.

This is a wide range of estimates. From six feet eleven inches down to six feet three inches. If I am just ranking methodology, I'd rank Green and Meldrum at the top and my contribution with Grover Krantz at the bottom (mine and Krantz's rely on some assumptions about camera distance, and a cast, which could be bigger or smaller than the actual foot). I think it is reasonable to say the subject of the film is very likely between six feet five inches and six feet eight inches.

In 2003, a man named Bob Heironimus came forward to announce that *he* was the guy in the bigfoot suit. I have had several people tell me, "That bigfoot film was found to be a hoax, the guy even admitted it." Bob Heironimus claimed to know Roger and alleged that Roger offered him $1,000 to go to California and wear a costume for "the hoax." Interestingly, when Bob Heironimus announced that he was the man in the suit, many people, as well as the many news outlets that covered that claim, simply thought, *Okay, there you have it, mystery solved*, without asking any real questions. I say, "Not so fast, I have some questions."

Why did Heironimus think Roger would pay him $1,000? Heironimus did know Roger, and he knew him well. This fact makes his claim odd. He certainly knew Roger could not pay him $1,000. Keep in mind that we are talking about 1967 dollars. Roger was chronically underemployed. He had no savings. The claim that Bob thought Roger was going to pay him $1,000 is, in my opinion, implausible.

Also, why did it take Mr. Heironimus thirty-six years to reveal that he was the guy in the suit? Remember, Roger died in 1973. Hard to understand the timing of this confession. *Was he thinking, Well, the estate is finally settled, I don't think Roger is going to pay me, I think thirty-six years is enough waiting.* Bob also released a book about the hoax in 2003, this may explain the timing of his confession.

How tall was Bob? After some sleuthing around, I found out that Bob was taller than average for a man in 1967. He was six feet tall and about 180 pounds back then. His height alone makes his claim somewhere between impossible and very suspect. The film could be a hoax, but I am pretty sure Bob Hieronimus was not the guy in the suit.

Personally, I think the film is convincing. But if all we had was the film, I would be less likely to put the *Patterson-Gimlin film* in the physical-evidence column. However, in addition to this film, several people had the foresight to make plaster casts of the tracks left at the film site, *and* we have some photographs of these purported sasquatch tracks as well. This physical evidence tells a compelling story.

This additional evidence tips the scales for me. I found the photos particularly interesting. While seeking permission to include these photographs in my book, I contacted the photographer, Lyle Laverty. Mr. Laverty, who was approximately eighty years old when we spoke, was in his mid-twenties back in 1967. He seemed like a nice guy and

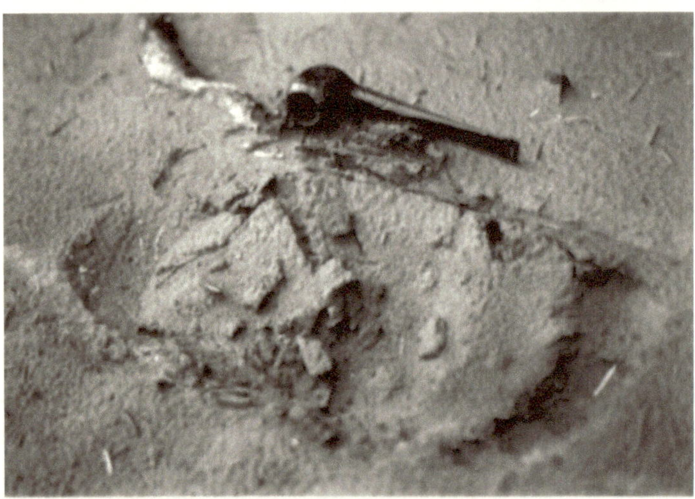

Photos taken by Lyle Laverty shortly after the *Patterson-Gimlin film* was shot. Notice the lack of uniformity on these two photos and the photo on the following page. Also notice the clear Midtarsal pressure ridge, particulary in the top photo that is often apparent in purported bigfoot tracks. I also think the pipe for scale is a nice touch in the bottom photo. (Courtesy of Lyle Laverty.)

was fun to talk to. He was not a bigfoot enthusiast at the time and still isn't. I asked him how he became involved with this famous footage. He said, "I wasn't involved at all." He didn't know anyone associated with the film. His vocation at the time was that of a timber cruiser. He had spent a chunk of the summer of 1967 camping in the area while preparing a larger timber sale. He was just driving down the "road," saw some guys milling about on the side of the road, and stopped. He saw the tracks, got out, took a few photos, and then went about his day. Turns out that those few photos were the best, perhaps only photos, taken of the trackway. (There are also some 16mm films of the trackway as well, but Lyle's photos are much better.)

Lyle's comment about the "road" surprised me a little. I had the false impression that this remote area was only accessible by horseback. Turns out, there was, in fact, access to the area via a logging road that was periodically back-bladed by a Cat. When I relistened to audio of Roger's account of the encounter, Roger does in fact say, "I watched it continue to walk down the road," after he ran out of film.

Lyle added that he was camping in the area for many weeks earlier that summer, and he did not see or hear anything unusual. These photos are interesting to me, as they show a pressure ridge that many believe is associated with a metatarsal hinge. They also show a depth that is consistent with what Bob Gimlin and Roger Patterson described. Gimlin said he was struck by track depth because he and Roger did not sink at all into the hard-packed sand. Because these tracks lack uniformity, if they were impressed using some fake foot, more than one fake foot would have been needed to make a series of slightly different tracks.

It takes a lot of mental gymnastics to explain this film and the tracks away as a hoax. The film is impressive, but the film coupled with multiple plaster casts by Bob Titmus, Roger Patterson and Bob Gimlin, as well as the random photos snapped by Lyle, make the hoax explanation a bit far-fetched in my opinion. Given the indigenous folklore and the thousands of sightings that predate this film, I think it is reasonable to conclude that large, hairy bipeds roamed the forest of BC and the Pacific Northwest in 1967. I, personally, have concluded that this film is real. I don't know if bigfoot still exists, but the evidence before me here is enough to convince me that the sasquatch *did* exist. I believe that Roger and Bob got some footage of one!

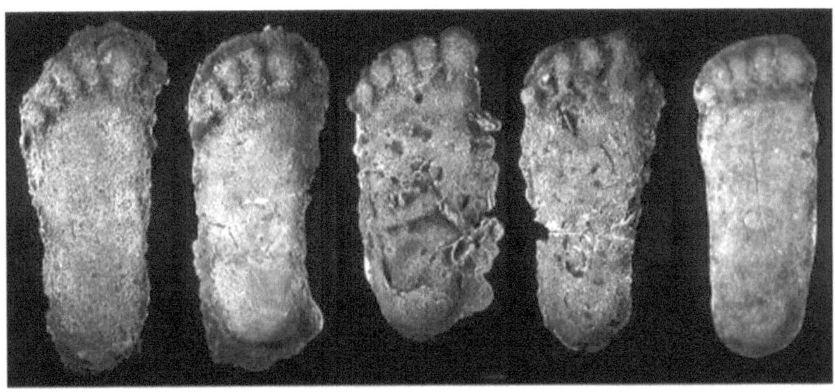

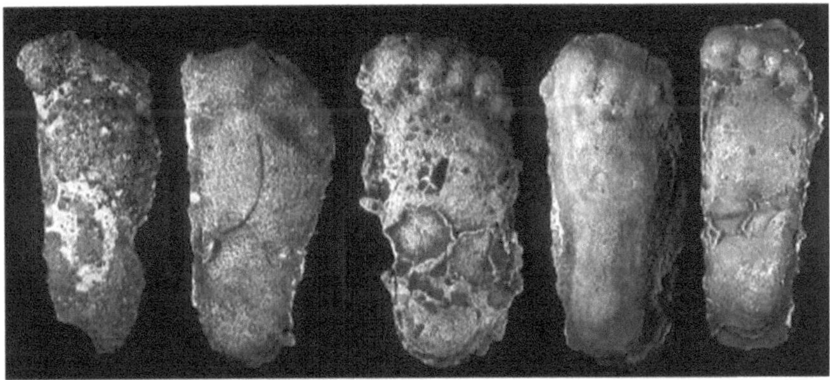

Bob Titmus took ten casts at the film site. He cast the most complete tracks he could find. (Courtesy of Jeff Meldrum.)

Appendix B

Theory of Knowledge: Ways of knowing

There are eight "ways of knowing" within the framework provided by the International Baccalaureate's "Theory of Knowledge" course.

Back in Chapter 5 I listed each "way of knowing." Initially, I included a brief description next to each way of knowing. This chapter and section were already pretty-damn tedious, and I was worried that I would lose readers if I made it any longer. So I made the call to move these "ways of knowing descriptions" into the Appendix.

I do think these descriptions are important so I'm very happy you had the stamina to turn to the Appendix. Here are some descriptions and limitations of the eight "ways of knowing."

Sense perception

We know because we see, hear, taste, smell, feel. If you dive even deeper into how we perceive the world, it is an amazing and complex topic. I am not going to dive too deep here. Both Diane Ackerman, *A Natural History of the Senses*, and Ed Young, *An Immense World*, have written fantastic books on this topic.

Interestingly, the beliefs of two different people will cause different people to interpret the exact same sensory input in different ways. Though not always reliable, we believe our senses over almost anything.

Memory

Memory, combined with sense perception, is how I know what I had for breakfast this morning. I know a lot of things simply because of memory. There is such a thing as false memory. I have had a few false memories in my life. My sister is very intelligent, and yet, she once insisted to me that when my son Max was born, he had black hair. He did not. Classic example of a false memory. If you spend time with someone with Alzheimer's disease, and I have, you will quickly see that memory is not a foolproof way of knowing. My interview with Larry and Dixie Wilson was dependent on their memory from an event that happened many years ago, and my reporting of the conversations was largely based on my memory as well. Memory is fallible, but it is also a very important way that we know stuff. Hard to know anything without recollection.

Faith

I would, and I will, argue that all knowledge is somewhat dependent on faith. Most people think of religious faith when they think of faith, and that is part of the equation but not the whole picture. Faith can be in a process or person. Faith is related to, but not the same thing as belief. Belief is a propositional attitude of truth, whereas faith is a trust in something without physical evidence. These are not the same thing. Faith is one of the most important ways of knowing, it is also the least reliable. Faith is complicated enough to get a good deal of discussion in the main text of my book, so I don't have to delve too deeply here.

Emotional

Emotional knowledge is often a reaction. Emotional knowledge is personal knowledge. I know it's wrong to kick a puppy, for example, because of how that makes me feel emotionally. I know that I love my wife and kids. This is emotional knowledge. Empathy involves emotional knowledge and imagination. We feel how we imagine someone else would feel.

Imagination

A thought experiment is an example of using imagination to gain knowledge. This is similar, but slightly different from intuition, which we will discuss in a bit. To creatively solve a problem requires imagination.

Coming up with a new way to approach an experiment is imagination. I think of imagination in the context of music and art as well. U2 guitarist The Edge once explained his process, "I drive myself crazy trying to get the sounds in my head to come out of the guitar." He imagines it *before* he makes the sound. A CEO with a vision for their company is also using their imagination. I had to imagine writing the concepts for this book for months before I could begin to write them. Perhaps the most important use of imagination has to do with the concept of empathy. What would it be like to be in someone else's shoes? You must imagine the feelings of others to have empathy. People lacking imagination struggle with empathy.

Language

Language is the structure we give to define the continuum of reality. Most people have a word to describe the white stuff that falls from the sky in the winter. It's, of course, snow. In the Inuit language, they have several words—at least ten, and by some accounts more—for "snow." Falling snow is different from snow on the ground. Crystalline snow has its own word. Snow suitable for making water is different from snow used for building igloos. Snow you can walk over has a different name than snow you sink into. Different language parameters cause us to look at this shared reality in a different way. The Innuit look at snow differently than those with different language parameters precisely because of language. We think about concepts within the context of our cultural language parameters.

Language also allows us to pass knowledge from person to person, even if a person has not personally used their sense perception to acquire that knowledge for themselves. Language is how I came to know about language, as a way of knowing. ☺

Logic/Reason

If you want to know if A = C, but all you know is that B = C and A = B, you can figure out that A = C using logic. Knowing some factual information allows us to infer other factual information using logic. Some people are very analytical by nature and use logic as a way of proving things to themselves. Logic, like all ways of knowing, has limits and pitfalls, but logic and reason can help uncover many truths about the reality of the world. Mathematics is a formalized discipline that relies heavily on logic as a way of knowing. You cannot build logic without known assumptions, axioms, or postulates. These assumptions come from other types of knowing. Logic is built upon other ways of knowing. When logic is used incorrectly, we get logical fallacies. These are easy to spot with a little training.

Intuition

I see Intuition at work when I teach physics. Some kid will be drawing a force diagram, and another kid will look at it and ask, "Why do you have the arrow going that way?" The kids will have some trouble understanding why the kid doesn't just intuitively know the direction the arrow should go. They will respond with, "Cause . . . that's the way it goes." Intuition is how we just know things.

We intuitively know right from wrong. Sure, some moral values are learned within a cultural context, but most people have intuition that can guide them in the arena of ethics.

In music, it can be how musicians come up with new unique melodies seemingly out of thin air. This is often intuition. (If they understand music theory, they could use logic as well.). In science, intuition directs discovery as well. Nickola Tesla's intuition led him to develop both the AC motor and the generator; he explained, "I saw it in a vision." Because of his intuition, the whole world now runs on AC power.

But I should also point out that it was also intuition that led Nikola Tesla to spend lots of time, energy, and money trying to transport electricity over very long distances without wires. Telsa would die penniless, but in love with his soulmate, a pigeon. Intuition is powerful, but like all ways of knowing, it clearly has limitations.

Appendix C

Paul Freeman

I first heard of Paul Freeman when I watched the documentary *Sasquatch: Legend Meets Science*. It was the companion documentary to Jeff Meldrum's book by the same title. This documentary showed a clip of the video that Paul Freeman recorded on August 20, 1992.

Paul Freeman was a big, tough guy. He had various jobs: bouncer, boxer, butcher, forest service patrolman. He was a little rough around the edges, which allowed some people to dismiss him as some country rube.

I had heard somewhere, I don't remember where, that he was a hoaxer. It may have been on some online forum or some other non-credible source, but that opinion stuck with me.

When I heard that Dr. Meldrum was convinced by a set of tracks that were initially found by Freeman, I was a little concerned that that these tracks came from this "known hoaxer." I later learned how this "known hoaxer" reputation was a fabrication; it was built on envy and mischaracterizations.

The envy part came from bigfoot "researchers" Peter Byrne and Rene Dahinden, and the mischaracterizations came from the TV show, *Good Morning America*.

Byrne dismissed Freeman on the basis that Freeman saw bigfoot on three separate occasions in his life, and he found tracks on several occasions. Byrne, on the other hand, had never seen bigfoot. And although he had spent a lifetime looking, he had only found tracks on one occasion. He therefore deduced that the only explanation for Paul's amazing luck was that Paul must be a hoaxer. Byrne was not a scientist, and his powers of deductive reasoning were, well, let's just say they were not airtight. Rene Dahinden's "analysis" was even weaker then Bryne's. Both Byrne's and Dahinden's opinions carried some weight in the bigfoot community. So when these two men didn't embrace Paul's evidence, it was a problem for Paul's reputation in the "bigfoot community."

A piece that aired on *Good Morning America*, October 29, 1987, was far more damaging. I just rewatched this story, and wow. If I was Paul, I'd be pissed. What follows is Steve Fox's damaging interview of Freeman, shot by shot.

Establishing shot of Steve Fox walking with "bigfoot skeptic" Mike Dennett.

Steve Fox: "Have you ever seen a case, or ever investigated a bigfoot sighting that seemed to be legitimate?"

Dissolve to close-up of Dennett.

Dennet: "No, never. Footprints can be faked; footprints have been faked, and we know of at least one person who claims he hoaxed bigfoot."

Cut to Fox: over-the-shoulder shot from Freeman's point of view.

Steve Fox: "You tried to make a fake foot, to make fake prints?"

Freeman: "Yes I did."

Cut to medium shot of Freeman.

Freeman repeats, "Yes I did."

Cut back to over-the-shoulder shot of Fox from Freeman's point of view.

Steve Fox: "So you admit to making fake prints, but you are saying that these are real."

Cut to close-up of Freeman's hands holding a cast as he talks about something related to that particular cast but unrelated to Fox's accusation.

Shortly thereafter, we go back to the GMA studios for a shot of a smirking Charlie Gibson.

Gibson: "Well, I don't know. If bigfoot is real, I wonder if he has a TV set. I wonder if he watches at 7:50 in the morning."

What is important, is what was *not* included in this edited version that the viewers of *Good Morning America* saw. In response to Steve Fox's question, "Have you ever made a fake track?

Freeman replies, "Yes, I have; *I have made tracks in my garden.*"

Freeman then went on to explain the importance of making fake tracks so you can see the type of track a fake foot would make, so you can see the difference between a fake and a potentially real track. Freeman continued to say that anyone who wants to see if a track is real needs to know what forgeries look like. He made some prints, but never to hoax as he explains. But that part of the interview was cut to, "Yes I have," giving the impression that Freeman is a hoaxer.

Dennett, the skeptic, was also misrepresented. He wasn't even referring to Paul Freeman when he mentioned "a known hoaxer." He was talking about Ray Wallace.

But in the piece the public saw and heard the interview cut together like this:

Dennet talking to Fox: "We know of at least one person who claims he hoaxed bigfoot."

Fox talking to Freeman: "You tried to make a fake foot, to make fake prints"

Freeman to Fox: "Yes I did."

Fox to freeman: "So you admit to making fake prints."

No rebuttal to that accusation was included in the GMA bigfoot story.

Everyone in the piece was made to look foolish, except "bigfoot skeptic" Dennett, who oddly chose to wear a tie for his walk in the woods with Steve Fox. Clearly this wasn't a serious discussion of bigfoot's existence. Bigfoot's existence didn't fit the narrative of this "news" story. This wasn't really a news piece anyway; it was an entertainment piece.

Micheal Freeman, Paul's son, refers to this GMA piece as "the hatchet job from hell." Charlie Gibsons glib dismissal of the whole story is just the cherry on top.

The GMA hit piece, coupled with Peter and Rene's dismissal of Freeman, somehow filtered into my brain—even though I hadn't personally watched the GMA video, or even heard Rene dismiss Freeman. Without even knowing why I thought, *Paul Freeman, I think I have heard of him, wasn't he hoaxer?* It is disturbing how easy it is to have our sense of reality infected by the half-truths that just float around in popular culture.

If he was not a hoaxer, and I don't think he was, then Paul Freeman

This image is one of many photos that Jeff Meldrum took of the trackway that Freeman showed him in the Spring of 1996. The trackway included many full tracks as well. I had a chance to examine these tracks. Notice the toe slippage. If they were a hoax, the toe slippage is a nice touch. (Courtesy of Jeff Meldrum.)

just happened to have a job in the forest service overseeing an area where possibly at least three different sasquatches lived. (I say three because a trackway was found in this area with three sets of Sasquatch Tracks. It was a seven-mile-long trackway with 122 clear footprints found in 1995.)

Perhaps the same sasquatch would reappear in 1996, when Jeff Meldrum photographed and cast the tracks of it.

The other thing that Paul Freeman is known for is a video from 1993 in the Blue Mountains. Many discounted this video due to "the hoaxer" reputation of Paul Freeman, which I have already explained is an unwarranted reputation. The quality of this video is not as good

The spring-of-1996-trackway included many full tracks as well. I had a chance to examine these tracks and their corresponding photos at Meldrum's office in Pocatello, ID. (Photo Courtesy of Suellen Swain.)

as the *Patterson-Gimlin film*, but for a crappy video camera, it is not bad. It seems to show a seven-to-eight-foot big something walking in the woods. I would say it is the second-best footage that exists. The tree that this alleged sasquatch walks by in the film was measured by a forest service ranger and found to be sixteen feet tall. Based on that measurement, Freeman estimated that the animal was about eight feet tall. They all could be lying; it could be a hoax and a guy in a suit. My opinion, for what it is worth, is that they are telling the truth about what they saw and recorded. If it was eight feet tall, the hoax seems implausible.

This footage will not convert a skeptic. But categorizing this footage as a simple hoax seems to me to be more daunting than the acceptance that maybe it is real. Paul's son Micheal spoke about how excited his dad was when he came home that evening after capturing the video, perhaps the happiest and most excited Micheal had ever seen his dad. There is a nice analysis of this film on YouTube by YouTuber Bob Gymlan—not his real name. Scan the QR code below to view the YouTube video. I think "Bob Gymlan" writes well, and his information is solid.

Appendix D

Frequently Asked Questions about Evolution

Evolution Q and A

During my twenty-five plus years teaching evolution at both the high school and college level, I received many good questions. By good, I mean they were useful as teaching tools because they illuminated some misconceptions about the topic of evolution. Here are some samples:

Q: "If we came from chimps, then why are there still chimps?"

When I look puzzled by their question, I have often noticed a smug gotcha look appear on the face of the asker. The reason I look puzzled is that the question itself is such an avalanche of misconceptions based on such a tiny kernel of truth that I often don't know where to begin. Their question is like asking: "So if Lutherans came from Judaism, then why are there still Jews?"

First, Lutherans did not come from Jews. The Christian religion arose/evolved from Judaism, The Old Testament is the companion book to the New Testament. The New Testament is the interpretations and teaching of Christ (a Jewish carpenter). One of the early versions of Christianity was the Catholic denomination. Martin Luther split off from this denomination during the reformation. Thus, Lutherans arose/evolved from the Catholic tradition, which arose out of the Judeo tradition. Lutherans did not replace Jews any more than chimps replaced humans. This "gotcha" question is more of a confession by the asker that they have a very limited understanding of the process and theory of evolution. We are related to chimps, but we did not "come from" them. In evolution, the "newer model" does not always replace the older model, sometimes it's just a different model. The more recent model might work better for a different situation. Think pickup trucks. The Toyota Tundra is a more recent model, but it did not replace the Toyota Tacoma. Though many design elements were conserved.

Q: "What are we going to evolve into next?"

My short answer is I have no idea. We, like all life, change in response to new selection pressures. How exactly that will play out is anyone's guess. The 2006 movie *Idiocracy* has some ideas that seem about as good as any. It is both funny and depressing (and unfortunately a little prophetic). It also does a good job explaining evolution.

Q: "Why are so-called 'primitive organisms' so complex?"

"Primitive" bacteria have evolved for their niche. Anything that is alive today is highly evolved. Bacteria did not just evolve a long time ago and then stop evolving. The fittest continue to survive and reproduce. Bacterial species are extremely well-adapted to their specific roles. Populations of bacteria have changed over time to inhabit and thrive in their particular niche, or into new niches with different selection pressures. Bacteria that resist antibiotics, for example, are a response to a new selection pressure. Primitive just means old; it does not mean inferior. Bacteria are just as "evolved" as a gorilla or person or squirrel. They have just evolved to their little niche. A squirrel could not live in your intestines, but bacteria thrive there. Some "primitive" bacteria thrive in boiling geysers; they have evolved to do so.

Q: "How can something as complex as the eyeball just suddenly evolve?"

Excellent question! "To suppose that the eye, with all of its inimitable contrivances . . . could have been formed by natural selection, seems, I freely confess, absurd in the highest degree." —Charles Darwin in *The Origin of the Species*

Sometimes creationists like to use this Darwin quote for their own agenda. But the operative word in the above quote is "seems." Even in 1859, Darwin was able to go on to explain that complex light-sensing organs did not appear out of the blue, but rather they began as less-complex organs that gradually became more complex over time. He pointed to anatomy in the living creatures we see today and imagined a line of ever-increasing complexity. This, he argued, would be refined as needed through natural selection. The things that worked were conserved, the parts that improved a particular type of useful vision were passed on, and those that were not useful were gradually lost. Of course, not all species have the same sensory needs, so "the eye" has become a different organ in different critters. But many critters evolved an eye with similar machinery to ours.

Fast-forward from 1859 to the modern era and we no longer need to even speculate. Some of the proteins in our eyes' light-sensitive cells, the rods and cones, are the same proteins found in other animals' light-sensitive cells. Light-detecting cells called photoreceptors are found in all animals that respond to light. These photoreceptors are made of proteins called opsins and chromophores, made, usually, from a derivative of vitamin A. In the animal world, just over 900 slight variations of opsin proteins have been identified. In 2012, Megan Porter compared these and found they all have a common opsin ancestor. The original opsin has not changed much. Evolution says, "If it ain't broke, don't fix it." The arrangement of the eye has subtle differences from one class of organisms to the next. The human eye is not the most amazing design, but it is pretty cool. Turkeys have better vision with a similar design, and birds of prey have spectacular distance vision. Trout have fantastic close-up underwater vision.

Insect eyes are arranged like a big retina on the outside. Still the same opsin proteins. They are great at seeing movement, and many can even see in the UV spectrum. The evolution of our human eye didn't happen out of the blue. Like all evolution, the human version of the eye was gradually selected for based on the needs of our species.

Q: "If bees die when they sting you, how could that evolve?"

Another excellent question. We must make a distinction between social bees and solitary bees. The bees that sting you and then die are typically social bees. Evolutionary pressures are different on social bees. A "worker" honeybee is a eusocial critter.

Eusocial means many members have given up the ability to reproduce and there is division of labor amongst the members of the colony groups—there are some other criteria as well. These species are very, very rare. Out of all the species of animals out there, we know of less than twenty critters or groups of critters that are eusocial. A few are mammals, and the rest are all in the phylum Arthropoda. The largest percentage, by far is the order Hymenoptera, and within that, the family of the ants. Thousands of ant species are eusocial.

But back to another order of Arthropoda, the Hymenoptera, or more specifically, the genus and species that we commonly call honeybees. Because only the queen bee and the male drone bees reproduce, from an evolutionary standpoint, it does not matter if the worker bee dies defending the colony. (Although, it might matter to that bee! ☺) Furthermore, only the older worker bees are assigned the job of defending the hive, so they were about to die anyway. It is best to think of the entire colony as a superorganism from an evolutionary point of view. Knowing that the colony has the capacity to defend itself ensures *the hive* will survive and reproduce, even if some old worker bees die sending a message to a mouse, a bear, or anything that seeks to do harm to the colony.

Evolutionarily, this makes perfect sense. The bees in a hive have the same genetics; their mom is the same girl. If the hive survives, the genetics continue to be passed on. And *individual* bees dying to defend the colony make it *more likely* that that *colonies* genetics will survive. The individual worker lacks the ability to mate and have offspring. Her sacrifice allowed the hive's genetics to survive.

Not so much a question but a comment . . . "Yea right. I evolved from a fish!"

You are in fact correct to say you did not evolve from a fish.

Most people have no problem with the process of evolution. They willingly accept that domestic dogs evolved from wolves, they are willing to accept and understand antibiotic resistance evolves in bacteria and pesticide resistance in weeds. Some even see the Galapagos finches as a pretty airtight case as well. What they have problems with are the big jumps.

People who accept all the empirical evidence for evolution understand the amount of time involved in the huge changes are almost unfathomable.

Even if the time frame is ninety years, that is too much for young kids. "Wait, you're telling me my grandpa once lived inside the uterus of a girl . . . no way." Yep, those are the facts, even if they seem crazy.

Most people, including myself, cannot fully get their head around numbers like 100,000 years. This expanse of time is just too far outside our experience. Social human societies go back around 10,000 years ago—that's a really long time ago, hard to fathom. It is very difficult to get your head around a time frame like 100,000 years ago, let alone the 13 million years of human evolution. Yes, you could trace back to when you had a common ancestor with a fish, but you would have to go back 250,000,000 years!

Big steps require some cognitive flexibility, as they are hard to imagine. If you remember the middle steps, things seem less unfathomable. For example, wolves to large breed dogs like elkhounds and huskies and German shepherds seems reasonable. Not a big leap. From there to full grown poodles, again, only a difference of a few genes. From there, selecting smaller and smaller poodles. Just some simple breeding and then, ta-da! . . . a toy poodle. Easy peasy!

You are in fact correct to say you did not evolve from a fish. But a long, very long, very, very long time ago, you and a fish had a common ancestor.

Acknowledgments

I have struggled with the question of which people to include in the acknowledgements section. So many people had a hand in my development as a human and thus the development of this book. The following is an admittedly incomplete list.

I'll just start by acknowledging my friends, as they are the most likely to buy my book, and the most likely to scan the acknowledgements for their names. Some, like Mark St. Andre, helped me write, some provided expertise, and all provided inspiration in one form or another.

I will list them in no particular order: Bruce and Blaine Adamson, Scoot and Sarah Hansen, Mark and Susie, Dave and Kelly, Rod and Julie Hesson, Rob Bradshaw, Ben and Leah Gapinski, Tim Walker, Dan Benson, Dan Simpson, Vic and Chris, Kori and Kate, Ellen and Doug, Ross and Mary Sue, Andrea and Chad, Dennis and LJ, Edona, Lydia M., Joe and Emily, Andy and Julianna, Mike and Ruthanne, Amy and Judd, Lisa and Jeff, Fred Roth, Kevin Gills, and Domnic and Racheal Davis.

Many of the students, and coworkers, that I taught with at WACO and Highland were also inspirations. I will not list them individually, but they certainly should get acknowledged for helping me refine my thinking on a variety of epistemological issues.

Obviously, my wife and my sons get a paragraph here. Suellen, Henry, and Max were and are my most important sources of inspiration, and encouragement. Suellen helped me edit as well. Her feedback was extremely helpful. My family has been a huge part of me becoming the person I have become. I love them so very much.

Jeff Meldrum should also get an acknowledgement. He was very gracious and helpful to me as I pursued the writing of this book. He had no reason to think I was ever going to finish this project, but he still returned emails and phone calls and even allowed my wife and I to visit his lab in Idaho. He recently passed away, so he never got to see the finished product. He was a kind and descent human.

My developmental editor, June Melby, was very instrumental in the production of this book. A mutual friend, Amy Margolis, put us in touch. I really needed some handholding to get my ideas and various voices to flow into some kind of narrative that was not just a jumbled, incoherent mess. If you still thought that this was a jumbled incoherent mess when you read it, let me assure you, it was much worse before! A special thanks to June. Speaking of editors, Sean Strain should also get a shout out. He did an excellent job with the final copy edit, if you still find any errors that is likely my fault.

As this was a self-published book, I relied on the expertise of Mayfly design to help me with the odds and ends of self-publishing. They helped with, layout, formatting, ISBNs, and a myriad of details that I was clueless about. So a big thanks to Julie, Molly and Ryan at Mayfly for helping me drag this project over the finish line. Renee Zukin also provided marketing advice along the way.

I will close out the acknowledgements with my mom and dad. They were fantastic parents and wonderful people. My dad had an enormous influence on my religious beliefs. He was a kind and wise person. I miss them both and I cannot thank them enough for their support and guidance over the course of my life.

Resources

Books

Campbell, Joseph and Bill Moyers. *The Power of Myth*. New York, New York: Anchor Books, 1991)

Freeman, Michael. *The Freeman Bigfoot Files*. Minneapolis: Hanger 1 Publishing, 2022.

Gomes, Peter. *The Good Book: Reading the Bible with Mind and Heart*. New York: William and Morrow Publishing, 1996.

Green, John. *The Sasquatch File*. Agassiz, British Columbia: Cheam Publishing Ltd., 1973.

Harari, Yuval N. *Sapiens: A Brief History of Humankind*. New York: Random House/Harper, 2011.

Jones, Alexander, ed. *The Jerusalem Bible: Reader's Edition*. Garden City: Doubleday & Company, Inc.,1966-1968.

Krantz, Grover. *Bigfoot Sasquatch Evidence*. Blaine, Washington: Hancock House, 1999.

Larson, Edward. *Summer for the Gods: The Scopes Trial and America's Continuing Debate Over Science and Religion*. Boston: Havard University Press, 1998.

Meldrum, Jeff. *Sasquatch: Legend Meets Science*. New York: Tom Doherty Associates, 2006.

Moore, Russell. *Losing Our Religion: An Alter Call for Evangelical America*. New York: Sentinel/Penguin Random House, 2023.

Pollan, Michael. *The Omnivore's Dilemma: A Natural History of Four Meals*. New York: Penguin Books, 2007.

Pyle, Robert. *Where Bigfoot Walks: Crossing the Dark Divide*. New York: Houghton Mifflin, 1995.

Sapolsky, Robert. *Determined: A Science of Life without Free Will*. New York: Penguin Press, 2023.

Wilson, Edward O. *The Social Conquest of Earth*. New York: Liveright Publishing/W. W. Norton, 2010.

Yong, Ed. *An Immense World*. New York: Random House, 2022.

Journals

Cristofori, I., S. Cohen-Zimerman, J. Bulbulia, B. Gordon, F. Krueger, and J. Grafman. "The Neural Underpinning of Religious Beliefs: Evidence from Brain Lesions." *Frontiers in Behavioral Neuroscience* 16 (2022): 977600. https://doi.org/10.3389/fnbeh.2022.977600.

Dunbar, Robin. "Managing the Stresses of Group-Living in the Transition to Village Life." *Evolutionary Human Sciences* 4 (2022): 1–39. https://doi.org/10.1017/ehs.2022.39.

Dias, B., and K. Ressler. "Parental Olfactory Experience Influences Behavior and Neural Structure in Subsequent Generations." *Nature Neuroscience* 17 (2014): 89–96. https://doi.org/10.1038/nn.3594.

Kennedy, Brian, and Alec Tyson. "Americans' Trust in Scientists, Positive Views of Science Continue to Decline." Pew Research Center, November 14, 2023.

Heijmans, B., E. Tobi, A. Stien, H. Putter, G. Blauw, E. Susser, E. Slagboom, and L. Lumey. "Persistent Epigenetic Differences Associated with Prenatal Exposure to Famine in Humans." *Proceedings of the National Academy of Sciences of the United States of America* 105, no. 44 (October 2008): 17046–17049.

Porter, M. L., J. R. Blasic, M. J. Bok, E. G. Cameron, T. Pringle, T. W. Cronin, and P. R. Robinson. "Shedding New Light on Opsin Evolution." *Proceedings of the Royal Society B: Biological Sciences* 279, no. 1726 (2012): 3–14. https://doi.org/10.1098/rspb.2011.1819.

Swire-Thompson, Briony, Nicholas Miklaucic, John P. Wihbey, David Lazer, and Joseph DeGutis. "The Backfire Effect After Correcting Misinformation Is Strongly Associated with Reliability." Journal of Experimental Psychology: General 151, no. 7 (2022): 1655–1665. https://doi.org/10.1037/xge0001131.

Vohs, K. D., and J. W. Schooler. "The Value of Believing in Free Will: Encouraging a Belief in Determinism Increases Cheating." *Psychological Science* 19, no. 1 (January 2008): 49–54.

Zhang, Y., and T. Harrison. "Gigantopithecus blacki: A Giant Ape from the Pleistocene of Asia Revisited." *American Journal of Physical Anthropology* 162 (2017): 153–177. https://doi.org/10.1002/ajpa.23150.

Online Resources

The Association of Religion Data Archives. "Belief in Bigfoot – Belief Statistics Topic." 2007. https://www.thearda.com/us-religion/statistics/beliefs?qsid=239.

Australian Museum. "Walking on Two Legs: Bipedalism." https://australian.museum/learn/science/human-evolution/walking-on-two-legs-bipedalism/.

Bays, Ruby, and Jennie Franco, told by. *The Yokuts Creation Story*. Visalia, CA: Tulare County Department of Education, Office of the Superintendent, 1975.

Chignell, Andrew. "The Ethics of Belief." In *The Stanford Encyclopedia of Philosophy*, Spring 2018 Edition, edited by Edward N. Zalta. https://plato.stanford.edu/archives/spr2018/entries/ethics-belief/.

Dawes, Gregory W. "Ancient and Medieval Empiricism." In *The Stanford Encyclopedia of Philosophy*, Summer 2023 Edition, edited by Edward N. Zalta and Uri Nodelman. https://plato.stanford.edu/archives/sum2023/entries/empiricism-ancient-medieval/.

The Editors of Encyclopedia Britannica. "Moral Majority." *Encyclopedia Britannica*, February 12, 2018. https://www.britannica.com/topic/Moral-Majority.

Hanks, Micah. "A Humanlike 'Living Fossil' Could Still Be Alive in Indonesia." *The Debrief*, February 15, 2023. https://thedebrief.org/a-humanlike-living-fossil-could-still-be-alive-in-indonesia-this-anthropologist-says/.

Ichikawa, Jonathan Jenkins, and Matthias Steup. "The Analysis of Knowledge." In *The Stanford Encyclopedia of Philosophy*, Fall 2024 Edition, edited by Edward N. Zalta and Uri Nodelman. https://plato.stanford.edu/archives/fall2024/entries/knowledge-analysis/.

Meldrum, Jeff. "Adaptive Radiations, Bushy Evolutionary Trees, and Relict Hominids." *Relict Hominid Inquiry* 1 (2012): 51–56. https://www.isu.edu/media/libraries/rhi/from-the-editor/Editorial_Bushy-Trees.pdf.

Murry, Conor. "Researcher Demoted by University of Pennsylvania Wins Nobel Prize for mRNA Discoveries—And Some Academics Urge Penn to Apologize." *Forbes*, October 6, 2023.

National Park Service. "Lakota Creation Story." https://www.nps.gov/wica/learn/historyculture/the-lakota-emergence-story.htm.

NSTA Board of Directors. NSTA Statement on the Nature of Science. 2020. https://www.nsta.org/nstas-official-positions/nature-science#:~:text=Science%20Is%20a%20Way%20of%20Knowing%3B,the%20Natural%20and%20Material%20World.

Pape, Robert. *American Face of Insurrection*. Chicago Project on Security and Threats. 2022.

Pardi, Paul. "What Is Knowledge?" *Philosophy News*, September 22, 2011. https://philosophynews.com/what-is-knowledge/.

Pew Research Center. *U.S. Religious Landscape Study: Questions about the Origins and Development of Life on Earth*. June 4–September 30, 2014.

The Smithsonian Museum, National Museum of Natural History. "Collections Overview." https://naturalhistory.si.edu/research/paleobiology/collections-overview.

The Smithsonian Museum. "Walking Upright." https://humanorigins.si.edu/human-characteristics/walking-upright.

Snyder, Laura J. "William Whewell." In *The Stanford Encyclopedia of Philosophy*, Winter 2023 Edition, edited by Edward N. Zalta and Uri Nodelman. https://plato.stanford.edu/archives/win2023/entries/whewell/.

Southern Poverty Law Center. "The New Dominionism Tries to Rule." June 4, 2024.

Steup, Matthias, and Ram Neta. "Epistemology." In *The Stanford Encyclopedia of Philosophy*, Winter 2024 Edition, edited by Edward N. Zalta and Uri Nodelman. https://plato.stanford.edu/archives/win2024/entries/epistemology/.

World History Encyclopedia. "Religion in the Ancient World." https://www.worldhistory.org/timeline/religion/.

Newspapers and Visual Media

Suk, Tom. "Officials Probe Reports of Bigfoot near Adel." *Des Moines Register* November 16, 1979.

Fox, Steve, reporter. "Bigfoot." *Good Morning America*, season 12, episode 216, October 29, 1987. ABC News Production.

Partland, Dan, director. *God and Country*. Produced by Rob Reiner. 2024. Anonymous Content / Castle Rock Entertainment.

Belton, David, writer and director. "God in America: One: A New Adam." Produced by Cathleen O'Connell. October 11, 2010. *Frontline / American Experience*. WGBH Educational Foundation.

Lesiak, Christine, writer, producer, and director. "Monkey Trial." February 17, 2002. *American Experience*. Nebraska ETV for American Experience.

Nasht, Simon, Annamaria Talas, and Sarah Holt, director and producer. *Alien from Earth*. November 11, 2008. WGBH Educational Foundation and Essential Media and Entertainment Pty Ltd, in association with Real Pictures and NOVA.

Kuhn, Robert L., writer and producer, and Peter Getzel, director. "How Do Belief Systems Work." Episode 10, #127. 2012. *Closer to Truth*. The Kuhn Foundation.

Levenson, Mark, director. *Particle Fever*. Produced by David Kaplan. March 5, 2014. Anthos Media, Abramorama BOND360.

Pierce, Charles B., director and producer. *Legend of Boggy Creek*. Written by Earl Smith. August 8, 1972. Howco Productions.

Puttkamer, Peter Von, director. *Sasquatch Odyssey: The Hunt for Bigfoot*. June 28, 2003. Bayview Films.

Beloff, Evan, director. Produced by Fredric Bohbot and Evan Beloff. *Bigfoot's Reflection*. 2007. Gaiam TV.

Young, Nic, director. Produced by David Upshal. "Reach for the Stars: Trial of Galileo/Yuri Gagarin's Flight." Season 2, Episode 6. November 15, 2004. *Days That Shook the World*. BBC Scotland.

Lorre, Chuck, and Bill Prady, writers. Directed by Mark Cendrowski. "The Raiders Minimization." Season 7, Episode 4. Produced by Kristy Cecil. October 10, 2013. *The Big Bang Theory*. Chuck Lorre Productions / Warner Bros. Television.

Kogen, J., and W. Wolodarsky, writers. Directed by M. Kirkland. "Homer the Heretic." Season 4, Episode 3. 1993. Executive producers J. L. Brooks, M. Groening, A. Jean, M. Reiss, and S. Simon. *The Simpsons*. Gracie Films; Twentieth Century Fox Film Productions.

Penn, Jillette, and Teller, writers. Directed by Star Price. "Cryptozoology." Season 4, Episode 4. April 20, 2006. Executive producer Star Price. *Bullshit!*. Showtime Network.

Frank, Kosa, writer. Directed by Lori McCreary. "Who Is God?" Season 1, Episode 4. April 17, 2016. *The Story of God with Morgan Freeman*. Revelation Entertainment.

TED Talks, Podcasts, Radio, and YouTube

Dennett, Daniel, and Robert Sapolsky. "Do We Have Freewill? / Daniel Dennett vs. Robert Sapolsky." *How To Academy*. https://www.youtube.com/watch?v=aYzFH8xqhns.

Dunn, Michael. "Guide to Theory of Knowledge (TOK): Ways of Knowing." Cambridge University Press Education, 2016. https://www.youtube.com/watch?v=oZv3q7udZYo.

Goodall, Jane, and Ira Flatow. *NPR's Talk of the Nation / Science Friday*. September 27, 2002.

McIndoe, Peter. "Birds Aren't Real? How a Conspiracy Takes Flight." TED Talk, 2024.

Tyson, Neil deGrasse, and Bryan Elliott. "Science Explains Everything: Neil deGrasse Tyson." *Behind the Brand*, 2021.

Tyson, Neil deGrasse, and Joe Rogan. "Neil deGrasse Tyson." Episode 1658. *Joe Rogan Experience*, 2024.

Vedantam, Shankar. "Our God Shaped Brains." *Hidden Brain*, June 17, 2023. Hidden Brain Media.

Notes

Section 1: Bigfoot

Chapter 1: Why Bigfoot?

Pierce, Charles B., director and producer. *Legend of Boggy Creek*. Written by Earl Smith. August 8, 1972. Howco Productions.

Chapter 2: Larry Wilson

Suk, Tom. "Officials Probe Reports of Bigfoot near Adel." *Des Moines Register*, November 16, 1979.

Chapter 3: Bigfoot and Epistemology

Penn, Jillette, and Teller, writers. Directed by Star Price. "Cryptozoology." Season 4, Episode 4. April 20, 2006. Executive producer Star Price. *Bullshit!*. Showtime Network.

Chapter 4: The Bigfoot Question

Zhang, Y., and T. Harrison. "Gigantopithecus blacki: A Giant Ape from the Pleistocene of Asia Revisited." *American Journal of Physical Anthropology* 162 (2017): 153–177.
The Smithsonian Museum. "Walking Upright." https://humanorigins.si.edu/human-characteristics/walking-upright.
Australian Museum. "Walking on Two Legs: Bipedalism." https://australian.museum/learn/science/human-evolution/walking-on-two-legs-bipedalism/.
Green, John. *The Sasquatch File*. Agassiz, British Columbia: Cheam Publishing Ltd., 1973.

Pyle, Robert. *Where Bigfoot Walks: Crossing the Dark Divide*. New York: Houghton Mifflin, 1995.

Krantz, Grover. *Bigfoot Sasquatch Evidence*. Blaine, Washington: Hancock House, 1999.

Meldrum, Jeff. *Sasquatch: Legend Meets Science*. New York: Tom Doherty Associates, 2006.

Puttkamer, Peter Von, director. *Sasquatch Odyssey: The Hunt for Bigfoot*. 2003. Bayview Films.

Beloff, Evan, director. Produced by Fredric Bohbot and Evan Beloff. Bigfoot's Reflection. 2007. Gaiam TV.

Green, John. *The Sasquatch File*. Agassiz, British Columbia: Cheam Publishing Ltd., 1973.

Campbell, Joseph and Bill Moyers. *The Power of Myth*. New York: Anchor Books, 1991.

Section 2: How Do We Know?

Chapter 5: What Does It Mean to Know?

Steup, Matthias, and Ram Neta. "Epistemology." In *The Stanford Encyclopedia of Philosophy*, Winter 2024 Edition, edited by Edward N. Zalta and Uri Nodelman. https://plato.stanford.edu/archives/win2024/entries/epistemology/.

Dunn, Michael. "Guide to Theory of Knowledge (TOK): Ways of Knowing." Cambridge University Press Education, 2016. https://www.youtube.com/watch?v=oZv3q7udZYo.

Dawes, Gregory W. "Ancient and Medieval Empiricism." In *The Stanford Encyclopedia of Philosophy*, Summer 2023 Edition, edited by Edward N. Zalta and Uri Nodelman. https://plato.stanford.edu/archives/sum2023/entries/empiricism-ancient-medieval/.

Chapter 6: The First Pizza of Empirical "Truth"

Levenson, Mark, director. Particle Fever. Produced by David Kaplan. March 5, 2014. Anthos Media, Abramorama BOND360.

Chapter 7: The Story of Galileo

Young, Nic, director. Produced by David Upshal. "Reach for the Stars: Trial of Galileo/Yuri Gagarin's Flight." Season 2, Episode 6. November 15, 2004. *Days That Shook the World*. BBC Scotland.

Lorre, Chuck, and Bill Prady, writers. Directed by Mark Cendrowski. "The Raiders Minimization." Season 7, Episode 4. Produced by Kristy Cecil. October 10, 2013. *The Big Bang Theory*. Chuck Lorre Productions / Warner Bros. Television.

Snyder, Laura J. "William Whewell." In *The Stanford Encyclopedia of Philosophy*, Winter 2023 Edition, edited by Edward N. Zalta and Uri Nodelman. https://plato.stanford.edu/archives/win2023/entries/whewell/.

Chapter 8: The Nature of Science

NSTA Board of directors. "NSTA statement on the Nature of Science". (2020). URL https://www.nsta.org/nstas-official-positions/nature-science#:~:text=Science%20Is%20a%20Way%20of%20Knowing%3B,the%20Natural%20and%20Material%20World.

Chapter 9: Misconceptions about Science

Pollan, Michael. *The Omnivore's Dilemma: A Natural History of Four Meals*. New York: Penguin Books. 2007.

Frontier Science vs. Established Science

Tyson, Neil deGrasse, and Joe Rogan. "Neil deGrasse Tyson." Episode 1658. *Joe Rogan Experience*, 2024.

Kennedy, Brian, and Alec Tyson. "Americans' Trust in Scientists, Positive Views of Science Continue to Decline." Pew Research Center, November 14, 2023.

Levenson, Mark, director. *Particle Fever*. Produced by David Kaplan. March 5, 2014. Anthos Media, Abramorama BOND360.

Chapter 10: Scientists and the Sasquatch

Meldrum, Jeff. *Sasquatch: Legend Meets Science.* New York: Tom Doherty Associates, 2006.

Goodall, Jane, and Ira Flatow. *NPR's Talk of the Nation | Science Friday.* September 27, 2002.

Tyson, Neil deGrasse, and Bryan Elliott. "Science Explains Everything: Neil deGrasse Tyson." *Behind the Brand*, 2021.

Chapter 11: Three Men and a Sasquatch

Murry, Conor. "Researcher Demoted by University of Pennsylvania Wins Nobel Prize for mRNA Discoveries—And Some Academics Urge Penn to Apologize." *Forbes*, October 6, 2023.

Section 3: Belief

Chapter 13: Definitions

Ichikawa, Jonathan Jenkins, and Matthias Steup. "The Analysis of Knowledge." In *The Stanford Encyclopedia of Philosophy*, Fall 2024 Edition, edited by Edward N. Zalta and Uri Nodelman. https://plato.stanford.edu/archives/fall2024/entries/knowledge-analysis/.

Pardi, Paul. "What Is Knowledge?" *Philosophy News*, September 22, 2011. https://philosophynews.com/what-is-knowledge/.

Chapter 15: Beliefs and Belief Systems—an Overview

Cristofori, I., S. Cohen-Zimerman, J. Bulbulia, B. Gordon, F. Krueger, and J. Grafman. "The Neural Underpinning of Religious Beliefs: Evidence from Brain Lesions." *Frontiers in Behavioral Neuroscience* 16 (October 2022): 977600.

Kuhn, Robert L., writer and producer, and Peter Getzels, director. "How Do Belief Systems Work." Episode 10, #127. 2012. *Closer to Truth.* The Kuhn Foundation.

Chapter 18: Entanglement of Nurture and Nature

Heijmans, B., E. Tobi, A. Stien, H. Putter, G. Blauw, E. Susser, E. Slagboom, and L. Lumey. "Persistent Epigenetic Differences Associated with Prenatal Exposure to Famine in Humans." *Proceedings of the National Academy of Sciences of the United States of America* 105, no. 44 (October 2008): 17046–17049.

Ressler, K., and B. Dias. "Parental Olfactory Experience Influences Behavior and Neural Structure in Subsequent Generations." *Nature Neuroscience* 17 (December 1, 2013): 89–96.

Chapter 20: Umwelt

Yong, Ed. *An Immense World*. New York: Random House, 2022.

Section 4: God and Religion

Chapter 22: Religion and God

Dunbar, Robin. "Managing the Stresses of Group-Living in the Transition to Village Life." *Evolutionary Human Sciences* 4 (September 2022):1-39.

Wilson, Edward O. *The Social Conquest of Earth*. New York: Liveright Publishing/W. W. Norton, 2010.

The Association of Religion Data Archives. "Belief in Bigfoot – Belief Statistics Topic." 2007. https://www.thearda.com/us-religion/statistics/beliefs?qsid=239.

Chapter 23: The Nature of God/Types of Belief Systems

Vedantam, Shankar. "Our God Shaped Brains." *Hidden Brain*, June 17, 2023. Hidden Brain Media.

Chapter 24: Overview of World Religions

Frank, Kosa, writer. Directed by Lori McCreary. "Who Is God?" Season 1, Episode 4. April 17, 2016. *The Story of God with Morgan Freeman*. Revelation Entertainment.

Pew Research Center's Forum on Religion and Public Life. *Global Religious Landscapes*. December 2012.

Pew Research Center. *Global Religious Landscapes*. June 2025.

Editors of World History Encyclopedia. "Religion in the Ancient World" https://www.worldhistory.org/timeline/religion/.

Section 5: Evolution

Chapter 27: Evolution and Theology

Pew Research Center. *U.S. Religious Landscape Study: Questions about the Origins and Development of Life on Earth*. June 4–September 30, 2014.

Chapter 28: Science of Evolution

Bays, Ruby, and Jennie Franco. From Bigfoot and other stories. Visalia, CA: Tulare County Department of Education, Office of the Superintendent 1975

National Park Service. "Wind Cave Creation Story." https://www.nps .gov/wica/learn/historyculture/the-lakota-emergence-story.htm.

Chapter 29: Evidence for the Theory of Evolution

The Smithsonian Museum, National Museum of Natural History. "Collections Overview." https://naturalhistory.si.edu/research /paleobiology/collections-overview.

Chapter 30: Human Evolution

Nasht, Simon, Annamaria Talas, and Sarah Holt, director and producer. *Alien from Earth*. November 11, 2008. WGBH Educational Foundation and Essential Media and Entertainment Pty Ltd, in association with Real Pictures and NOVA.

Harari, Yuval N. *Sapiens: A Brief History of Humankind*. New York: Random House/Harper, 2011.

Smithsonian Institution, "Homo floresiensis." Smithsonian National Museum of Natural History, Human Origins Program. https:/ /humanorigins.si.edu/evidence/human-fossils/species/homo -floresiensis.

Meldrum, Jeff. "Adaptive Radiations, Bushy Evolutionary Trees, and Relict Hominids." *Relict Hominid Inquiry* 1 (2012): 51–56. https:/ /www.isu.edu/media/libraries/rhi/from-the-editor/Editorial _Bushy-Trees.pdf.

Hanks, Micah. "A Humanlike 'Living Fossil' Could Still Be Alive in Indonesia." *The Debrief*, February 15, 2023. https://thedebrief .org/a-humanlike-living-fossil-could-still-be-alive-in-indonesia -this-anthropologist-says/.

Chapter 31: The Book of Genesis

Jones, Alexander, ed. *The Jerusalem Bible: Reader's Edition.* Garden City: Doubleday & Company, Inc.,1966-1968.

Chapter 33: Scopes "Monkey Trial"

Lesiak, Christine, writer, producer, and director. "Monkey Trial." February 17, 2002. *American Experience*. Nebraska ETV for American Experience.

Larson, Edward. *Summer for the Gods: The Scopes Trial and America's Continuing Debate Over Science and Religion*. Boston: Havard University Press, 1998.

Section 6

Chapter 34: Responsibility and Free Will

Sapolsky, Robert. *Determined: A Science of Life without Free Will*. New York: Penguin Press, 2023.

Dennett, Daniel, and Robert Sapolsky. "Do We Have Freewill? / Daniel Dennett vs. Robert Sapolsky." *How To Academy*. https://www.youtube.com/watch?v=aYzFH8xqhns.

Vohs, K. D., and J. W. Schooler. "The Value of Believing in Free Will: Encouraging a Belief in Determinism Increases Cheating." *Psychological Science* 19, no. 1 (January 2008): 49–54.

Chapter 35: Epistemic Responsibility

Chignell, Andrew. "The Ethics of Belief." In *The Stanford Encyclopedia of Philosophy*, Spring 2018 Edition, edited by Edward N. Zalta. https://plato.stanford.edu/archives/spr2018/entries/ethics-belief/.

Gomes, Peter. *The Good Book: Reading the Bible with Mind and Heart*. New York: William and Morrow Publishing, 1996.

Chapter 36: Political Beliefs

Chapter 37: Christian Nationalism

Partland, Dan, director. *God and Country*. Produced by Rob Reiner. 2024. Anonymous Content / Castle Rock Entertainment.

Southern Poverty Law Center. "The New Dominionism Tries to Rule." June 4, 2024. https://www.splcenter.org/resources/reports/new-dominionism-tries-rule/.

The Editors of Encyclopedia Britannica. "Moral Majority." *Encyclopedia Britannica*, February 12, 2018. https://www.britannica.com/topic/Moral-Majority.

Chapter 38: Theological Origins of Christian Nationalism

Belton, David, writer and director. "God in America: One: A New Adam." Produced by Cathleen O'Connell. October 11, 2010. *Frontline / American Experience*. WGBH Educational Foundation.

Chapter 39: George Whitefield

Belton, David, writer and director. "God in America: One: A New Adam." Produced by Cathleen O'Connell. October 11, 2010. *Frontline / American Experience*. WGBH Educational Foundation.
Moore, Russell. *Losing Our Religion: An Alter Call for Evangelical America*. New York: Sentinel/Penguin Random House, 2023.

Chapter 40: Who Are the Christian Nationalists?

Pape, Robert. *American Face of Insurrection*. Chicago Project on Security and Threats. 2022.

Chapter 41: So, Are We Responsible for Our Beliefs?

Chapter 42: Birds Aren't Real

McIndoe, Peter. "Birds Aren't Real? How a Conspiracy Takes Flight." TED Talk, 2024.
Swire-Thompson, Briony, Nicholas Miklaucic, John P. Wihbey, David Lazer, and Joseph
DeGutis. "The Backfire Effect After Correcting Misinformation Is Strongly Associated with Reliability." Journal of Experimental Psychology: General 151, no. 7 (2022): 1655–1665. https://doi.org/10.1037/xge0001131.

Appendix

A. *Patterson-Gimlin film*

B. Theory of Knowledge: Ways of knowing

C. Paul Freeman

Fox, Steve, reporter. "Bigfoot." *Good Morning America*, season 12, episode 216, October 29, 1987. ABC News Production.

Freeman, Michael. *The Freeman Bigfoot Files*. Minneapolis: Hanger 1 Publishing, 2022.

Gymlan, Bob. *The Freeman Footage: Best Bigfoot Evidence*. YouTube video, https://www.youtube.com/watch?v=d_Fnp03gbes.

D. Frequently Asked Questions about Evolution

Porter, M. L., J. R. Blasic, M. J. Bok, E. G. Cameron, T. Pringle, T. W. Cronin, and P. R. Robinson. "Shedding New Light on Opsin Evolution." *Proceedings of the Royal Society B: Biological Sciences* 279, no. 1726 (2012): 3–14. https://doi.org/10.1098/rspb.2011.1819.

Wilson, Edward O. *The Social Conquest of Earth*. New York: Liveright Publishing/W. W. Norton, 2010.

Harari, Yuval N. *Sapiens: A Brief History of Humankind*. New York: Random House/Harper, 2011.

About the author

Will Swain is a science educator with over 30 years of experience teaching students across a wide range of ages and settings. He taught undergraduate courses such as Human Biology, Evolutionary Biology, and Principles of Animal Biology at The University of Iowa, where he also administered research programs for undergraduate students, precollege students, and science teachers. At the high school level, he taught Physics, Geology, Astronomy, Chemistry, Biology, Environmental Science, and Human Biology. He also served as the regional director of the Iowa Junior Science and Humanities Symposium and as a member of the National JSHS Regional Director's Executive Council.

His interest in the relationship between science and religion began early in life and has followed him ever since. Growing up surrounded by family and friends with differing views on faith and science sparked a lifelong curiosity about belief formation. These questions ultimately led him to write *Certainly Uncertain*, a research-informed and personal exploration of how beliefs, and knowledge itself, take shape—and how understanding their limits and tentative nature can lead to more thoughtful and compassionate conversations.